NORMAN MARK'S CHICAGO

WALKING, BICYCLING & DRIVING TOURS OF THE CITY

NORMAN MARK'S
CHICAGO

3rd EDITION

PHOTOGRAPHS BY
BOB LANGER
FOREWORD BY
MIKE ROYKO

CHICAGO REVIEW PRESS

To Grace Arons, whom I love; Anne Arons, the daughter who is no longer "step"; and Geoff and Joel, sons who accept the changes in my life.

With special thanks to Curt Matthews, publisher who understands how to get manuscripts on time; Mary Munro, the editor of my dreams; Donna Neuwirth, a researcher who goes back to places she didn't want to visit in the first place; Bob Langer, photographer; Emmett Dedmon for his notes for his book *Fabulous Chicago;* Herman Kogan, for all his help and his writings; and the literally thousands of Chicagoans who gladly shared their time, advice, direction, notes, ideas and their ability to give the straight scoop to a wondering, wandering writer.

Library of Congress Cataloging-in-Publication Data

Mark, Norman.
    Norman Mark's Chicago.

    Bibliography: p.
    Includes index.
    1. Chicago (Ill.)—Description—1981–   —Tours.
I. Title.
F548.18.M33   1987   917.73'110443   87-10315
ISBN 1–55652–003–4

Third edition

Published by Chicago Review Press, Incorporated
814 North Franklin
Chicago, Illinois 60610

CONTENTS

1	South Michigan Avenue Walk	1
2	Mid-Michigan Avenue Walk	14
3	North Michigan Avenue Walk	29
4	Oak Street Walk	43
5	State Street Loop Walk	54
6	Dearborn Street Sculpture Walk	68
7	Wacker Drive River Walk	84
8	Suhu Gallery Walk	92
9	Gold Coast Walk	102
10	Lincoln Park Walk	114
11	Oak Park Walk	125
12	University of Chicago Walk	136
13	Museum Walk	147
14	Museum of Science and Industry Walk	158
15	Brookfield Zoo Walk	169
16	Lake Front Bike Tour	178
17	North Side Drive	188
18	South Side Drive	201
19	Rush-Division Pub Crawl	217
20	Streets of Food	225
21	Greek Town Pub Crawl	236
22	Old Town Pub Crawl	242
23	Armitage-Halsted Walk	250
24	South Lincoln Avenue Pub Crawl	255
25	North Lincoln Avenue Pub Crawl	261
26	North Halsted Walk on the Almost Wild Side	266

FOREWORD

BY MIKE ROYKO

In fine detail and entertainingly, Norman Mark is going to tell you what you can expect to see while walking in various parts of Chicago. But it is the unexpected that can turn an ordinary stroll into something memorable.

Everytime I take a walk, I expect to see something unexpected. I don't know what it will be, of course, but I do know that it or he or she will be there.

Depending on the part of town, it might be an imaginative panhandler, reciting a dramatic story of hardship. We don't have a great many panhandlers in Chicago, because Mayor Daley believed the poor should be neither seen nor heard, but merely registered to vote. But a few manage to duck the paddywagons.

Always listen them out. It's worth the time and a few coins. Most tell such good lies, you'll be amazed that they avoided becoming advertising executives.

My favorite was Willie the Weeper, who sobbed and wailed and tore his hair while telling strangers that he needed train fare to get his penniless little brothers and sisters (waiting at Union Station) back home, wherever that was.

If you asked him for specifics, he wailed louder, bent as if in agony, and his answers were so racked with hickups and gulps that he was incoherent.

But the tears were somehow real—huge, glistening drops that poured down his cheeks and soaked his shirt. They were irresistible. At the end of the day, the weeper usually had enough in his pockets to fly a family to Vegas for a weekend.

The last time I saw Willie, he had grown both as a performing artist and a physical specimen. I told him: "Kid, I gave you a dollar when you were just a tyke. Now you are six-feet tall. You ought to consider getting a new act."

He choked off a sob, wiped away a tear, and said: "Hey man, beat it or I'll stomp you."

Which reminds me of a prudent rule in taking Chicago walks. Norman Mark will advise you not to carry large sums of money. That's good advice. But do not carry too little, either. Chicago respects the work ethic, and if someone goes to the trouble of trying to rob you, he might be damned disappointed and frustrated if you produce only 65 cents. Twenty or thirty dollars is a small price to pay to avoid having your hair parted down to the nose.

Not that you should walk in constant dread. I've lived here all my life and have been robbed only once, not counting when my local tax bills arrive. Just avoid dark deserted streets at night, neighborhoods that are obviously mean, lawyers' officers, and you should be just fine.

Also, don't wander into just any tavern when your feet get tired and your throat dry. Chicago's taverns are among the world's finest and friendliest, and you shouldn't hesitate to visit them. They can provide some of the best unexpected sights. I once saw a man lift a jukebox and dance with it. In another, I saw a woman win a bet by eating the contents of a one-gallon jar of pickled pig's feet, and that was long before Paul Newman did the same with hardboiled eggs. If you cheer for the home team on TV, don't order fancy mixed drinks or try to cash a check, avoid expressing liberal views on racial or political matters, and don't call the bartender "fellow" or "my good man," you will be accepted. But a little common sense is required. Don't ever walk into a bar from which people or bottles are being thrown. Keep out if you have to climb over somebody lying in the entrance.

While you are walking, someone might unexpectedly try to sell you something. It might be a flashy wristwatch, a flashy young woman, a flashy young man, or tickets to a church raffle. As a general rule, decline politely and keep walking. Whatever he is selling, you can probably get it cheaper at a regular retail outlet, or even free if you have decent teeth and bathe regularly.

Someone might unexpectedly rush up to you and shake your hand near an elevated station or a factory gate. Don't be alarmed. He is a candidate for office, and if you assure him that you think he is wonderful and your entire family is voting for him, he'll be happy and will go bother somebody else.

If somebody unexpectedly walks up to you and tries to hand you a dollar, it probably means that it is election day in Chicago, you are near a polling place, and he is a precinct captain. Just tell him you have already voted somewhere else and he'll leave you alone. On the other hand, he might raise the offer to $2, in which case you will have to make up your own mind.

When in Rome, you might get away with it. But around here, it isn't a good idea to get loudly amorous at the sight of a good looking woman. You'll be mistaken for a fiend and might wind up being charged with a dozen or so unsolved sex crimes. Or she might just spray your face with Mace.

A few other simple rules. Stay out of strange pool halls, don't intervene in domestic quarrels that spill into the street, and never argue with a Chicago cop. Nelson Algren, the city's finest writer, once advised against eating in places called "Mom's." I would advise against eating in the swinging restaurants with cutesy-poo names.

Visitors will find that Chicago, while having much that is beautiful, has its share of the ugly. Try not to be offended. It is what gives this city so much of its character. And nobody ever explained this as well as Algren:

"It isn't hard to love a town for its greater and lesser towers, its pleasant parks or its flashing ballet. Or its broad and bending boulevards, where the continuous headlights follow, one dark driver after the next, one swift car after another, all night, all night and all night. But you never truly love it till you can love its alleys too. Where the bright and morning faces of old familiar friends now wear the anxious midnight eyes of strangers a long way from home."

Have a nice walk.

PREFACE

This book offers Chicago as a gift. It presents the city in a book to you the way I think that Chicago should be shown to everyone—tourist, casual visitor, suburbanite, and city dweller.

A city is people.

Lots of people.

Good people, bad people, strange people, but mostly ordinary folks walking quickly to appointments, looking as if they didn't get enough sleep, with either happy, set or energyless faces. People of different colors, costumes and smells, and occupying different spaces and times. People who bump into each other or avoid each other. Just people.

A city is not a location, or a river, or a cathedral, or famous places. It's a bunch of people getting together and agreeing to become a city. If they all disagreed, they'd go elsewhere and all the rivers or cathedrals in the world wouldn't create a city. They'd create a ghost town.

Chicago is not a ghost town.

It is alive with lovers, laughers and folks who sometimes walk with an aura of happiness around them. It's also a city with people who will lie, cheat and steal your last false tooth.

Immediately after your first walk, you'll begin to know Chicago, under its skin, where it lives, breathes, and smells.

You'll know it in an "unword" way. You may never be able to describe what you know about Chicago. But you'll be able to shake your head, smile, and say, "That's Chicago," the next time Chicago does something stupid or generous and you read about it in a newspaper or see it on television.

The single most important fact to remember about Chicago is this:

People came here to make money.

They stay here to make money.

Money—and power or clout—runs this town.

Novelist Henry B. Fuller wrote that Chicago was "the only great city in the world to which all its citizens have come for the avowed purpose of making money. There you have its genesis, its growth, its object; and there are but few of us who are not attending to the object very strictly."

They tell the story of Augustus Swift, the Chicago packer, who asked his son, George, then age five, how much was 12 plus 13. The child didn't know and cried, "That's too hard for a little boy."

Swift yelled, "Now, George, listen! If you had 12 cents and I gave you 13 cents, how much would you have?"

George beamed and said, "Oh, a quarter, of course! Why didn't you say you meant money?"

People do not come to Chicago for the climate. Although there are balmy days which make the spirit soar, often Chicago's climate is awful. It's so hot in summer it can buckle pavement, and so cold in winter that the wind has a name—"The Hawk." If people want climate, they go to Arizona.

The same goes for scenery. Chicago's lake front is an American jewel, but few people stay here for that. If they want scenery they go to Montana, San Francisco, Michigan or Wisconsin.

While making money, while surviving the summers and the winters, Chicagoans have created scenery and, if the air conditioning works, climate.

But they have done something more important. They have created themselves. They have created monuments to the individual.

Chicago doesn't lust after fads the way New York does. The city isn't as diffuse or as vague as Los Angeles is. We don't breathe as well as Denver is supposed to, we aren't as smugly or energetically liberal as is San Francisco, we aren't convinced we know what America is the way Dallas or Houston do, and we do not have great scenery locked in our back yards the way Portland or Seattle do. (Then again, Chicago isn't as dead as Indianapolis or Cincinnati or as vacant as Milwaukee.)

But Chicago does revere the individual. The late Mayor Richard Daley telling reporters to kiss his ass. Mike Royko's daily columns filled with outrage and respect.

Chicago individuals—Daniel Burnham saving the lakefront, Al Capone slaking our thirst for beer and violence, Clarence Darrow defending the loathed, Jane Addams decreeing that poverty wasn't a sin, Montgomery Ward battling for our parks, Marshall Field saying the customer is always right and meaning it, and some guy in Bridgeport saying he's fed up working for someone else and becoming a restaurant or bar owner.

Individuals. Resisting the crowd. Creating the new path. Becoming famous or notorious by being heroic, or a genius, sometimes being the biggest and best scoundrel around, using their talents to argue, write, take bribes, help others, kill, pander, create, lead or be a fine follower.

Chicago, by now, has many traditions and, during these walks, you may encounter a few of them. For instance:

• Political corruption. There were charges of vote fraud during Chicago's first mayoral election in 1837, and they have continued ever since. By 1856, there were 1,500 more votes cast than there were eligible voters in town.

• Immorality. It was said in 1857 that one resident of a Chicago whore house had been neither sober nor outdoors for five years, and had been nude for three of them.

Chicago tends to accommodate immorality more often than it fights it. During the 1893 World's Columbian Exposition in Chicago, local politicians made a deal with our pickpockets, who agreed not to rob people at the entrance to the fair grounds. This would guarantee that the rubes would have money to spend once they got in the gates. In return, the pickpockets arrested in the downtown area between 8 a.m. and 4 p.m. would merely be taken to a police station and quickly released.

• Telling it true. A local headline about a hanging once blared "Jerked to Jesus." Another legendary headline is alleged to have proclaimed "Headless Body of Blond Found."

During that same 1893 fair, the Infanta Eulalia of Spain once refused to dine with the Potter Palmers, saying "I prefer not to meet this innkeeper's wife." Mrs. Palmer waited a few years until she was invited to meet the Infanta in Paris. Mrs. Palmer wrote her regrets this way, "I cannot meet this bibulous representative of a degenerate monarchy."

• A desire to be first, the best, the biggest or the richest and most powerful. Perhaps those emotions encouraged the infamous Herman Mudgett, who as H. H. Holmes murdered over 200 people, setting a one-man world record. He went to the gallows in 1896, leaving a South Side murder castle (since destroyed) with trap doors, lime pits, a dissecting table and a wrack, which he used to attempt to stretch a human being to twice his length. He failed.

Chicago, of course, has other, more positive traits. It can be overwhelmingly friendly, meaning that asking directions might result in an information overload. And the city usually forces its residents to greet life with a sense of humor. Remember: In Chicago, police once aided burglars and a report once noted that the longer a child stays in Chicago schools the more he or she is intellectually harmed. Read news like that every morning and the Chicagoan either laughs or cries, or both.

Before venturing into this wonderful, beautiful, outrageous, crazy, hilarious, vicious, silly hell of a town, most people have a few basic questions, such as:

1. *Is it safe?*

Chicago is safer than you believe it is. Chicago's crime statistics usually go down—which means only that the statistics are going down, not necessarily that there are fewer actual crimes.

You will be walking through a big city, so be sensible.

Don't hold your purse as if it contains a million dollars. If you do, someone might believe you and take it away.

If you are walking down a street and you do not feel safe, you may be right. Quickly return to the better-lit main streets.

Women, young or old, should not walk alone at night. It is preferable to have a companion during the daytime.

Do not worry about the crime syndicate. Although 1,000 syndicate-related deaths occurred from 1919 to 1967 and although The Boys seem to be once more hiring killers, they seldom take amateurs for rides.

Your safety has been a major factor in the creation of these walks. Local residents and police were constantly consulted about the routes. I want my kind of town to welcome you. And I want you to experience Chicago as a town of incredible ethnic diversity, of joyous experiences.

You can only know a city by walking through it. Chicago responds to the casual stroller better than most cities. Besides, walking is good for the heart and waistline and saves money on gasoline.

If you do the daytime walks when there is still sunlight and avoid sidestreets during the nighttime pub crawls, you should have many thoroughly enjoyable, even expansive, experiences. Chicago is far less dangerous than its reputation says it is.

2. *What should I wear?*

If you will walk close to the lake, it will generally seem cooler than the weather forecast indicates. If it is winter, dress warmer than you think you ought to. If it is summer, dress in lighter clothes than the joking TV weathermen indicate. If it is raining, wait. It will probably stop before the day ends.

3. *How can I find my way?*

Chicago has a simple street system. Except for some old, diagonal, Indian trails, such as Lincoln or Milwaukee Aves., Chicago streets form a regular grid pattern. State and Madison is zero, with numbers going up to the north, south, east and west of that. If the numbers are going down, you are heading towards the center of the city. If they are going up, you are gradually leaving town.

4. *Is it necessary to act like a Chicagoan while walking?*

No. However, if you want to, talk through your nose, believe you know everything, dress a little out of style, and every so often say, "Yah, but the city works."

Enjoy.

Norman Mark
Chicago
1987

1 SOUTH MICHIGAN AVENUE WALK

BUCKINGHAM FOUNTAIN TO THE LIBRARY

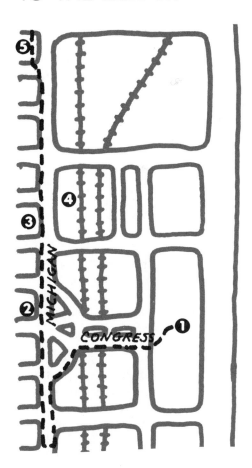

1. Buckingham Fountain
2. Auditorium Building
3. Orchestra Hall
4. Art Institute
5. Chicago Public Library (Cultural Center)

Time: About two hours, less if you walk quickly.
To get there: Take a Number 2, 126, or 149 bus to Congress Pkwy., also known as the Eisenhower Expressway, get off and walk east to the fountain, about a block away. Or take a 145, 148 or 154 bus, get off at Congress and Michigan, walk east two blocks past the Equestrian Statues to the fountain. Or take the

1

subway to Van Buren or Harrison, walk to Congress and then east.

If you drive: Exit Lake Shore Drive at either Balbo, turning right on Columbus, or Jackson, turning left on Columbus. Look immediately for a parking space. If you do not find one, go east on Congress (Eisenhower Expressway), bear right and, just over the bridge as you near the refurbished Equestrian Statues, take a right and park in the city's underground lot.

Buckingham Fountain and Grant Park

We begin at Buckingham Fountain because all explorations of Chicago should begin and end at its lakefront, its glory.

Buckingham Fountain, given to Chicago by Miss Kate Buckingham in 1927, is, according to some Chicagoans, the largest fountain in the world. Modeled after the Latona Fountain in Versailles, sitting in a section of Grant Park also modeled after Versailles, Buckingham Fountain is 280 feet across the bottom of the pool. The central spout shoots 135 feet in the air and the pool contains 1,500,000 gallons of water.

What's more important than all those mind-boggling statistics is the fact that Buckingham Fountain can become your secret pleasure spot on earth, where man's and nature's beauty combine in a unique manner for you. The Fountain has a delicate, cooling, lung-filling, inspiring beauty all its own, a lakefront jewel set off by a comprehensible skyline.

The fountain operates daily from 11:30 a.m. to 10 p.m. from May 30 to Sept. 30, with major, no-holds-barred, challenge-the-rainbows color displays from 9 to 10 p.m. It's something to see, day or night.

Face the skyline, look to your right and you can see, through the trees to the north, the Petrillo Bandshell, where there are many free summer concerts.

Less than a half mile from you, just south of the bandshell, Robert Bartlett flew the largest hand-launched kite, a monster 83 feet long with 820 square feet of cloth. It happened on April 24, 1974, as part of the WIND-AM Annual Kite Fly.

Now walk west, towards the skyline along Congress Pkwy., past the Equestrian Statues on each side of Congress Plaza. They were created by Ivan Mestrovic and unveiled in Oct., 1929. Turn left (south) on Michigan and continue to walk along Grant Park.

Up ahead, you'll see the Augustus Saint-Gaudens statue of Gen. John A. Logan, unveiled in 1897 and given lasting fame during the 1968 Democratic Convention riots, when peace marchers (or hippies or yippies) attempted to climb the statue and were beaten by police.

The park brings Wednesday evening, Aug. 28, 1968, back to memory—the alleged "police riot." The surging crowds in front of the

Conrad Hilton. The nightsticks, tear gas and screams. The harsh television lights. Writer Shana Alexander described the scene this way: "The baby-blue helmeted police operate like a wolf pack, cutting out one or two demonstrators at a time from the swirling, heaving throng and pounding them into the pavement of Michigan Ave. as the mob with an inarticulate roar falls back into the bright-green park . . ."

Conrad Hilton Hotel

Cross the street to the Conrad Hilton, the subject of a $180 million restoration. This grand hotel now anchors South Michigan Avenue looking even better than it did when it opened in 1927 as the Stephens Hotel with 3,000 rooms. The Hilton became luxurious army barracks for a while, and now has 1,680 rooms, many with two baths.

Look up to the top three floors, known as The Towers, where corporate executives have their own lobby, concierge, honor bar and twice-daily maid service.

At the very top, there are the Imperial Suites and their names can be justified because Queen Elizabeth slept there in 1959, during her trip to America to open the St. Lawrence Seaway. They were added to the hotel when helicopters plunked down the pre-fabricated suites prior to the Queen's visit.

The suites cost $1,500 a night, but that includes spectacular views of the lake and two bedrooms.

But there are even better deals. For $4,000 a night ($6,000 for two nights on the weekend), you could rent the Crown Imperial Suite, with three bedrooms, five baths, an enormous living room with a grand piano and a see-through fireplace which looks into the study-bar, a jacuzzi capable of seating six people in comfort. The suite comes complete with a butler in a formal tuxedo and a downstairs maid wearing a tasteful black dress with white lace collar and cuffs. The hotel will offer free use of a chauffeured limousine with the suite.

By the way, in case the President should want to use the suite, there is a private switchboard which is already hooked up to lines going directly to the White House.

On the weekends, the suite comes with a dinner for 20 or cocktails for 50 of your closest friends. Don't worry, the dining room table can seat that many.

If you are hungry, or thirsty, there are four restaurants in the Hilton: Buckingham's, which has a gourmet menu and a harpist; the Pavillion, which is open round the clock; the Lakeside Green, which offers high tea at 3 p.m. and chamber music in the evenings; and the Fast Lane, a deli.

Before leaving the Hilton, do look around the ornate lobby featuring murals on the ceiling and gorgeous soft carpeting.

Next turn north, and notice the Blackstone Theater, at 60 E. Balbo, to see what play is currently there. It's probably among the best in town.

Sheraton-Blackstone Hotel

After crossing Michigan at Balbo, walk west towards the Blackstone Theater a few feet and enter the Sheraton-Blackstone Hotel, to be greeted by a lobby with huge chandeliers, sculptured plaster and wood. Reflect for a moment that no one will ever build a lobby like this again (and perhaps reflect why anyone would want to in the first place).

This hotel, the temporary home of ten presidents, is also the site of the original smoke-filled room, suite 404-5-6. Around 2 a.m. on a warm evening in 1920, Warren G. Harding was called to these rooms, was told that the nomination for president might be his and was ordered, "We think you should tell us, on your conscience and before God, whether there is anything that might be brought up against you that would embarrass the [Republican] party . . ."

Many presidential candidates would have been insulted at the suggestion contained in that order, but Harding took about ten minutes, perhaps considering his mistress(es), illegitimate child or the rumor that he had Negro blood. Harding said there wouldn't be any impediment to his becoming president.

Later, the *New York Times* described Harding as "the firm and perfect flower of cowardice and imbecility of the Senatorial cabal," but that didn't prevent him from being elected and leading the second most scandal-prone Republican administration in American history.

Spertus Museum of Judaica

Walk diagonally across the lobby, down some stairs and out the Michigan Avenue door. Turn left (north), continue up Michigan Avenue to the Maurice Spertus Museum of Judaica, at 618 S. Michigan.

This museum claims to have the only permanent room dedicated to the memory of the 6,000,000 Jews killed in Nazi Germany, the Bernard and Rochelle Zell Holocaust Museum, which displays a concentration camp uniform and soap made from human fat.

The Museum, with its exhibits of Jewish traditions, and holidays, is open Monday through Thursday 10 a.m. to 5 p.m. and Friday and Sunday 10 a.m. to 3 p.m. It is closed Saturdays. Admission is $1 for adults, 50 cents for children.

Americana Congress Hotel

Walking past Columbia College, a school with an excellent communications curricula, at 600 St. Michigan, we find the Americana Congress Hotel, at 532 S. Michigan, where industrialist J. Pierpont

Balcony view of the Auditorium Theater

Morgan is supposed to have imbibed a bit much and fallen into the crystal fountain. The Presidential suite, complete with a bathroom larger than most hotel rooms, is available for $450 a day. Franklin D. Roosevelt rehearsed his acceptance speech here in 1932.

Auditorium Theater

Now cross Congress, with its always growling traffic rushing away from or towards the lake, and turn left, walking west towards a large sign saying "Auditorium." Enter the foyer and ask the person in the ticket window for either a free brochure about the Auditorium Theater or buy a ticket to a future event. Look above the lobby doorways to the six stained glass windows there, allegedly the first public works of Frank Lloyd Wright.

You can peek through the windows into the lobby, but the warmth of the Auditorium itself will escape you. Unless you are part of a group of ten or more and arrange a tour, the only way to see the Auditorium is to buy a ticket for an event there. It costs too much to light it up so it can be seen properly by individuals requesting tours.

But remember, you are standing in and near a tribute to the indomitable wills of at least three people—the 1889 architects Louis Sullivan and Dankmar Adler (with an assist from Wright, at a $25 a week salary), and Mrs. Bea Spachner, who helped raise the money to restore what Frank Lloyd Wright called "the greatest room for music and opera in the world—bar none."

The Auditorium Theater was first opened to great fanfare in 1889. On Nov. 25, 1910, Mary Garden performed *Salome* there and the chief of police almost closed the show, saying, "Miss Garden wallowed around like a cat in a bed of catnip . . ." Billy Sunday, the preacher famed for attempting to close Chicago down, condemned Miss Garden on Monday and took her out for an ice cream soda on Tuesday.

(For true nutty behavior by an opera performer, we must remember P. Brignoli, a Chicago favorite who flourished just before the Auditorium opened. Brignoli never allowed prima donnas to touch him, never did anything on Fridays, was frightened of the number 13, and carried an old stuffed deer's head with him as a child would a teddy bear. After talking and singing to it, he would place it on his window sill and order it to bring good weather. If the weather the next day turned out well, Brignoli would pet his deer. On lousy days, he would box its ears and refuse to speak to it. By all accounts he was a good singer, so no one cared what he did to his mangy deer's head.)

The Auditorium has featured the performances of Rosa Raisa, Marian Anderson and Adelina Patti. On Nov. 18, 1919, Amelita Galli-Curci premiered there in "Rigoletto." The audience made her famous overnight because it "rose up, shouted, screamed, stamped, stood on its figurative head and otherwise demeaned itself as no staid, sophisticated Saturday afternoon audience ever (had) acted before or since," one reviewer noted.

Then came World War II, and Adler and Sullivan's acoustically perfect hall was painted red, turned into a home for miniature golf and bowling, and wrecking crews waited in the wings.

They were defeated by Mrs. John V. (Bea) Spachner, a short lady, blessed with unyielding determination. With architect Harry Weese

6

cutting corners and paring budgets, Mrs. Spachner and others raised $3,000,000, restored the Auditorium and reopened it on Oct. 31, 1967 with a performance by the New York City Ballet.

Now retrace your steps, returning to Michigan Avenue, turn left and enter Roosevelt University. Try to ignore the modern-looking chandeliers in the lobby and imagine what that grand staircase before you must have looked like in 1889!

Fine Arts Building

Return to Michigan Avenue, walk north (to your left again) to 410 S. Michigan and enter the Fine Arts Building, which proclaims above its doorway, "All passes—Art alone endures."

Walk inside and, on your left, read the list of tenants, which should include a few opera companies, a modern dance studio, teachers of piano, guitar, cello and art, churches, architects, hypnotists, yoga practitioners, the Fine Arts Denture Clinic and assorted kooks. The Fine Arts Theater lives up to the name by presenting the finest artistic films around, some with subtitles and some with impossible English accents which need subtitles! Outside, George Mitchell's Artists Snack Shop has a sidewalk cafe with astro turf and white tables and chairs. A nice place to sit and observe Michigan Avenue or listen to opera singers practicing in the Fine Arts.

Opened in 1893, the Fine Arts Building was once the center of Chicago culture. Frank Baum and W. D. Denslow created the "Wizard of Oz" here. *The Little Review* was published here by Margaret Anderson. Despite four orders from the U.S. Post Office that the magazine be burned, Ms. Anderson continued printing sections of James Joyce's *Ulysses,* and the censorship battle, which began in 1918, continued for three years.

The Little Theater movement in America was founded here in a 91-seat Grecian Temple, where Chicagoans got their first views of works by Shaw and Strindberg. And there are still art studios on the 10th floor, where sculptor Lorado Taft once worked.

Now continue to walk north on Michigan.

Railway Exchange Building

As you stand at Jackson and Michigan, look to the west to the Railway Exchange Building, the 17-story structure at 80 E. Jackson. Notice that this once-dusty building is now clean, handsome and grand. Thank you, restorers.

In 1904, architect Daniel Burnham's workroom was located on the top floor of this building and, in 1909, Burnham and Edward H. Bennett released "The Plan of Chicago," which attempted to mold the future of the city. Burnham, as fine a salesman as he was a city planner, said, "Make no little plans. They have no magic to stir men's blood."

Burnham envisioned the lakefront as a playground for Chicagoans with manmade islands there for recreation. He saw a modern highway system, railroad tracks coming into the city in an orderly manner, and so on. Eventually, before the Depression, World War II and greed stopped things, about half his vision became reality. Because of Burnham, Michigan Avenue was widened, new bridges were thrown over the Chicago River, railroad tracks were sunk below ground level, the shoreline was changed and new park lands were bought.

The lake- or river-fronts of almost every other major city on the globe are either devoted to shipping, industry or private ownership. Most of Chicago's lakefront is parks. Burnham wrote, "The lakefront by right belongs to the people. It affords their one great unobstructed view, stretching away to the horizon, where water and clouds seem to meet. No mountains or high hills enable us to look over broad expanses of the earth's surface; and perforce we must come even to the margin of the lake for such a survey of nature. These views calm thoughts and feelings, and afford escape from the petty things of life . . . Not a foot of its shores should be appropriated by individuals to the exclusion of the people." Alas, his words are too often forgotten.

Orchestra Hall

Continuing up Michigan Avenue, we pass Orchestra Hall, at 220 S. Michigan, home of the world renowned Chicago Symphony Orchestra, with the names of Bach, Mozart, Beethoven, Schubert and Wagner over the entrance. This has not always been a peaceful place. Desire DeFauw, conductor from 1943–47, was driven out of town by criticism of his programs, conducting, musicianship and clothes. Chicagoans take their music seriously!

The Art Institute

You'll see the Art Institute across the street. It's guarded by two lions designed in 1894 by Edward L. Kemys, a dentist who became a sculptor. It is not true that they only roar when a virgin walks by.

You may be getting tired by now and should probably save an Art Institute tour for another day. However, if you're feeling energetic, the riches of the Art Institute are available to you through a free pamphlet at the information desk titled "Not to Be Missed." Suggested admission is $4.50 for adults, $2.25 for students, children and senior citizens, but Tuesday is free.

The maps in the pamphlet will guide you to Grant Wood's "American Gothic," and paintings by El Greco, Rembrandt, Renoir and others. But the maps are terrible, which is an advantage. Because of

Georges Seurat's *Sunday Afternoon on the Island of La Grande Jatte* in the Art Institute

the confusion they cause, you will see many more paintings than you thought you would.

Refreshments are straight ahead in the Art Institute, through Gunsaulus Hall and down the stairs. When you've found Louise Nevelson's "American Dream", you will be in front of the delightful Garden Restaurant and McKinlock court, with its "Fountain of the Titans" by Carl Milles. This outdoor dining area is open May 23 to Labor Day, with the typical Chicago provision "weather permitting." There is also The Promenade restaurant near the transplanted Stock Exchange room.

The Art Institute is justly famous for its riches. There are rooms with walls overfilled with paintings by Manet, Degas, Corot, Renoir, Cezanne, Monet, Gaugin, Seurat, Matisse, etc.

Many of these paintings were collected with typical Chicago hustle. Many rich Chicagoans saw no reason to collect masterpieces any differently than the way they bought hogs. One trustee, using techniques perfected by Gustavus Swift in the stock yards, bought four works of art before breakfast and before an agent from the Louvre could get to them.

In 1890, some Chicago collectors confessed to a New York newspaper that they weren't sure what they bought (the paintings they brought back included works by Rembrandt, Franz Hals and Meindert Hobbema). The paper concluded that the paintings probably cost "$1,000 a foot" and that Chicago would greet them "in huge floats, drawn by a team of milk-white Berkshire hogs . . ."

Continuing up Michigan Avenue, you'll pass the Chicago Association of Commerce and Industry offices at 130 S. Michigan, where polite folks will answer questions about hotels and tours of Chicago.

Buildings by Wright and Sullivan

Walking north, you will shortly be at Monroe and Michigan. If you look to the northwest, you'll see the 14-story, Tudor Gothic building known as the University Club, built in 1909. Frank Lloyd Wright called this structure "an effete gray ghost."

The facade of the Gage Building, at 18 S. Michigan, was designed by Louis Sullivan, who said "form follows function," meaning what's going on inside the building should be reflected on the outside. Sullivan was a master at intricate adornment of buildings. He was also egotistical, arrogant, tactless, and died in a South Side flophouse in 1925 convinced he was a failure.

History: Ward Defends the Lakefront

Crossing Madison Street, we come to the Tower Building, at 6 N. Michigan. And it is here that we should remember A. Montgomery Ward, another individual who stood against nearly everyone in his time to win something valuable for generations to come.

In 1890, Ward looked down on Michigan Avenue from his offices in the Tower Building and saw, to the east, shacks, garbage, circus litter, rotting freight cars and an armory used for masquerade balls thrown by Chicago aldermen and featuring fallen women (or, rather, ones then in the midst of falling). Ward is supposed to have shouted to his lawyer, "Merrick, this is a damned shame! Go and do something about it." They found a notation on an ancient map, scribbled by the commissioners who created the Illinois and Michigan Canal. The ground between Michigan Avenue and the lake from Madison Street to 12th Street had the notation, "Public Ground—A Common to Remain Forever Open, Clear and Free of Any Buildings, or Other Obstruction Whatever."

To make that come true, Ward spend $50,000 and 20 years of his life. He was repeatedly in court and he eventually won. The Illinois Supreme Court ruled that no building could be built east of Michigan Avenue unless all property owners along the avenue agreed to its construction (that's a major reason why a Grant Park Bandshell has been there since 1933).

The Art Institute was allowed to remain east of Michigan Av. only after the signature of Mrs. Sarah Daggett, the one owner who refused to agree to its being there, was forged by her husband. The courts of the 1890s upheld a husband's right to do this.

Ward hated publicity and didn't particularly like it when the *Chicago Tribune* called him a "human icicle." In 1909, when the issue was finally decided, Ward gave out a single interview. He said, "I fought for the poor people of Chicago, not the millionaires . . . Here is park frontage on the lake, comparing favorably with the Bay of Naples, which city officials would crowd with buildings, transforming the breathing spot for the poor into a showground of the educated rich. I do not think it is right." He then added, perhaps wistfully, "Perhaps I may yet see the public appreciate my efforts. But I doubt it."

Chicago Public Library Cultural Center

From here it is a short walk to the Chicago Public Library Cultural Center, at 78 E. Washington, which ends this tour.

Today, the Cultural Center, built in 1897, is a joy to behold. This wasn't always so. When Nobel Prize-winning author Saul Bellow studied there in the '30s and '40s, the inside of the Chicago Public Library Main Building was over-heated, painted an ugly green and dirty. A depressing place.

That began to change in 1973, when the library announced plans to move its books from its central location to the Mandel Building, hidden behind the Equitable Building, about a mile north of you. Chicago has lots of books and, at present, it's difficult to find most of them, although the city often announces new plans for a central library. There was discussion involving using the old Goldblatt's State Street store, but that only led to controversy.

The old Central Library building stands on historical turf. Dearborn Park, where Abraham Lincoln spoke in favor of the new Republican Party and against slavery in 1856, was on this property until 1892. There was a grandstand across Michigan Avenue for the Chicago White Stockings, who became Anson's Colts and eventually, because they were so young, the Chicago Cubs. Thus, the White Stockings are ancestors of the Cubs and not the Chicago White Sox. Over 100,000 people cheered the White Stockings when the team came home after beating Memphis 157 to 1 in the 1880s. In 1876, with the help of a player named Billy Sunday, the team won the National League championship.

Enter The Cultural Center by walking to your left (west) on the north side of Washington. This entrance resembles a Roman temple. The Randolph Street entrance is more Grecian. Ideas for bits and

11

Preston Bradley Hall in the Chicago Public Library Cultural Center

pieces of the entire building were taken from famous buildings elsewhere—it was the style of the day.

Just inside the door, above you, the stairway forms a Venetian Bridge. The Carrara marble is decorated with rare, dark green marble from Connemara, Ireland, with designs by the House of Louis Tiffany. Today, after a soap-and-water bath, the place sparkles. Notice the mosaics under the landings and the sea green lights if you walk to the far right or left before going up the stairs.

Walk slowly up to the third floor and then just look at that huge Tiffany dome, magnificent, overdone, a little ugly, but utterly original and back lit after being covered over for decades. Sit down in a comfortable chair in Preston Bradley Hall (named after a local minister who served on the library board for over 50 somnolent years).

Take the elevator to the fourth floor, ponder the $12,000,000 spent by the Public Buildings Commission to bring this building into the 20th century (thank you, Commission, for the air conditioning), walk by the iron fourth floor landing, modeled after the Bridge of Sighs in Venice and walk to the south end of the building.

The doors you walk through, everyone is told, are "very like" those in the Erechtheum at Athens. The second room you'll pass through, the children's library, is modeled after an assembly hall in the Doge's Palace in Venice. If you look closely at the "pillars" in the center of the wall facing the windows, you'll see an almost indiscernible line about 12 feet above the floor. When the old wall radiators were taken down because modern heating was installed, it was discovered that the false pillars on the walls did not extend below the radiators. New "ancient" pillars were built to approximately match the old ones and the line indicates where they were joined.

Now walk down to the second floor and the location of the old GAR Museum, where you'll see a second Tiffany Dome, with more yellow in it and with more of a spidery design. Walk on down and out the Randolph side, having seen a 19th century building gloriously entering the 20th century.

This ends your South Michigan Avenue tour.

Rest. Your feet deserve it!

2 MID-MICHIGAN AVENUE WALK

RANDOLPH TO ONTARIO

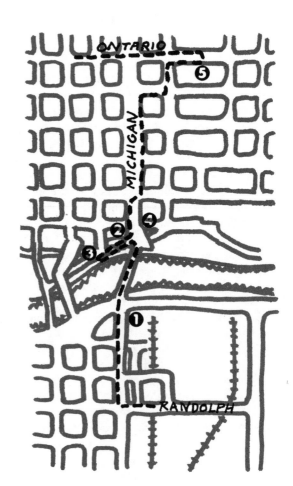

1. Fort Dearborn Massacre Site
2. Wrigley Building
3. Sun-Times
4. Tribune Tower
5. Museum of Contemporary Art

Time: About two hours, more if you find a restaurant you enjoy.
To get there: Many CTA buses go by Michigan and Randolph, where this walk begins, including the 1, 2, 3, 16, 58, 131, and 157 buses. In addition, the Illinois Central stops there, and the

CTA subway stops at Randolph and State, just two blocks west of Michigan. There is also city parking for cars in lots with entrances just off Michigan.

Prudential and Standard Oil Buildings

This walk begins with huge buildings and ends with paintings and fine restaurants. It is a stroll up an avenue built for walking while looking smart, carefree and sassy.

The Prudential Building looms before you, as you stand at Michigan and Randolph, with Prudential's trademark, as 65-ton sculpture of the Rock of Gibraltar, as part of this building. This building is the home of Leo Burnett, one of the largest advertising agencies in the world. They have represented McDonald's, United Air Lines and Green Giant.

Beaubein Court, the one-block street just west of the Prudential Building, and next to the Chicago Bar and Grill, is named after a wildly irresponsible, but charming, early Chicagoan, Mark Beaubein, who had 23 children by three wives. When he was supposed to be running the ferry across the Chicago river, he was off racing horses. When he opened the town's first hotel, which was in existence when Chicago incorporated in 1833, he let the kitchen run itself, often sang an endless ballad about the fall of Detroit, and said, "I play the fiddle like the devil and keep the hotel like hell." His beds consisted of a blanket, which he'd give to new guests, only to steal it back from them as soon as they went to sleep, so as to have it available for the next guest. Mark never ran out of beds. Sounds like the kind of guy who only deserves a one-block street.

The Standard Oil Building, behind (to the east of) the Prudential Building, is the world's tallest marble-clad building, with 8,000 tons of Carrara marble covering this structure. A strike of marble cutters in Italy in 1974 stopped construction of this building and it stood half nude for several months.

The sculpture in the reflecting pool is a bunch of rods which is supposed to "produce an infinite variety of mellow and lingering musical chords." Harry Bertoia's work does make clanging noises when the wind blows, but stands mute on calm days.

History: Jake Lingle Shot

Return to Michigan Avenue and note the entrance to the Illinois Central Railroad platform, off Randolph near a busy newsstand against the Cultural Center. Ric's Newsstand is owned by Ric Graff and his dog, Rocky. It is one of Chicago's busiest, and it is open from 5 a. m. to 9 p. m. Most days he offers 111 different comic books. If you wish to hear a salty tale, ask Ric to describe the last time he

15

Standard Oil Building

captured a mugger or sodomite. His language might fry the gym shoes off a passing little old lady.

Chicago Tribune crime reporter Jake Lingle was shot in this IC underpass by a tall, young, blond man on June 9, 1930. Chicago criminals had always been warned they would be in serious trouble if they killed a policeman or reporter, so Lingle's death was shocking. Then it was discovered that, on a salary of $65 a week, he had a suite in a downtown hotel, a West Side home and a Wisconsin summer home. He wore tailor-made suits, English shoes and had a $100,000 account with his stock broker. Clearly, this young man knew how to save money.

It was later whispered that Lingle, a close pal of Al Capone, took $25,000 of the Syndicate's money and, instead of bribing a judge, lost it on the stock market. Lingle allegedly later told "the boys" that they "can't touch a newspaperman." It was a serious mistake.

Muffins on Michigan Avenue

Walk north on Michigan Avenue. Illinois Center, across the street to the east, is one of several recent additions to Michigan Ave. If it is raining, dash inside and explore the confusing passageways which connect this multi-building development, allowing you to walk dry shod to the east towards the lake.

However, if the weather is good, stroll up Michigan Avenue, and perhaps have a "fine gourmet muffin" at Newbury Muffins, 320 N. Michigan, one of the earliest places to capitalize on Chicago's recent muffin craze. It obviously filled a need, but it was one Chicagoans didn't even know they had before 1985.

Continue north, stopping in the 333 N. Michigan Building to see the Art Moderne elevator doors by Edgar Miller (unless Art Moderne elevator doors bore you, in which case you can skip this particular thrill).

Illinois Center

Walk north to Wacker Drive and turn east. If you go up the stairs, you will be standing between the One and Two Illinois Center Buildings, two, huge, simple boxes designed by Ludwig Mies Van Der Rohe. These buildings are over the Illinois Center air rights, which extend from where you are standing nearly to the lake. The railroad owns the land for its tracks, but won permission to sell the air above the land (air is free nearly everywhere but in Chicago). Some day dozens of huge simple boxes will be built to the east of you, meaning that someday air and boxes will make lots of people rich. It boggles the mind.

WFMT

If you continue east, to 303 E. Wacker, you will find the home of WFMT, the finest classical music station in America. It insists that its advertisements contain no jingles and that its own announcers read all commercials. It broadcasts the Chicago Symphony, the

Lyric Opera and single-handedly supports folk music and Chicago comedy with its "Midnight Special," heard each Saturday on 98.7 FM at 10:15 p.m., or maybe 10:20, or maybe 10:10, depending on newscasts.

Studs Terkel, author of *Division St. America* and *Working,* is host of a daily interview program on WFMT. Studs' office is decorated with an enlarged newspaper story from Bangkok, saying "A police spokesman said the battle began when the bandit gang, disguised as policemen, challenged a group of policemen disguised as bandits." Studs, ever ready to enlist his raspy voice in a good cause, points to that story and regularly shouts, "That's Chicago!"

Hyatt Regency

The structure immediately to the east is the Hyatt Regency Hotel, which has a waterfall in its lobby. The constantly running water causes the help to go to the washroom a lot. There are five restaurants here: Mrs. O'Leary's, a turn-of-the-century saloon; Capt. Streeter's; with a buffet; Stetson, a steak and seafood restaurant; Scampi, which is surrounded by fountains and a pond with a piano player or string quartet performing from 7 a. m. until midnight; and Skyway, located in the walkway between the two buildings. Just before Christmas, the Hyatt is host to "the world's largest Christmas party," an event sure to be in the Guinness book some day.

Fort Dearborn Massacre

Return to Michigan and Wacker, look at your feet and you'll see the outlines of Fort Dearborn etched in the pavement. The fort was evacuated on Aug. 15, 1812, and everyone who left was involved in the subsequent massacre.

The fort was surrounded by Pottawatomie Indians friendly to the British and the troops weren't very happy about leaving. As they opened the gates at 9 a.m., they struck up the "Dead March." Famed Indian scout Capt. William Wells blackened his face, symbolic of the fact that he was already a dead man. It was not the happiest parade Michigan Avenue has ever seen.

About 500 Indians attacked the 18th Street and the Lake, killing 24 soldiers, 12 civilian men, two women and a dozen children. The Indians lost only 15 braves and were still bragging about the victory 125 years later.

The wife of the commander of the fort was eventually bought back from captivity for a mule and ten bottles of whiskey, which sounds cheap unless it was good whiskey.

Later the white man got his revenge on the Pottawatomie by gypping them out of everything but their loin cloths by 1835.

The Wrigley Building and the site of Fort Dearborn

Cross the Michigan Avenue bridge. The north side of this bridge was the beginning of an Indian trail which once led to Green Bay, Wisconsin. Any trace of this trail has been obliterated.

Wrigley Building

Cross to the west side of Michigan and pass between the two Wrigley Building Towers, the approximate site of the home of Jean Baptist Point Du Sable, a black, and Chicago's first settler. Some historians say that Jean Baptist Guillory or Guyari or Guary or Gary was here first, but he didn't stay long and no one knows too much about him, so First Settler Award usually goes to Du Sable. Du Sable's cabin was 40 feet long and he owned 44 hens, 38 hogs, 30 cattle, two calves and two mules—Chicago's first tycoon.

The Wrigley Building, once the home of such radio shows as "The WBBM Air Theater," "Ma Perkins," and "The Guilding Light" is the corporate headquarters of the world's largest chewing gum manufacturer. It is not generally known that the 16th floor board room of the William Wrigley Jr. Chewing Gum Co. also houses the world's finest chewing gum wrapper museum. It's a secret collection, not open to the public, and the result of salesmen around the world sending sample wrappers back to the home office.

William Wrigley Jr., founder of the chewing gum empire, began as a soap salesman who gave away baking soda as a premium. Folks loved the baking soda so much that he began selling the stuff, and gave away gum as a premium. When that got popular, Wrigley began an empire, and the world lost a soap salesman.

Wrigley taught the world to chew gum. He died in 1932, a man who was expelled from eighth grade, who began business life with $35 in his pocket, and who left a $200,000,000 estate and lots of people with gum on their shoes.

His Wrigley Building has been described as "a luscious birthday cake down whose sides someone had drawn his fingers." The building is floodlit at night, creating a beautiful area—the Michigan Avenue bridge over the Chicago River reflecting the Wrigley Building.

Chicago Sun-Times

Now proceed between the two towers and into the little plaza in front of the *Chicago Sun-Times* (and the former *Chicago Daily News*) Building. Isn't this a most relaxing spot in the bustling city?

Next enter the *Sun Times* Building. There is a long corridor before you, where you can see the huge presses to your left or an exhibit of photos or posters to your right.

Mike Royko, Sidney J. Harris, Ann Landers, John Fischetti, Irv Kupcinet and others have worked in this building which, because it

A sunny day in the Equitable Plaza

once housed the *Chicago Daily News,* has inherited a 100-year-old tradition of fine journalism produced by quirky employees.

In 1876, the paper editorially supported the Indians in their massacre of Custer and the *News* almost went under. In the '20s, a foreign correspondent was not recognized by a guard, who didn't let him in the *News'* building. So he went around the corner and filed a 12,000-word story by telegraph—collect.

When Richard Loeb, who with Nathan Leopold committed the "Crime of the Century" by killing Bobby Franks, was stabbed in Stateville Prison during an alleged homosexual quarrel, *Daily News* reporter Robert J. Casey wrote, "Richard Loeb, who graduated from college with honors at the age of 15 and who was a master of the English language, today ended his sentence with a proposition."

Retrace your steps back through the plaza. You will see Don Roth's River Plaza Restaurant, which has outdoor dining in the summer and lots of wood, different levels and semi-secluded nooks for dining indoors in the winter. It is just west of a McDonald's. Ubiquitous. Ubiquitous.

Riccardo's: Watering Hole for Writers

The Wrigley Building Restaurant is also before you. Every time I eat there, I have the feeling incredibly important deals are being made at the next table. Often they are. Down below the plaza is Riccardo's, a watering hole for local journalists and a fine Italian restaurant owned by Greeks. Do read the newspaper story near the cloakroom about the men of a small Greek village who came to Chicago, who own dozens of local restaurants and who support many relatives back home. Behind the bar of Riccardo's there are seven murals commissioned in 1935 by the original Ric Riccardo. Ivan Albright and Aaron Bohrod, two WPA artists, are among those represented. In addition, when journalists gather at Ric's on a cold Friday evening, sometimes a man and a woman will begin singing "Indian Love Call" from opposite ends of the bar.

You'll also note a small area in front of Riccardo's, the outdoor cafe. Here local writers exchange bon mots while looking out at two parking lots, the underside of Wabash Avenue, and while smelling car exhausts and the fumes of the Bommer Chocolate Co., a local factory. A Campari and soda here, for some reason, is the height of local sophistication.

History: Indian War Dance

The last great Indian war dance in Chicago history began very near the corner where Riccardo's stands. The Indians had given up all their claims to land in and around Chicago, and, on Aug. 18, 1835, had to leave town.

About 800 braves gathered near Riccardo's, naked except for loin cloths, their faces streaked with war paint accented with black, their hair adorned with hawks' and eagles' feathers. They made their way into the city, leaping, crouching, creeping, yelling, howling, stopping at every home to scare the daylights out of the residents. Some local newsmen, when leaving Riccardo's, do the same thing today.

One witness, Judge Dean Caton, wrote, "Their countenances had assumed an expression of all the worst passions . . . fierce anger, terrible hate, dire revenge, remorseless cruelty . . . Their muscles stood out in great hard knots . . . Their tomahawks and clubs were thrown and brandished in every direction . . . and with every step and every gesture they utter the most frightful yells in every imaginable key and note, though generally the highest and shrillest possible . . . this raging savagery glistening in the sun, reeking with steamy sweat, fairly frothing at the mouths as with unaffected rage. . ." The city was not to see a parade of its like until the Shriners began coming to town in the 20th century.

In 1962 an anthropologist noticed a Pottawatomie reservation near Topeka, Kansas. He learned that these were the descendants of the original braves who attacked the Fort Dearborn inhabitants. They still had some handcrafted silver made by a local pioneer, John Kinzie, and they remembered stories about their wonderful victory in 1812.

Billy Goat Tavern

Walk down the steps to Rush Street and take a right on Hubbard, which is in front of Riccardo's. Yes, this is a dark, dank, slightly frightening area but it will take you to a dark, dank, delightful bar called the Billy Goat Tavern, which was either "est." or "born" (depending on which sign you read) in 1934.

Here reporters, printers and all who can find the place come for "Cheezborger, cheezborger, no Pepsi, Coke," a phrase heard here years before the late John Belushi said it on Saturday Night Live.

Read the many stories written about the Billy Goat, all lovingly preserved on the walls, including novelist Bill Granger's tribute calling it the "best tavern" in Chicago and Mike Royko's hilarious account of the determined streaker in the tavern at 1:30 a.m. one night.

But take special note of the stories about an important event in 1945, a day which darkened Chicago history for four decades. Sam "Billy Goat" Sianis tried to take Savonia, his goat, to the Cubs' World Series game. Despite having box seat tickets, the goat was tossed out of the game, leaving an angry Sam to pronounce a curse on the Cubs: They would not again appear in any World Series until his goat was allowed back in the game.

Later, when the Cubs lost that 1945 World Series, Sam sent a telegram to the team owner, Phil K. Wrigley, asking, "Who smells now?"

The curse was quite effective. The poor Cubs not only remained out of the World Series, they generally stayed in last place until 1982, when a goat was invited back to a Cubs game. The Cubs have been doing somewhat better since then, but they have yet to be in a World Series.

Reflect on the power of the curse, enjoy a dark, cold draft of beer, eat lots of fresh pickles with a "cheezborger, cheezborger," note that the washrooms are labelled Nanny or Billy, and then continue our

A gargoyle on the fourth floor beneath the balcony of Tribune Tower

trek by going east (left) on Hubbard to the corner, taking another left and going up the concrete stairs, which have needed repair for decades. You emerge on Michigan Avenue, where you will proceed north.

Tribune Tower

When you reach the east side of Michigan Avenue, you will be standing before the Tribune Tower. If you walk around to the rear of the Tower (the south east corner), notice the stones of famous buildings imbedded in the tower, allegedly including bits of the Alamo, the Great Pyramid, Notre Dame, the Parthenon, Pompeii Baths, the Colosseum, St. Peter's, Hamlet's castle, the Great Wall of China and Westminister Abbey. Along the east side of the building, you'll also see 18 famous *Chicago Tribune* front pages, from Lee surrendering at Appomattox to "Assassin Kills Kennedy." The Trib's most famous front page, the one saying that Thomas Dewey had been elected president, isn't there.

When you are reading the front pages, the Mandel Building is to your right. The Chicago Public Library is now on the 12th floor of this building. It is easy *not* to find.

Return to Michigan Avenue, and consider Tribune Tower (you may have to step back to the Michigan Avenue bridge to do so). The *Tribune* held a competition in 1923 and the design you see won $100,000 for Howells and Hood, although many preferred the second-place submission designed by Eero Saarinen of Finland. Louis Sullivan said, of the Gothic flying buttresses at the top of the building (which hold up nothing in particular) that they look as if the designers crowned the tower with a monstrous, eight-legged spider. The *Tribune,* called its building "a symphony in stone," but Sullivan said it was "an imaginary structure . . . starting with false premises it was doomed to a false conclusion."

After the *Tribune* was bought by Joseph Medill in 1855, it helped found the Republican party and to elect Abraham Lincoln as president. In return for that favor for Lincoln, the *Tribune* got the right to name the postmaster of Chicago in 1861 so as to "extend the influence of the *Tribune.*"

Medill believed America belonged to the Anglo-Saxon race. The *Tribune* editorially supported lynchings of communists and strychnine or arsenic for tramps. Prior to World War II, the paper gave space to Chicago's Nazi vice-consul, and later saw one of its foreign correspondences broadcasting messages for the Third Reich.

The *Tribune* changed in the '70s and eventually it even asked President Richard Nixon to step aside. Today, the paper is modern, fresh and young.

If you walk into Tribune Tower, you'll see many inscriptions about newspapers and the First Amendment. If you look behind you over the revolving doors, you'll see a magnificent stone screen with such oddly discordant figures as Robin Hood, the *Tribune* editors during World War I, Zeus, a parrot and a porcupine. It's all highly symbolic. True to its Gothic traditions, the building also has gargoyles, especially to the right and left of the entrance arch.

For years the *Tribune* printed "Injun Summer," a cartoon about that last Pottawatomie war dance by John T. McCutcheon, and

Chester Gould came down on Mondays to work on his cartoon "Dick Tracy." Harold Gray's "L'il Orphan Annie," Frank King's "Gasoline Alley" and Milt Caniff's "Terry and the Pirates" were all created at the *Trib*. Ring Lardner worked here in the '20s, and Claudia Cassidy, once the most feared critic in America, issued her barbs from this building.

Floyd P. Gibbons set off on a *Tribune* assignment of his own making in 1917—to find a ship being sunk by the Germans. His luggage included a life preserver, fresh water, a flashlight and a flask of brandy. He needed all that when he went down with the *Laconia* on Feb. 26, 1917 and gave the world an unforgettable story.

Walk a few feet north and you'll see Nathan Hale Court, with a statue to that American patriot. At one time the building behind Hale was the home of the *Chicago American,* which died Sept. 14, 1974, after giving Wrong Way Corrigan his name and creating a tradition of slam-bang, big headline, find-the scandal journalism.

Hotel Continental

If you walk north to 505 N. Michigan, you'll see the Hotel Continental, which began life in 1929 at the Medinah Athletic Club and which still has a 25-yard swimming pool in its 16th story. There aren't many hotels with a swimming pool decorated in a Moorish, Hawaiian theme and now called a "natatorium."

Walk into the first entrance you find, and look at the ceiling. Or walk up the stairs, go past the elevators, walk up a few more stairs to the right, and look at the ceiling and ornamentation of the Cabaret Continental.

Possibly the most hilarious moment for this grand old hotel occurred in 1946, when the National Pickle Packers convened in the then Sheraton-Chicago. They hired World War II bombardiers to throw pickles from the 42nd floor into a barrel on the sidewalk. There were a number of direct hits.

Sayat Nova

Walk north and turn right (east) on Ohio. You will pass the Sayat Nova, at 157 E. Ohio, run by Leon and Arsen Demerdjian, and a favorite restaurant of local media types. Try the raw *kibbie,* which resembles tartar steak and which is only made when the meat is absolutely fresh. Or try the *beoreg* (cheese pastry), a *taboule* (cracked wheat salad) and the sauteed lamb. This is a family-run downtown restaurant with a reputation for great food.

Museum of Contemporary Art

Continue east, turn left on St. Clair, walk one block to Ontario. Take a right and go to 237 E. Ontario, home of the Museum of Contempo-

Workmen ready to install plate glass on Michigan Avenue

rary Art. Claes Oldenburg's mural of green pills is on the wall of the building next door.

Originally founded, in part, because Chicago's Jews were often excluded from the upper reaches of the city's cultural Establishment (such as the Art Institute), this museum has flourished on the experimental. It was wrapped in tarpaulin by Christo, and survived.

Adult admission is $3, children under age 16 are charged $2, and under age six are admitted free. Hours are Monday, Tuesday, Wednesday, Friday and Saturday 10 a.m. to 5 p.m., Thursday 10 a.m. to 8 p.m., Sundays and holidays noon to 5 p.m. Closed Mondays.

Once you leave the museum, you'll see a large building to your right, with the letters "CBS" on it. This is the home of WBBM-AM-TV, which are owned by CBS and which are housed in a former skating rink.

More Shopping and Eating on Michigan Avenue

Return to Michigan Avenue and visit Hammacher Schlemmer, at 618 N. Michigan. Wander past the solar powered pith helmets; the rolling gardener's seat; an electric blanket for plates; the Schmeckenbecker putter equipped with compass, candle, level, rabbit's foot, air horn and tape measure; the Las Vegas one-armed bandit; the pre-natal-sound lamb; a sonic rodent eliminator; a talking bathroom scale with a memory (who needs that!); and the automatic scoring dartboard. For one Christmas, the most expensive item was a mini-fire engine, 12 feet long and six feet high for $45,000, but that was only found in the New York store.

This ends the mid-Michigan Avenue walk. But you are in the midst of a wonderful collection of restaurants. So end by eating at Lawry's, where puppet operas were performed for many years and where the roast beef is superb; at the Lower East Side, where the relish trays can't be beat; or at the Szechwan House for spicy Chinese food. You could also wander back for an Armenian meal at the Sayat Nova; an Italian meal carefully prepared by Greeks at Riccardo's; or a cheezborger at Billy Goat's. Then reflect on art, newspapers and buildings topped with spiders.

3 NORTH MICHIGAN AVENUE WALK

HURON TO OAK STREET

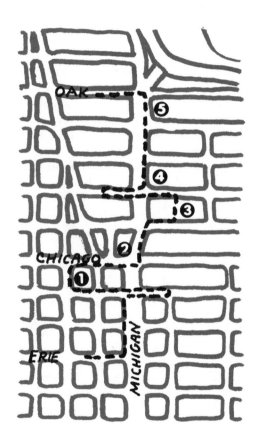

1. Holy Name Cathedral
2. The Water Tower
3. Ritz Carleton Hotel and Water Tower Place
4. John Hancock Center
5. The Drake

Time: Less than two hours.

To get there: Buses plying N. Michigan Avenue and stopping at Huron and Michigan include numbers 145, 146, 147, 151, 153, plus numbers 11 and 125. Parking is almost impossible in this area, although there are lots just west of Huron and Michigan on Rush Street.

The Magnificent Mile

This is the Magnificent Mile, containing men's and women's shops, little boutiques and some of the world's best and most expensive stores.

It is a place to go with your credit cards locked somewhere else.

We start at Michigan and Huron, with Saks' Fifth Avenue to the south and the Allerton Hotel to the north. For seven years, until the program ended in 1969, "The Breakfast Club" was broadcast from the Regency Room of the Allerton. Audience members marched around the breakfast table and sang, "Good morning breakfast clubbers, good morning to ya, we got up bright and early, just to how-dy-do yah." Sam Cowling presented "Fiction and Fact from Sam's Almanac," Fran Allison was Aunt Fanny and Don McNeill, the host, said, "Be good to yourself." McNeill recalled that "The Breakfast Club" was previously broadcast from two other Chicago hotels, the Sherman and the Morrison, and both are no more. "If you want your hotel knocked down, just invite the Breakfast Club," he said.

It is said that, in 1946, Mel Torme came to the Allerton to write the "Christmas Song" with "chestnuts roasting on an open fire." Today, the Allerton has the L'Escargot Restaurant, which warms its patrons both with its wood panelling and its French food. The Penthouse Suite, which was the home of the late Byron Wrigley, a member of the chewing gum family who was also a painter, rents for $450 a day.

Stuart Brent's Book Store

Across the street to the south you will see Stuart Brent's Book Store, a must stop because Brent knows books and people. Brent has been described as a "battler with a hint of Norman Mailer in his face."

Brent grew up on Chicago's West Side, taught school, came back from World War II to open a book store called The Seven Stairs (it had eight, actually), and started his life's work. He told Nelson Algren to name his book "The Man with the Golden Arm." He showed Ernest Hemingway the joys of Rush Street, had tea with Noel Coward in Woolworth's, toured Chicago with Ben Hecht and allowed Nelson Algren and Simone de Beauvoir to tryst in his store.

Brent is an irascible original, who proudly states, "After all, I am the single most successful personal bookseller in all America." And he does mean personal. He refuses to sell many books including "The Joy of Sex." He has been known to throw seekers after trash out of his store.

Brent has summed up his life by telling the *Sun Times*, "So I sell books. When you buy a book, a corner of your heart will grow a little larger. It's what makes you alive, kid."

Expensive Shopping

Now let's walk north, on the east side of the street, plunging onward into deepest credit card land.

We first see Gucci, with its surprisingly modern chandelier on the outside. Go inside to inhale the scent of expensive leather: the bags, the umbrellas, the shoes.

Next door is Tiffany. You only need walk a few feet inside to know that you are far from the home of the blue light specials. Notice the marble on the walls and the gigantic peach vases.

Elizabeth Arden is at 717 N. Michigan. It is here that many Chicago ladies come to have it all done—makeup, hair, the works.

At Superior and Michigan, just to the east, you can see the sign proclaiming that Gino's East, at 160 E. Superior, has the "world's most celebrated pizza." It was once the second best thick-crust pizza in Chicago according to *Chicago Magazine*. The best, at the time, was Giordano's, a 6253 S. California, which was called "the Cecil B. DeMille of pizza."

Neiman-Marcus, at 737 N. Michigan, has a grand archway and the fancy goods we have come to expect of this store.

Holy Name Cathedral

However, we will go west of Michigan Avenue on Superior, walking two blocks to State Street and Holy Name Cathedral, whose 1,200 pound doors look like the gnarled roots of an ancient tree and whose interior features a statue of Christ suspended in mid-air.

Historians record that this ground was given to the Catholic Church as a political payoff. William B. Ogden and Walter L. Newberry owned a lot of North Side property and they wanted a bridge over the river at Clark Street so folks could get to their land. They gave the block on which Holy Name now stands to the Catholic Church so as to get the Catholic vote for the bridge. It worked. Catholics got a church. Chicago got a bridge. And perhaps even heaven profited.

This area also has a bloody history. Dion O'Banion, who was arranging flowers in his shop for the funeral of murdered Mike Merlo, first president of the Unione Siciliane, was killed at 738 N. State on Nov. 10, 1924. O'Banion, who allegedly knowingly let Johnny Torio get caught with 13 truckloads of beer in a federal raid, was busy creating Torio's $10,000 floral piece for Merlo, plus Capone's $8,000 worth of flowers. Three men entered his shop, located across the street from where you are standing, and pumped five bullets into him.

After that, local newspapers called O'Banion an "artist in crime who mixed bootlegging with roses, murder and funeral wreaths" and who died "crashing back . . . into a showcase full of chry-

Holy Name Cathedral

santhemums and roses." Thus the Chicago artistic community lost a contributor to fairs and balls. O'Banion's flower shop was razed in 1960.

Two years after O'Banion's death, again within sight of where you are standing, Hymie Weiss, formerly Wajciechowski, who took over O'Banion's gang, was machine gunned while he was with attorney W. W. O'Brien. The cornerstone of Holy Name Cathedral was chipped in the attack, but has since been repaired.

After considering the odd way religion and violence have occupied this area, and after visiting Holy Name, walk north to Chicago Avenue (to your right as you leave the front doors of the church), then take a right and go east.

Park Hyatt Hotel

Be sure to notice the doorman in front of the Park Hyatt Hotel, at Rush and Chicago. He is, very probably, the best dressed doorman in Chicago. If the weather is cold, he will be wearing a $10,000 custom-made (by I. Magnin), black diamond, full-length mink coat, cape and hat. Fred, one of the doormen, shares the coat with his brother, Steve, another doorman. Fred says that the coat is a little long on him and a little short on Steve, but things work out well enough for both of them.

This is one hotel which knows about the grand manner. A 1965 Silver Cloud III Rolls Royce is available to take guests to the nearest deli, if they choose to use it.

The Penthouse Suite, which goes for $2,500 a night weekdays and $1,600 a night on weekends, has been the home away from home for Elizabeth Taylor, Yul Brynner (who couldn't bring his dog), Mitzi Gaynor, Red Buttons, Phyllis Diller, Eddie Murphy, Paul Anka, Dudley Moore and Barry Manilow. The $2,500 includes champagne (Dom Perignon), caviar (Beluga), and rooms furnished with an 1898 Steinway grand piano, a Louis XV writing desk, antique Oriental silk cushions, a Chinese temple statue in the master bedroom, three baths, and a fine view of Michigan Avenue and the lake.

The LaTour Restaurant in the Park Hyatt is the subject of much critical praise (four stars according to more than one discerning diner) and it offers a relaxed view of the Water Tower park.

High tea in the lobby of the hotel includes finger sandwiches, pastry or cake, scones and the tea of your choice. I am also told that the ladies' room in this hotel is one of the nicest in town, with each stall being complete and private. I did not personally check this out.

Water Tower Survives the Chicago Fire

Leaving the Park Hyatt, we next walk across the street and through the park in front of the Water Tower, the most artistically beautiful

Water Tower and the John Hancock Center

standpipe ever created. This structure survived the Chicago Fire of
1871 and Chicagoans love it. Oscar Wilde called it "a castellated
monstrosity with pepper boxes stuck all over it."

The fire, which spared the Water Tower and made it a symbol of

survival, began south and west of here, in Patrick O'Leary's barn at 137 DeKoven, now the site of the Chicago Fire Academy. One of the O'Learys, Big Jim, later became an important gambler and politician, which proves that tragedy need not prevent someone from becoming a success.

There were only five inches of rain in Chicago that entire summer and the city was almost entirely built of wood—streets, sidewalks and homes. No one knows for sure what happened in that barn on the evening of October 8, 1871. People blamed tramps, neighborhood boys who were smoking, the carelessness of a neighbor or, according to one reformer, the combustibility of the entire Midwest due to a comet depositing flammable elements in our soil years ago. Since almost everyone believes Mrs. O'Leary's cow did it by kicking over a kerosene lantern and since the cow never said that it didn't, that's the story most people accept.

When the fire started, citizens called the fire department. So did a watchman in City Hall, who gave the wrong address for the blaze. The fire units rushed to an area a mile away from the O'Learys'. By the time the firemen found the right barn, the fire had spread and was uncontrollable.

And the city burned. 300 people died. A third of the city was left homeless. The fire generated heat of more than 3,000 degrees, which created a fire storm that shot burning timber through the air, over the Chicago River, and spread the fire.

Thousands of rats ran along the gutters. Horses stampeded. Hoodlums sacked stores and attacked citizens. A woman knelt at Wabash and Adams, holding a crucifix as her skirt burned.

They say that the first structures to go up after the fire were gambling dens and brothels. Maybe so. With the infusion of money from insurance companies, Chicago rebuilt. The fire, which was a disaster, actually helped the city by destroying aging structures and allowing for the greatest building boom, with the most creative architecture, any city had ever seen.

Incidentally, on the same night Chicago burned, Peshtigo, Wisconsin, was also destroyed with a loss of life set at 800 people. Chicago had the telegraph wires and so the Chicago fire got the newspaper coverage, plus a place in the history books. Few people today remember the Peshtigo fire. Even disaster sometimes needs a good press agent.

Horse-Drawn Carriages

If you look across the street, you will see I. Magnin & Co., where the furs become artistic creations.

You can, if you wish, hire a horse-drawn carriage at the corner of Pearson and Michigan, just north of the Water Tower, for a romantic ride through the city. Weekdays, it costs $20 a half hour. Night time and weekends it's $25 a half hour. Yes, the horses wear a form of a diaper, which, according to experts, captures more than 90 percent of what the horse drops.

On Sept. 1, 1983, a taxi somehow got its rear bumper entangled with the right hoof of Elwood, a four-year old carriage horse, who was dragged 80 feet along Michigan Avenue. The horse screamed, the two passengers (a man, age 42, and a woman age 28) were shocked, and the never-ending battle between the City Council and the horse carriage operators got hotter. As a result of Elwood's mishap (and no one knows if the horse bumped the taxi or the taxi backed into the horse), the carriages were banned during evening rush hours from 4 to 6 p.m.

If you do not take a carriage ride, cross the street to the pumping station east of the Water Tower where WGN radio and TV present Here's Chicago! a multimedia promotional view of the city costing $3.75. There is also a gift shop inside where all the souvenirs you have ever wanted are available.

Water Tower Place and the Ritz-Carlton

Next, continue north on Michigan, crossing the street and entering Water Tower Place, the tenth tallest building in the United States, costing $195 million to build. What we have here is shoppers' heaven, with 125 stores in the Atrium Shopping Mall, 11 restaurants and 7 movies.

In addition to Lord & Taylor and Marshall Field's, you will find Banana Republic, with its perpetual safari look; Bigsby & Kruthers, for men's suits; Eddie Bauer, for the camper who doesn't have everything; the Gap; M. Hyman & Son, for big and tall men; Laura Ashley, for the women who love paisley; and a McDonald's with a tiny fountain all its own.

There are also Godiva chocolates and Mrs. Fields Cookies, and several book stores, including Kroch's & Brentano's on the fourth floor and Rizzoli International on the third floor. It's the kind of place where a casual visitor can actually lose track of time.

Next, somehow wander out of Water Tower Place (not easy to do), go east on Pearson to the Ritz-Carlton.

Enter the elevator and go to the main lobby on the 12th floor (the elevators stop at one, two and twelve). Notice that there are chandeliers in the elevators. That's class.

Get out of the elevator, walk straight ahead to an area known as the Green House, which is just beyond a fountain with a sculpture showing three birds standing on top of each other. If you have the money, sit in a wicker chair, look at the plants and order a drink. Warning: It will be expensive. But you are now in the lap of luxury.

Tea is served from 3 to 5 p.m. weekdays on The Terrace, which is, as you face the elevators, around and to your right, just beyond an indoor waterfall with real trees.

In this hotel, it is possible to rent the State Suite for $2,500 a night, which has five baths, a kitchen, library, Italian silk sheets costing $600 a set in the four bedrooms, hangers padded with silk in the closets, 22-foot-high living room ceilings, and matchbooks covered with silk and emblazoned with your name in gold letters. It is rumored that Michael Jackson, Roger Moore, Mick Jagger, Lionel Richie and Tina Turner enjoy the comforts away from home here.

Otherwise, in the rest of the hotel, single rooms rent for $155 to $190 per night and doubles go for $180 to $215 on weeknights.

The Ritz-Carlton also features one of Chicago's fanciest brunches on Sundays in an elegant setting for $22.50 per person, and tea for $9.50 in The Greenhouse weekdays from 3 to 5 p.m.

John Hancock Center

Next, return to ground level and exit on Pearson, going west to Michigan Avenue, taking a right and going north to the John Hancock Center.

Cross its plaza and go down the stairs and towards the back (east) to take the tower elevators to the observation deck. The trip costs $2.50 for adults and $1.50 for children and, on a clear day, it is well worth the price. As you zip upwards, announcer John Doremus automatically tells you that you are speeding along at 1,800 feet per minute, that you will soon be 1,030 feet above the ground and that on a clear day you can see four states.

There is another way to see the same thing. Walk towards the Chestnut side of the Hancock Center, enter the doors saying "The Ninety-Fifth" and take the elevators there. The Ninety-Fifth is a restaurant, but there is also a bar, called Images, where domestic beer is $3.50 and fancy mixed drinks are $5.00. In other words, for a $1 more than the $2.50 you'd spend to go to the observation deck, you get the same view and a beer. The best times to go to the Ninety-Fifth are at sunset or during lightning storms, when the clouds are often below the 95th floor of the Hancock. The best view, I am told, is from the ladies' room!

The Ninety-Fifth, with its harpist entertaining nightly, is one of Chicago's most expensive restaurants with entrees ranging from $16.50 to $28.00. Everything is a la carte. But the view is unsurpassed.

As you return to the main floor, note that you are passing 47 floors of apartments, from floors 45 to 92. A four-bedroom condominium in the John Hancock Center might sell for as much as $1,500,000.

Streeterville Plaza Named for Cap Streeter

When you return to the ground floor, you are in Streeterville Plaza, named for one of the most colorful characters in Chicago history. On July 11, 1886, Capt. George Wellington Streeter stranded his steamboat, the *Reutan,* bound for Honduras where Cap hoped to sell guns to South American outlaws, on a sandbar here. Within a few days the sandbar built up around the *Reutan,* and soon Cap and his wife, Ma, were on dry land. "Found land," he called it.

Cap invited local contractors, who were building homes for the rich on Chicago's North Side, to dump whatever they wanted on his land. Within a few months, Cap could lay claim to 186 acres. He stood on his rights. It was his land. He did not recognize the sovereignty of the City of Chicago or the State of Illinois for his "District of Lake Michigan," which only bowed to the federal government.

Ordinary folks called the area Streeterville, but rich people didn't like squatters dirtying up their front yards, and so began a 30 years war between Cap and the Chicago establishment. Most of the time, Cap won.

Ma, using her axe, clipped off the heel of one rich dude who tried to throw Cap off his property. When sheriff's deputies invaded Cap's property in 1894, Ma poured boiling water on them. During another raid, Ma's axe almost severed the arm of one policeman and nine of the city's finest were wounded by Cap's birdshot. During yet another raid, one policeman was killed, but Cap was acquitted of murder when he proved that he only used birdshot, never bullets and the man died of a bullet wound. One of Cap's friends stabbed another cop with a pitchfork, killing him, and was acquitted on a plea of self defense.

Then 100 hired gunmen (or maybe it was 500—accounts differ and grow with each passing year) invaded Streeterville. Cap and Ma looked done for, until the gunmen found Cap's liquor supply. They got drunk, Cap rounded up his friends and, during a brisk one-sided half-hour's battle, wounded 33 members of the invading army. Cap then loaded the still living into his wagon, drove them to the Chicago Avenue police station and demanded that they be charged with trespassing, assault and battery. Cap was eventually captured by police, who couldn't hold him because shooting at a Chicago police officer wasn't considered a crime then.

Finally, a frontier gunfighter named John Kirk was mysteriously murdered and Cap was found guilty of the crime. Nine months later, Cap was ordered pardoned, but things became more difficult in Streeterville. Ma died and was replaced by Alma, Cap lost an eye in yet another gun battle, during which he shot a police captain.

The courts and Cap's desire to do a sinful thing—sell beer on Sundays—finally ended his stay in Streeterville. On December 10,

Quigley Preparatory Seminary North's second floor chapel

1918, Cap was thrown off his property. Cap retired and operated a hot dog stand on Navy Pier until his death on January 21, 1921 at age 84, an honored citizen who fought the establishment and lost. His land was the subject of continuing court battles until 1940, when the last of his heirs and those he sold property to for as little as $1 had their suits dismissed in federal court.

Cap Streeter's land is conservatively worth over $1,000,000,000 (one billion) today. And all he wanted to do on it was serve beer on Sundays and squat.

More Ramblings on Michigan Avenue

Walk west on Chestnut, cross Michigan and go to 103 E. Chestnut, the Quigley Preparatory Seminary North, a school for young men interested in the priesthood. If you ring the bell, someone will answer the door. Ask to see the chapel, which is at the end of the hall to the right on the second floor. If it is afternoon, the rays of the setting sun will be the only illumination through the deep reds and blues of the stained-glass window. There is an awe-inspiring silence. A moment to contemplate, and to escape the city.

Now return to Michigan Avenue. You are near Crate and Barrel, with its mugs and a new high tech office look. Walking on the west side of the street past the Fourth Presbyterian Church, which was built in 1912. Cross Michigan at Delaware and walk in front of the Westin Hotel, which one restaurateur said has the best food service of any hotel in the country.

Knickerbocker Hotel

You will soon be in front of the Knickerbocker, 919 N. Michigan.

The name changes, alone, indicates that this place has quite a history. It began in 1927 as the Davis Hotel, became the Knickerbocker in 1931, changed to the Playboy Towers in 1970, and returned to the Knickerbocker after 1979, when $5 million was spent to remodel the place.

It still has the lighted dance floor in the grand ballroom, with 760 fluorescent lamps under the feet of those dancing the light fantastic.

We are told that the 14th floor of the Knickerbocker was once a speakeasy during the sinful days of Prohibition. According to the general manager, Mike Cooper, there is a hidden staircase from the 12th to the 14th floors. It's now covered by wallpaper, but when the hotel was originally built, by gentlemen who were fronting for the Purple Mob of Detroit, the 14th floor had two casinos. Only one elevator serviced the 14th floor. In case of a raid, gamblers and drinkers could dash down the street staircase to the 12th floor and get a different elevator out of the building.

Drake Hotel

Next walk east on Walton, and enter the Drake Hotel, which prides itself on its dignity. It has housed Winston Churchill, Queen Elizabeth and Edith Rockefeller McCormick, who died in her Drake Hotel suite in 1932, still hoping her husband, Harold, might return. Harold's name had been linked with Ganna Walska, Betty Noble, Pola Negri and Baroness Violet Beatrice von Wenner, who accompanied him during his whistling concerts.

The Drake opened in 1921, has employees who average over 14 years of service, and offers such conveniences as human elevator operators and windows which can open and shut, a rarity in hotels these days.

View from the Hancock Center

As you enter the Drake, walk to your left into the arcade, with its
flower shop, beauty salon, drug store and, finally, the Cape Cod
Room, where you ought to taste the Bookbinder red snapper soup
with sherry in a room famous for its fish dishes.

Next walk upstairs to the lobby, with its open fire place, comfy
chairs and expansive feeling. This is a great hotel in the old style.

Continue to Oak Street, and notice that traffic heading towards
Lake Shore Drive goes into an underpass. In 1962 Chicagoans suc-
cessfully prevented an elevated highway interchange from being built
here. It would have ruined the view of the lake.

Mayfair Regent Hotel

To end this walk, go east or right less than a half block to the Mayfair

Regent Hotel, one of the most elegant and secret places in town. If it is late in the afternoon, do stop for tea in the beautiful room to your left off the lobby, The Mayfair Lounge, with its Chinese murals, a woodburning fireplace and lace table cloths.

If it is Sunday, by all means take the elevator to the Ciel Bleu, a restaurant with a view of the sweep of Lake Michigan from Oak St. Beach to the north. The champagne brunch is not well known to most Chicagoans, but the range of choices in the buffet is staggering and the staff will make us feel like gentlemen and ladies.

What better place to rest, to think about the expensive shops we have just strolled by and to marvel at the view before you. It rivals any beach, any lake- or ocean-front in the world in its beauty.

4 OAK STREET

SHOPPERS' PARADISE WALK

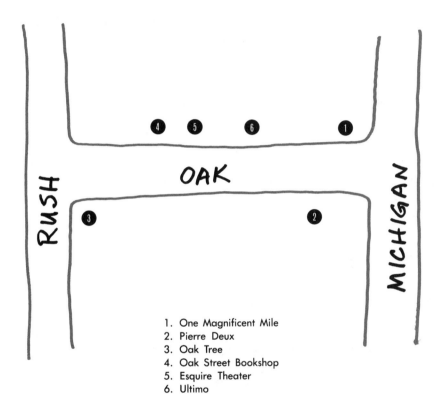

RUSH

OAK

MICHIGAN

1. One Magnificent Mile
2. Pierre Deux
3. Oak Tree
4. Oak Street Bookshop
5. Esquire Theater
6. Ultimo

Time: Two hours, depending on how intensely you want to shop.
To get there: The 145, 146, 147 or 151 CTA bus stops at Walton and Michigan, one block south of the beginning of the walk. However, since we're going to look at expensive, designer clothing, perhaps a cab ride is more fitting, especially since it should cost less than $3 to get to Oak and Michigan from State and Madison or many other Loop locations.

Start at One Magnificent Mile

Oak Street, from Michigan to Rush, is the mecca for shoppers who enjoy spending money and who must know what are the latest styles from Italy and France.

This is the walk for the fashion conscious and, even if you are here to look rather than to buy, it is fun to see what the rest of the world considers to be the ultimate in taste.

Like so many areas of Chicago, Oak Street is in transition. Today, the street still has a neighborhood feel, with the various shop owners tending to know and like each other. But that may not last for long. Rents have been soaring on this street, many of the smaller shops are thinking of moving elsewhere because their profitability is affected, and there is a danger of Oak Street becoming an extension of Michigan Avenue, with its huge, powerful, fashionable stores.

If some of the boutiques mentioned here have disappeared by the time you take the walk, do take a moment to mourn their passing. It means that the street is changing, and perhaps not for the better.

Putting aside such melancholy thoughts, let us begin this walk celebrating the many ways the human body can be draped by entering One Magnificent Mile, at the corner of Oak and Michigan. Take the escalator to the second floor and enter Spaggia, an elegant restaurant with doors with huge marble handles. This also has a wonderful view of Michigan Avenue and the park at Oak Street.

The South Side of the Street

Once you have resisted the temptation to begin a shoppers' walk by sitting and drinking or eating, retrace your steps, exit One Mag Mile and walk west on Oak Street on the south side of the street. This simple walk will consist of strolling up one side of Oak Street for one block, crossing the street and then coming back on the other side.

Benetton's, at 121 E. Oak, is part of a chain of Italian-made knit-ware stores. The franchise, named after Luciano Benetton, offers mohair, angora and cashmere sweaters for around $65 and up. It is the winter place to go, especially if you have begun the walk feeling a little chilly.

A little farther west, at 113 E. Oak, Pierre Deux is a discovery. The front of the shop offers pillows and trays, clothing and purses with a distinctive Laura Ashley visits India look. The room to the rear holds bolts of fabrics from which the dresses and pillows are created.

You have entered a French provincial shop featuring fabrics from Tarascon, an obscure village in Provence. Here La Souleiado, a textile firm, creates fabrics from designs originally imported to France from India for royalty.

Bolts of fabric in the back room at Pierre Deux

There are actually two men named Pierre behind Pierre Deux, Pierre Moulin and Pierre LeVec, who met while working with the Marshall Plan after World War II. Moulin is very, very French and LeVec is a former paratrooper and G-man from Missouri.

They opened an antique store in Greenwich Village in New York in 1967, but didn't start having great success until 1969. Pierre Moulin, who was also installing x-ray equipment in hospitals, returned from France with pillows made from French Provencal fabrics. The pillows were sold out in 48 hours, and the two Pierres began thinking more about fabrics and less about antiques.

Today, with 18 stores on such desirable streets as Rodeo Drive in Beverly Hills, Sutter Street in San Francisco and Oak Street in Chicago, they have a $20 million a year business, 10 percent per year growth rate and 15 percent annual profits. Princess Diana was seen with one of their handbags in *Time Magazine,* the same bag noted in *The Preppy Handbook.*

Continue west, past Deutsch Luggage, 111 E. Oak, to the Water Mark, 109 E. Oak, where Cristi and Nancy Gross, a mother-and-daughter team, provide thank-you notes, wedding invitations, Christmas cards, Bar Mitzvah announcements and a small freezer with Miss Grace's Lemon Cakes from Beverly Hills.

Bottega Veneta, at 107 E. Oak, imports Italian leather goods from Vecenzia, which is near Venice. The shop is known for its woven

Video fashion show at Gianni Versace

leather bags (just feel how soft they are), luggage, billfolds, its $4100 handbags and its $3100 crocodile or alligator attache cases.

If you are a career woman and need that certain power suit, visit Ann Taylor at 103 E. Oak.

Or take a look at the perpetual video fashion show on the TV set as you enter Gianni Versace, at 101 E. Oak. Here is where the Miami Vice look can be assembled. Men's suits start at $700, women's dresses at $350 and up, and women's suits at $700 and up.

The Versace shop, the largest in the world devoted to that Italian designer, is owned by Jim Levin, 27, who also owns the Tru-Link Fence Co. The kick-off fashion show for the shop was held March 26, 1986, at the Field Museum, where Iman, one of the highest priced models in the world, paraded the designs under the watchful eye of Versace, then 39 years old.

After looking around the Versace shop and noting that a three-story building was turned into a two-level store to give higher ceilings, continue walking west to 65 E. Oak, where Jackie Renwick, an attorney, offers suits and dresses for the executive woman.

As the walk continues, you will pass In Chicago, a sportswear shop at 63 E. Oak; Divine Knits, at 61 E. Oak; and the Brass Boot, which imports Italian shoes and $600 lizard boots at 55 E. Oak.

When you visit Jeraz, at 51 E. Oak, be sure to ask for Jerry Frishman, who says, "My wife's the owner. I work for her." Here is a

Jerry Frishman with racks of Italian suits at Jeraz

man with a quick wit, an easy manner and extensive knowledge of his Italian suits designed by Canali, Corneliani, Valentino and others.

Most of the suits here come from Milan in Northern Italy because, Frishman observes, "In Southern Italy, all they do is fish, sit outside, drink coffee and watch the broads go by." Frishman has five tailors, suits from $450 by the best Italian designers and a way of cutting through fashion nonsense to make sure that his customers get what they want.

47

Lori Ganet shows her wares at A Capriccio

Walking down a half a flight of stairs at 47 E. Oak, you'll find A Capriccio, the place to go for leotards, tights, swim suits, and ballet shoes. Lori Ganet, the owner, was a special education teacher in Lake Forest and Elmhurst. Then she taught a child who should have been transferred to regular classes but was kept back because the school needed the special ed funding. The world lost a teacher and gained a delightful shop owner.

Lori continues to sell leotards (especially the sexy French cut) because "with all the leotard stores going out of business, someone who needed a leotard had to have somewhere to go." She proudly states that "any leotard you see in Shape Magazine, you can buy here."

Ilona of Hungary, at 45 E. Oak, is a skin care institute where the staff provides very private facials, manicures, pedicures and massages. Owned by Ilona Mezzaros, the clinic also has outlets in New York, Denver, Houston and Dallas.

The manager of Ilona of Hungary here is Hanna (Jakubczak) of Poland, who says that over 40 percent of the customers are men because "men are so into skin care that they are now the leaders of women when it comes to beauty."

Cross the Street and Head Back East

This half of the walk ends at the Oak Tree, 25 E. Oak, where we can have a $5 or $6 sandwich in a busy outdoor cafe. If you are not hungry, cross the street, walking towards the Burger Ville, and start heading back to Michigan Ave.

Jean Charles, at 30 E. Oak, features "the best French and Italian shoes in town," according to the owner's sister, Juliette Kevorkian, who adds, "They are. I'm being modest and I'm not being prejudiced."

If you walk through a passageway in the back of the store, you will enter another Jean Charles shop at 1003 N. Rush, which features men's and women's clothing.

My Sisters Circus or Isis (the store has both names), at 38 E. Oak, began as the Bikini Zoo in another location. Later, the two sisters changed the Bikini Zoo to My Sisters Circus and sold one-of-a-kind dresses for 14 years. When they amicably parted, one sister, Suzanne Fey Gantz, opened Isis, named after the Egyptian goddess of womanly goods, adding that name to the previous Circus name. Isis features fun sportswear.

Musicraft, at 48 E. Oak, is an electronic store with new equipment and a startlingly good, dependable selection of used amplifiers, speakers, etc.

Whatever you do during your Oak Street walk, you must stop by the Oak Street Bookshop at 52 E. Oak and say hello to Carol Stoll, who identifies herself as "the living legend." When she last saw me, she correctly chastised me, "I've been waiting 20 years for you to visit." It is not a mistake I will make again.

Carol Stoll, sipping coffee, smoking a cigarette and chatting, oversees a narrow, crowded store devoted to readers. In 1985, director Bryan Forbes wrote in the *London Times* about the "culture in an ill-read neighborhood." He remembered when an imposing dowager demanded a book on do-it-yourself brain surgery and Carol replied, "Wouldn't you know? We're right out of it. Had a run on that one this

Carol Stoll of Oak Street Bookshop

week." He added, "Every community should have its Oak Street Bookshop, presided over by someone who cares to keep the flame alight. Carol Stoll loves books, and with her love of books comes a rare hope for us all in a world where the real quality of life is under constant attack from the yahoos."

When I was last there, Carol was complaining about the rent ($2000 a month) and observing that, on Oak Street, "We all love each other. I buy everything on this street because I want to support the others here and because they buy from me. Everyone wants everyone else to succeed."

Carol Stoll is one of a kind, the queen of her special world from the confines of a book store with soul, and I am sorry that I took 20 years to visit!

Moving east, past the Esquire Theater (which may be torn down by the time you read this) and the Haagen Dazs, at 70 E. Oak, where you can have ice cream and sit in a little room overlooking Oak Street; enter Clown, 72 E. Oak, a children's clothing store for kids who really need a $200 suede and leather jacket at ages four to six.

Coralee Lavery, Clown's owner, has created the shop for the mother and grandmother who want their children to be in style. Walk upstairs to the Oak Street Beach Club, also owned by Coralee, and you can get jogging outfits with a sailing theme, and especially the sweatshirts and t-shirts with the unique Beach Club logo.

At Stuart Chicago, 102 E. Oak, owner Stuart Goldin is proud of his collection of men's Italian suits, ties and shirts. He quickly took a German suit coat off the rack, put it on me to illustrate the latest trend in men's styling. "Guys have been working out so much and their chests have gotten so much larger that now the suits are being specially tailored for the in-shape male," Goldin said.

Botega Glasseia, at 106 E. Oak, features custom tailored clothes designed to make a women of any size and age look gorgeous. Good customers may also be picked up in a Rolls Royce and refreshed with champagne during the arduous trip to this unassuming little shop.

Upstairs there is the Ultimate Bride, Seno's formal wear and a plastic surgery clinic.

Down the street at 110 E. Oak, Sugar Magnolia is always busy. There is a happy, intense energy here, with blaring rock music and younger women rifling through trendy sportswear.

They try to keep Chicago in step with New York at Ultimo, 114 E. Oak, where owner Joan Weinstein offers incredible service—15 people in the alterations department, meaning that they can totally remake blouses or cut suits down three sizes, if need be.

Ultimo carries the latest and the best. If you open a Vogue or Harper's Bazaar magazine and like something you see, often the only place to get it in Chicago is Ultimo.

As you enter Ultimo, you see no clothes. Instead you feel as though you have walked into the vestibule of a rajah's palace, with opulent fabrics, carpets and flowers greeting you.

Ultimo originally opened as a men's store, until the late Jerry Weinstein suggested that his wife, Joan, "do something upstairs." Thus, the famed women's department was born. Here, dresses are bought in small quantities so that, heaven forfend, two women will not show up at a society benefit wearing the same $3000 dress.

John Jones, men's department buyer, said that he has had sales of over $40,000 to a single customer on more than one occasion. How-

Street view of Ultimo

ever, he has never waited on that famed shopper Imelda Marcos.

The store has been renovated three times since it opened in 1969, but always with the same decor, originally designed by photographer Victor Skrebneski. The sensual feel of the place is enhanced by the hundreds of yards of fabric placed in a way to remind the customer of a seraglio waiting for its veiled harem girls to arrive.

Joan Weinstein, who now runs the entire shop, has added a new section with "lower priced things because we don't want anyone to feel intimidated. Chicago is a friendly city which won't put up with the kind of elitism you might find in New York. And we are a friendly store." But only a visit there can prove it to you.

Conclude with a Burger at the Acorn

Conclude the Oak Street walk by entering the dark and friendly confines of Acorn on Oak. Before you walk by the bar in this narrow restaurant, look for the reprint of the Time Magazine "American Best" issue of June 16, 1986. There it is, printed in black and white, proclaiming that the Acorn on Oak serves one of the four best hamburgers in America (others are in New York, New Orleans and Maine). And it costs around $5. If you stay late, Buddy Charles begins performing at the piano six days a week around 11 p.m. (he takes Sunday off) and his songs and kibbitzing have been going on there for a dozen years.

You have just visited many stores with the designs that are the height of style. It is estimated that this one block takes in over $100,000,000 worth of business a year. And that is a lot of Italian suits and dresses.

5

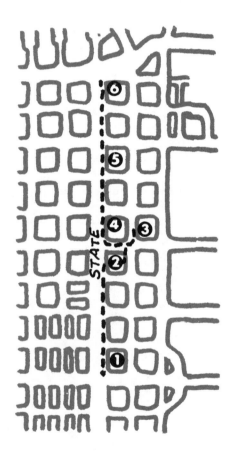

1. Sears Roebuck Store
2. Palmer House
3. Kroch's and Brentano's
4. Carson Pirie Scott & Co.
5. Marshall Field & Co.
6. United of America Building

Time: Two hours, less if you're not in the mood to look at clothing stores.

To get there: Nearly every form of public transportation known to man stops along or near State Street. The corner of State and Congress, where the walk begins, is a stop for the 2, 6, 145, 62, 99, 162, 164, 146, 44, 62, 15, 36, 29 buses. The subway stops at Jackson or Harrison and State St. and there is parking for cars in city lots south of Congress on State Street.

From Trail to Mall

Everyone knows State Street is "that great street." Well, it wasn't—at least not for many years.

Then in 1979, the new State Street Mall was opened to great fanfare. State Street, that fading street, had trees, shrubs and maybe a new life.

As it is today, State Street is a vital merchandising area, bustling with people, slightly tacky in spots, needing to be revitalized, but still an exciting place to visit. The word is that State Street is on the edge of a great revitalization and that soon State Street will again be the Great Street it once was.

State Street was originally a trail laid out by the legendary Gurdon Hubbard, trapper, trader, nicknamed "Swift Walker" because he could cover 75 miles in a single day and out-walk and out-run any Indian. He was the husband of a 14-year-old Indian lass named Watseka. He also became Chicago's first meat packer when he collected hogs during the winter of 1828–29, piled them on the river front where they froze, awaiting sale the following spring.

Hubbard was an uncanny investor, buying lots for $66.33 in 1829 and selling them for over $80,000 seven years later. He did it again in 1835, when he bought more property for $5,000 and sold it four months later to New York sharpies for another $80,000. History records that he eventually "cast aside" Watseka for someone called a "legal helpmate."

Hubbard Trail became State Road in 1834, when road commissioners marked Swift Walker's old, straight path with milestones. State Road originally ran from Vincennes, Indiana, to Chicago. Eventually, State Road was abandoned, except for its path through Chicago, which became known as State Street. The entire street was then worth about $60.

As you stand at Congress and State, you are in front of the former Sears Roebuck Store, built by William LeBaron Jenney in 1891. Jenney's use of a steel skeleton allowed him to create huge windows which let in more light to show off the merchandise in the building. It shows off little merchandise today because it is the People's Gas offices. But, if you look closely, you'll see the name "L. Z. Leiter" carved into the parapet. Levi Leiter, who commissioned this building for $1,500,000, formed a partnership with Marshall Field to create that department store before branching out on his own. This building, which is called the Second Leiter Building in architectural guide books, is known for its simple design.

Walk north on State Street towards the ugly elevated structure which is over Van Buren.

The Old Vice District

It is hard not to notice that the west side of the street is a parking lot. But this has not always been so.

In 1896, Mickey Finn, an ex-pickpocket, opened the Lone Star Saloon in this area and later invented a knockout mixture which subsequently made him famous. The area was then known as Whiskey Row and in the early 1900s one Johnny Rafferty planned his confidence games here. If you saw "The Sting," you saw an approximation of some of the stunts pulled on gullibles from Terra Haute or Galena. In the 1870s, State and Van Buren was the beginning of "Satan's Mile," a vile vice district. One turn of the century reformer described the goings on as "only conceivable in Sodom and Gomorrah."

A bit of that tradition continues to this day. Notice the State Street News, at 350 S. State, that slick-looking porno store. A scandal developed here when it was discovered that the City of Chicago owned this property and that somehow this store was operating here rent-free.

Continue along the east side of State. After crossing Van Buren, you will be passing by the Goldblatt Store, built in 1912, originally known as Rothschild's, later the Davis Store (part of Marshall Field & Co.), and once part of a Chicago-based chain of department stores.

This store was supposed to be converted into Chicago's new downtown public library. The city bought the store, saving Goldblatt's from bankruptcy, but then the controversy and the arguments became heated in the wake of media investigations. It was said that the fire sprinklers didn't work and that the floor couldn't hold the load of all those books. Let's hope that this issue is settled quickly and Chicago gets a good, clean, central place for its main library.

If you look to the west, across State Street, between Jackson and Adams, there is a cul de sac which has the Everett McKinley Dirksen Federal Building blocking its west end. Here you will find McDonald's, Wendy's Hamburgers, Aurelio's Pizza and Popeye's Famous Fried Chicken vying for your attention. Think of that. An entire mews devoted to fast food. And who says that State Street isn't that Great Street?

The Palmer House

Continue strolling north on State Street. In slightly less than half a block you'll reach the entrance to the Palmer House, the oldest continually operating hotel in the country. It is safe to say that State Street wouldn't be here if it were not for Potter Palmer, builder of the original Palmer House and the man who invested $7,000,000 in the street in 1866. He widened it, leased a store to Marshall Field and

Palmer House arcade

Levi Z. Leiter, founders of Marshall Field & Co., and built a fine hotel which opened on Sept. 26, 1871.

That was not the most auspicious date to open a 225 room hotel costing $300,000. It burned to the ground in the Great Chicago Fire just 13 days later.

A second, allegedly fireproof, hotel was built in 1873, and Palmer invited his competitors to "build a fire in the center of any chamber or room of the Palmer House proper." Palmer bet that, after the room was closed for one hour, the fire would not extend beyond that single room. No one ever took him up on his challenge.

The current hotel was rebuilt in sections in 1925 through 1927, and completely replaced the "old" Palmer House, where John Coughlin got a job as a rubber in the baths as a youth and became "Bathhouse John," a memorable crooked Chicago alderman, for the rest of his life.

Today's hotel is part of the Hilton chain. In 1975, President Gerald Ford stayed in the Presidential Suite. In 1976, candidate Jimmy Carter stayed in a regular room and carried his own luggage.

Walk into the Palmer House, go about halfway through the arcade and take the escalator to the lobby. Look up and be dazzled by the painting on the ceiling featuring three panels of nudes looking graceful and bashful.

If you walk towards the stairway at the rear of the lobby you'll approach the Empire Room, once the finest big-name entertainment spot in Chicago, and now a restaurant. Veloz and Yolanda, a dance team, worked there for 34 weeks in 1935, and the room saw the talents of Eddie Duchin, Ted Weems, Sophie Tucker, Hildegarde and Maurice Chevalier.

Walk up the stairs towards the Empire Room, do not be taken aback by the maitre d' and look inside the Empire Room, with its black and gold trim and its huge mirrors behind pillars at either end of the room. Like thousands and thousands of others, I took the most beautiful girl in my high school class here after our Senior Prom. The Empire Room may have seen more strapless evening gowns and unforgettable nights than any other spot in Chicago.

Return to the escalator, go down, take a left and exit on Wabash Avenue, so-named because Indiana teamsters from the banks of the Wabash River would stop there. It was once paved with stove lids because it was so muddy. The Mid-Continental Plaza Building is in front of you, but you can't see most of it because of the Elevated or "El" structure, which no one likes, which everyone would like to see replaced and which occasionally is the scene of an accident. That doesn't happen often enough to be worried about it.

Kroch's and Brentano's

Go left and walk north to Monroe Street, crossing to the east and entering Kroch's and Brentano's book store, the largest in the city. They have an uncountable number of paperbacks in the basement, perhaps as many as 30,000 titles. According to the publishers, Kroch's windows are the most fought-after pieces of real estate in the city.

A little farther north, at 17 S. Wabash, in a 95-year-old building, is Iwan Reis & Co. tobacconists, the city's oldest company continuously owned and operated by the same family. The store always has that distinctive fresh tobacco scent and boasts a fine collection of antique pipes.

Carson Pirie Scott

Now return to State Street by walking west on Monroe. When you arrive at State and Monroe, you are in front of the Carson Pirie Scott & Co. Store, an architectural landmark. Walk to the State and Madison entrance, one block north (to your right), noticing both the plaque explaining the building's historical interest and the way architects Louis Sullivan (1899, 1904), Daniel H. Burnham (1906) and Holabird and Root (1960) designed and redecorated this store. Sullivan's ornamentation of this building is both delicate and unsurpassed.

This store's roots go back to Samuel Carson and John T. Pirie, who sailed for America from Northern Ireland on Aug. 26, 1854, saw their ship wrecked off Newfoundland, worked for family friends in small Illinois towns and earned enough money for Carson to bring his bride, Elizabeth Pirie, his partner's sister, back from Belfast within two years. Later, Mr. Pirie married Mr. Carson's sister to keep everything in the family.

Carson and Pirie, to be joined by John E. Scott in 1890, opened their first Chicago store in 1864, and were burned out in the 1871 fire. But Andrew MacLeish, general manager, stood in the store as the flames approached and offered fleeing Chicagoans, "fifty silver dollars for every wagonload of merchandise you save out of this building." About 40 percent of the inventory was saved.

Enter the store through the State and Madison doors. You'll find a department store which is constantly updating itself. The Corporate Level, in the basement, has everything for the executive man and woman, including fashions, a bank and a post office. On the second floor, Metropolis is an in-store shopping mall with the largest Liz Claiborne shop in America, plus fashions from Esprit, Anne Klein and others.

Crowds and History at State and Madison

Return to State and Madison and consider several more facts while standing at allegedly "the world's busiest corner."

At one time, because of the hill on which Fort Dearborn stood, the Chicago river entered the lake here probably not far from where the information booth now stands.

A little later, in the 1830s, you could buy lots on this corner, now valued at "beyond expectations," for $6.72 an acre. Still later, in the McVicker's Theater near this corner, Chicagoans saw the acting of Joseph Jefferson, Edmund Keane, Edwin Forrest and, in 1862 in Shakespeare's "Richard III," John Wilkes Booth.

On November 11, 1924, after the assassination of the beloved Dion O'Banion, local flower arranger, bootlegger and patron of culture, one Louis Alterie told reporters that he wanted a shoot out at the corner of State and Madison with the guys who killed O'Banion, specifically with certain members of the Capone gang. Alterie was always loyal to his pals, although that shoot-out never occurred. According to *Chicago Magazine,* when his buddy "Nails" Morton died after a fall from his horse, Alterie rented the nag, shot it through the head and called the stable owner, telling him, "We taught that god-damn horse of yours a lesson. If you want the saddle, go and get it." It is reported that the horse never threw a rider again.

In addition to all this history, there's a good small French restaurant only a few feet from you, Le Bordeaux, at 3 W. Madison, next door to the Mosley Bras and Girdles, which displays shampoo, jewelry and silly hats, but no underwear in the window.

Cross Madison, continue walking north, and you'll be in front of Wieboldt's Department Store, 1 N. State St. By this time, you should have passed several fruit, flower and popcorn vendors, perhaps a few street musicians and, in the winter, even someone selling hot chestnuts. When Richard Daley was mayor, such entrepreneurs were energetically frowned upon. Now they are legal, and Chicago enjoys their presence even though the hot chestnuts seemed like a New York idea.

Do stop at the Hot Tix Booth, 24 S. State, to learn about half-price tickets to many Chicago theaters. What a great idea—you can get these tickets only on the day of performance, but they can not only save you money, they fill the empty seats of local theaters.

Karoll Building

There is a masterpiece in a state of decline on the west side of State Street at Washington, a half block north. The Karoll Building, formerly the 32 North State Street Building, formerly the Reliance Building, is dirty and, from the outside, looks decrepit. Yet, if you walk toward the entrance near the Charles Shops Exotic Lingerie Store window, which is usually filled with undies with holes in them, you'll see a plaque put up in 1957 by the Chicago Dynamic Committee. The plaque lavishly praises this building, designed in 1890 by Daniel H. Burnham, and calls it "a glass tower . . . witness to the best architectural spirit of the 19th century . . ." Today it is grimy, but glorious.

Crosby's Opera House

On the north side of Washington, just west of State Street once stood Crosby's Opera House, where, in 1868, the Republicans nominated Gen. Ulysses S. Grant for President. But that is not what Crosby's Opera House is famous for.

On January 21, 1867, it was the scene of the greatest lottery—and possibly the most skillful swindle—in Chicago history.

The opera house's opening night, in 1865, was delayed several days because of the assassination of Lincoln. Financial difficulties continued to beset the theater and finally Crosby had to sacrifice it. He chose to do so by actually giving it away, by lottery.

Chicagoans loved the idea. Thousands bought the $5 lottery chances, which came with a book of engravings, suitable for framing and displaying. When Jan. 21 arrived, "the city was taken by storm," according to one newspaper. Thousands of strangers arrived, filling the hotels, the Armory and saloons, and looking over the opera house with a smug proprietary air. Courts, businesses and even the Board of Trade closed when the drawing was scheduled.

The 210,000 chances, plus the 25,593 held by Crosby, were put into a giant wheel. Another, smaller wheel held 302 prizes ranging from the opera house to worthless decorations. It took 113 spins of both wheels before the opera house was awarded to ticket number 58,600. But no one stepped forward to claim that number.

The mystery of who was the owner lasted for three days, until a letter appeared in a St. Louis newspaper from a "Col. Abraham Hagerman Lee" of Prairie du Rocher, Ill. "Lee," a person no one in Prairie du Rocher knew, claimed he was very excited by the news but that he couldn't leave his sick wife. On January 26, another letter from "A. H. Lee" appeared in the *Chicago Republican* newspaper. That letter claimed that "Lee's" wife was better, thank you, and that "Lee" had come to Chicago in secret—and he had accepted Crosby's offer to buy back the opera house for $200,000.

Oh, the suspicious minds! People said that Crosby drew all the best stuff anyway—two paintings and a bust of Lincoln. Furthermore, Crosby sold $900,000 worth of chances. Even if "Lee" existed and he was paid $200,000, Crosby was doing pretty well.

Things got so hot for Crosby that he had to leave town. His uncle, Albert, was managing the opera house when Grant was nominated there.

(Crosby fared better than Chicago's first season of opera in 1853. Rice's theater, on the south side of Randolph, was presenting Bellini's *La Sonnambula,* when the theater burned to the ground. One drunken opera lover sat in his seat applauding what he thought was a fake fire until he was dragged to safety. Total time for the first season of Chicago opera: One hour.)

Marshall Field clock

Marshall Field & Co.

Once you reach Randolph and State St., you are standing under the
7¾-ton, cast-bronze, Marshall Field's clock, one of the most famous
meeting spots in Chicago. Even though there is an identical clock on
the Washington Street side of the store, "I'll meet you under the

Field's clock," means the one on the Randolph Street side every time.

Enter Field's through the door nearest Randolph Street, walk to the center of the store and look up to the skylight. Each Christmas this open area becomes everyone's vision of what a downtown Christmas should be, with a huge tree and many traditional decorations.

Walk straight ahead, escalate to the third floor and take a left to the Crystal Palace, an old-fashioned ice cream parlor, whose ice cream took fourth place in a recent judging. The Crystal Palace is a symphony of olde tyme furnishings, a pink hue covering counters and chairs and stained glass filling its arches.

Return to Randolph and State, and think about history.

History at Randolph and State

In 1847, Long John Wentworth, the six-foot-six inch mayor of Chicago, got angry at the signs overhanging this area, so he ordered the police to take them all down and pile them in the center of Randolph near State. As Chicago's first Republican Mayor, Long John, during his second term, fired the entire police force on March 26, 1861, because the new police board might take over some of his powers. A captain, six lieutenants and 50 patrolmen were fired at 1:40 a.m. By 10 a.m. the next morning the police board hired back most of them, despite the fact that there were 1,500 applicants for their jobs.

Wentworth, who was an energetic mayor, also charged into the Sands, a vice district near Chicago Avenue and State, with axes, crowbars and teams of horses with hooks and chains. All the shanties were pulled down or burned while their owners were away enjoying a dog fight.

Randolph and State was the center of gambling in Chicago in the 1870s and 1880s. To the west, the area between State and Dearborn along Randolph was known as "Hairtrigger Block" because of the many gun battles there.

It was also in this general vicinity that Gentle Annie, known as the fattest madame in town, fell in love with Cap Hyman, a gambler. Refusing to take no for an answer, Gentle Annie stormed into Cap Hyman's gambling house on Sept. 23, 1866, dragged him from the sofa, knocked him down the stairs and chased him up the street with a whip. The couple was married only a few weeks later, proving that love will have its way.

Vaudeville and Movie Palaces

If you look to the west, just beyond Randolph and State, you'll see the Oriental Theater, once one of Chicago's grand movie palaces.

Today that electronics store is stuffed into part of the lobby of the old theater, which stands on a parcel of ground with a tragic history. On December 20, 1903, at about 3:30 p.m., Eddie Foy was appearing in the Iroquois Theater there in *Mr. Bluebeard*. Almost 1700 people, including many children, attended this special performance in what was then a marble palace. In the midst of a number titled "In the Pale Moonlight," an overloaded electric circuit flashed and the flame caught some flimsy drapery on the side of the stage.

Foy made sure his eldest son, Bryan, got out the stage door and then he urged the orchestra, "Play, play anything, but for God's sake don't stop, play on!" It didn't work. There was a panic. People piled up at the exits, jamming the doors shut.

Estimates vary, but between 571 and 603 people died that day, including 212 children. It was a scene of horror as scores were smothered, untouched by the flames. Over 200 bodies were found in a single narrow passageway. It was the second greatest fire death toll in American history—only exceeded by the 800 people killed in the Peshtigo, Wisconsin, fire.

Investigations and indictments followed, but there was no legal punishment for what happened. Today's Chicago fire code demands that all theater doors be made so as to open outward. The "panic bars" you see on theater doors today are a tribute to the Iroquois Theater fire victims.

Also, just west of where you now stand, at 64 W. Randolph, a Chicago Tin Pan Alley flourished after the turn of the century. Most people do not know that the following songs were written in Chicago: "Let Me Call You Sweetheart," "Down by the Old Mill Stream," "Memories," "Sweet Sue," "I'll See You in My Dreams," "My Buddy," and "My Blue Heaven."

As you walk north on State Street, you'll pass the former Loop Theater which played Russ Meyer's *The Vixen* in the late '60s. This was the first adults only film on State Street and it paved the way for other, sleazier movies. This helped hasten the decline of the Loop (so called because the elevated trains "loop" around the central business district). Of course the kung fu films which followed *The Vixen* didn't help matters.

Across the street, you'll see the building which housed the old State Lake Theater, another former popcorn palace, built in 1917 as part of the Orpheum Circuit. Ernie Simon, the Curbstone Cutup, presented his live sidewalk TV interview shows from under that marquee in the late '40s.

If it ever becomes time to write an epitaph for such grand theaters, perhaps the most fitting was found by author Ben Hall in the Paradise Theater in Faribault, Minn. A sign there read:

"Please do not turn on the clouds until the show starts.

"Be sure the stars are turned off when leaving."

As long as the nostalgic mood is upon us, the Chicago school of television, which pioneered minimal sets and using real people as hosts, had one of its finest practitioners at 190 N. State, where WLS-TV now has its home. Burr Tillstrom's "Kukla, Fran and Ollie" was once broadcast from this address. How many of you can remember three other KFO characters and their theme song?

Today, the station employs Oprah Winfrey, a TV talk show host, and the 190 N. State building is being refurbished.

If you continue a few feet north, you will be standing under the marquee of the Chicago Theater. Here, at last, we have a movie palace story with a happy ending.

Built in 1921, the Chicago Theater was the flagship of the Balaban and Katz theater chain. It was supposed to be awe inspiring, and it was.

Every important performer appeared there for four decades, often earning astronomical salaries even by today's standards. For instance, in 1935, Rudy Vallee earned $13,125 for a week's work, while the next week Sally Rand did her fan dance for $4,375. Jack Benny got $10,900 in 1940, the same year the Marx Brothers and Bob Hope earned over $13,000 per week.

By 1942, The Andrews Sisters got $8,250; Tommy Dorsey and his band, $10,500. In 1946, Frank Sinatra earned $26,250 (out of which he had to pay Skitch Henderson and the Pied Pipers).

Dean Martin and Jerry Lewis earned $21,000 for the week of Nov. 23, 1950. Nine months later, after becoming national hits in comedy and singing, they earned a record $62,201.25. To compare, that same year, Red Skelton earned $26,250 a week; the Mills Brothers, $7,551.25; Billy Eckstine, $14,152.50; Dinah Shore, $21,000 (she had the Will Mastin Trio with her); and Peggy Lee, $7,469.87. The last live act there, Eydie Gorme, played the Chicago Theater the week of Aug. 29, 1957 and earned $13,355.

For years after that, the Chicago Theater was slowly declining, until 1982, when a demolition permit was requested. There was an immediate uproar because the theater had been placed on the National Register of Historic Places.

Then a $26 million package was put together. This included the purchase of the Page Bros. Building just to the north, in which the interior of the building was completely gutted and rebuilt. In other words, the outer brick structure of the Page Building is used as a facade to hide a new wooden office building inside.

Over $4 million was spent to clean the old movie palace. Three inches of filth were vacuumed from some areas. The entire theater was scrubbed. The gold leaf was oiled and brought back to life. Chandeliers were found from other now-dead movie palaces and brought here. (Do look up at the magnificent 2400-pound fixture in the lobby.) The organ was restored. All the ropes used to fly curtains and scenery were replaced. The mice were ousted from the seats, and the chairs were refurbished. False ceilings were removed to reveal the beautiful plaster you can see above you in the hallway to the left of the lobby.

Then, on September 10, 1986, Frank Sinatra stepped on stage. He was backed by the Count Basie Orchestra, augmented by a dozen strings. He sang "My Kinda Town" and the Chicago Theater was officially back to life.

Do step inside and look around after purchasing a ticket to a musical or a star attraction. Notice the B & K emblem on the huge stained glass window facing State Street and the balcony below it overlooking the lobby. Here pianists and other performers would entertain the throngs waiting to enter the theater.

Think what Chicago would be missing if this were a parking lot. Sometimes even old theaters have the happiest of theatrical endings.

The Corner of State and Lake

Walk out of the theater and go to State and Lake, under the elevated tracks. This corner is historically interesting because here Long John Wentworth picked a fight with a Scottish roughneck named Allan Pinkerton, Chicago's first detective. Wentworth was bigger, but drunker, than Pinkerton, who destroyed him with punches to the belly. Pinkerton quit his job and later went on to fame and fortune as protector of President Abraham Lincoln and the person in charge of Union spies during the Civil War.

In 1849, Lake Street was excavated down to lake level and planked in the hopes that sewage would run off under the street. That didn't work, the water and refuse gathered under the planks and the street smelled.

Engineers then advised that the only way to get Chicago out of the mud, which was sometimes posted with warning signs saying "Bottomless," was to jack up the entire town 10 or 12 feet. Chicago was built on a gigantic mud lake.

Work began in 1855. George M. Pullman, who later built railroad sleeping cars, once lifted an entire block, using 600 men and 6,000 jack screws. Nothing was disturbed in the block as each man turned his 10 screws a quarter turn to gently raise the building, after which a new stone foundation was inserted under it.

Meanwhile, people moved their homes (as long as they were going to be jacked up anyway) hither and yon. Accounts of the time tell of people watching a jail with prisoners inside, moving down the street.

The State Street walk ends at Wacker and State, where pioneers in prairie schooners got supplies before moving west in the 1830s.

Heald Square, with a statue of George Washington, Robert Morris and Haym Salomon, is just around the corner, to your right. Morris and Salomon both helped finance the Revolutionary War and both died broke. The statue was dedicated on December 15, 1941, the 150th anniversary of the ratification of the Bill of Rights. Chicago's Mayor Edward J. Kelly praised our rights and then, because it was just eight days after Pearl Harbor, declared that our rights were in danger from "blood-mad gangsters, hordes of yellow enemies."

Parts of the State Street you have just seen are rotten and awful. But you are sure also to see construction cranes and new buildings. State Street isn't that Great Street—yet.

6

DEARBORN STREET SCULPTURE WALK

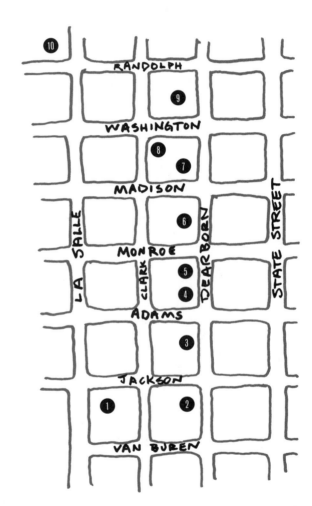

1. Board of Trade
2. Monadnock Building
3. Calder
4. Marquette Building
5. Xerox Building
6. Chagall
7. Henry Moore
8. Miro
9. Picasso
10. State of Illinois Dubuffet

Time: Two hours.

To get there: 156 LaSalle bus will let you off at Quincy and LaSalle, one-half block from the Board of Trade. Otherwise, State Street buses will drop you at Jackson and you can walk west.

Chicago Board of Trade

Without really planning it or announcing it in advance as a glorious civic intention, Chicagoans have created one of the great modern, outdoor sculpture walks. Within three blocks along Dearborn Street, anyone can see major works by Calder, Chagall and Picasso, plus architectural landmark buildings, while touching the financial section of Chicago and observing some of its churches.

Let's begin two blocks west of Dearborn, at LaSalle and Jackson, where we can begin to understand the powerful commercial interests in Chicago. The building blocking LaSalle Street is the Chicago Board of Trade, 141 W. Jackson.

The relatively youthful Chicago of Options Exchange, which was born on April 26, 1973, as the first securities exchange in the world established expressly for trading stock options, is located on the eighth floor. The viewing rooms, from which you can see a floor filled with price-displaying TV sets and aswarm with young brokers rushing about to early heart attacks because of the tensions of their jobs, are open from 9 a.m. to 3 p.m. weekdays.

The Chicago Board of Trade visitors center, on the fifth floor, is open from 9:15 a.m. to 1:15 p.m. weekdays. Polite guides there will tell you why all the men in blue, green and red jackets are yelling so frantically about wheat, soybeans, corn, oats, silver, gold, plywood and mortgage-backed certificates.

The Chicago Board of Trade was founded in 1848. Today, it is said that fewer than 500,000 Americans have ever traded a futures contract. Some of them are smiling and living in Palm Springs. Some aren't.

Both the Chicago Board of Trade and the Options Exchange are the big leagues, where fortunes can be made or lost. It is said that once upon a time Philip D. Armour, the packer, decided to drive the price of wheat to a new low. He called an old pal of his, George Seaverns, locked the door to his office, swore Seaverns to secrecy and tipped him off that wheat was "bound to rise." Seaverns put everything he had into wheat, mortgaging his house and bringing several of his friends into the deal. Then the market collapsed. Armour called his friend and is supposed to have said, "George, I knew you'd tell." Then he made out a check to cover Seaverns' losses.

As of today, the Board of Trade Building, which is 526 feet high and topped by a statue of Ceres, Greek goddess of grain, is partly a landmark and partly not. The Chicago City Council Cultural and Economic Development Committee decided, in 1977, that the Art Deco lobby and a few other sections of the building were landmarks. The rest could be remodeled at will, which is just the victory the Board of Trade lawyers wanted.

Continental Bank

Walk north on LaSalle past the solid columns of the Continental Illinois Bank and Trust Company of Chicago, and remember a time when they were not so solid, indeed.

In fact, this, the largest bank in Chicago and the seventh largest in America, was the subject of a $4.5 billion federal government rescue in July, 1984, the largest government takeover of a bank in history.

However, with a new management and almost $12 billion in guarantees from a safety net of other banks, the Continental began to come back to life. In 1986, the Federal Deposit Insurance Corporation announced that it would begin to sell its shares of the Continental in an attempt to recoup its losses becauses of the rescue. The government estimated that it would lose close to $1 billion to save this bank.

The Rookery

Remembering to change your mind about banking being a dull profession, continue walking north to The Rookery, at 209 S. LaSalle St., which was designed by Burnham and Root in 1886, with the lobby remodeled by Frank Lloyd Wright in 1905. It is, according to a plaque in the lobby, Chicago's oldest skyscraper.

It's named The Rookery because a temporary city hall, located here from 1872 (after The Chicago Fire) to 1884, attracted a lot of pigeons. The old Rookery was built around an iron water tank, which survived the fire and which housed Chicago's first public library.

After looking and marveling at the decorations in the lobby-court, notice the stairway starting above the second floor landing. A semicircular tower, jutting into the court, encloses this stairway, making it useful as an indoor fire escape.

The Rookery was once the scene of John W. "Bet-a-Million" Gates' whist and bridge games. The card games would begin on Saturday nights and $100,000 would change hands before Monday morning.

Next, retrace your steps back to the Board of Trade. When you get to Jackson, walk east past the front of the Board of Trade.

A Modern Jail

Stop at Clark and Jackson and look to your right at a strangely beautiful monolith, the Chicago Metropolitan Correctional Center, that triangular building which looks like a huge, concrete computer punch card, at 71 W. Van Buren. Designed by Harry Weese and built in 1975, this jail holds about 400 federal prisoners awaiting trial or sentencing, or serving brief terms. Rob Cuscaden, an architectural critic, called it the best designed building of 1975.

The indoor fire escape of the Rookery creates a nautilus shell effect

The idea that this was to be a prison without outside bars created that computer punch card appearance. The windows are 7½ feet tall, but only five inches wide, to prevent escapes.

A Bit of History

You are now one block from LaSalle and Adams, where the last wild bear was shot in the corporate limits of Chicago on October 6, 1834 by Sam George, a man trivia buffs should remember.

Continue east to Dearborn, two blocks away. As you pass Clark and Jackson, notice "Ruins III" by Nita K. Sonderland (1978) almost hidden in the southwest corner of the Federal Building Plaza. It looks real strange, like two chess pieces overseeing some columns. In 1841, a child was lost at this, the corner of Dearborn and Jackson, in grass taller than his head. A horseback rider saved the child from

71

certain death only because he saw the grass waving a bit as the boy walked through it. And that was less than 150 years ago!

Dearborn, the street, and the old Chicago Fort, were named after Henry Dearborn, a Secretary of the Army. One historian wrote that Dearborn "was one of the most ineffective leaders the nation has ever had to put up with." During the War of 1812, Dearborn organized an expedition to capture Montreal, but did not get across the border. His later efforts were even more feeble and indecisive and he was finally fired in 1813.

Monadnock, Manhattan, and Fisher Buildings

Before you, at 53 W. Jackson, is the Monadnock Building, with walls said to be 72 inches thick at the base. Built in 1891, designed by Burnham and Root, it is the highest building ever created of masonry construction.

Owen F. Aldis, the client for whom the building was created, often rejected Root's sketches as being too ornate, which is why the gently rippling front of Monadnock looks so spare and modern today. Architecture writer Ira Bach mentions a test of the building when there were doubts that its walls could stand Chicago's gusty winds. When winds of 88 miles an hour hit the city, engineers rushed to the Monadnock and measured the structure's vibrations. They were not more than ⅝ of an inch.

As you stand at Dearborn and Jackson, if you look to your right (to the south), you can see the Manhattan Building at 431 S. Dearborn, the first 16-story structure in the world. The Fisher Building, an architectural landmark designed by Daniel H. Burnham, is a little closer to you at 343 S. Dearborn.

Calder Stabile

Begin to walk resolutely north, which should be to your left, until you approach the glass-and-steel Federal Government Center, 219 S. Dearborn, designed by that great 20th Century architect, Mies van der Rohe, and opened in 1964.

You can't miss the Alexander Calder stabile, titled "Flamingo," in the Federal Center Plaza to your left (west). Both the Sears lobby and Federal Center Plaza Calder structures were dedicated on the same day, Oct. 25, 1974. Calder had a great time, riding down State Street in an orange and gold circus bandwagon, accompanied by calliopes.

Calder's 53-foot "Flamingo" reminds me of a giant praying mantis. In spring, when it is time to pay income tax, that isn't a bad symbol for government, especially if we mis-spell "praying" and make it "preying."

72

Calder stabile in the Federal Center Plaza

Indians, Hoodlums and Chicago's Last Cowpath

Continue north crossing to the west side of Dearborn and entering the Marquette Building, at 140 S. Dearborn. The mezzanine balcony is decorated with tile mosaics of Chicago history showing Indians extending a friendly greeting to Father Marquette, who discovered Chicago in 1673, preached here and died nearby in 1675. Everyone seems so dignified and friendly in the mosaics one wonders how the massacre came to be.

You will soon reach the corner of Dearborn and Monroe. Roger Plant's notorious "Under the Willows" brothel was located only two blocks west of here in the 1860s. Plant, an early believer in the power of advertising, painted in gold letters on every blue shade on every window of his building the tantalizing question, "Why Not?" After the Civil War, Plant retired as a successful panderer, bought land, farmed it and was a respectable patron of fashionable race tracks in town. Chicago has always respected money.

The offices of Mike McDonald, the hoodlum of the 1880s who first said, "You can't cheat an honest man," are only a block west of you. McDonald, adept at saying memorable things, also said, "Never give a sucker an even break." The Chicago Loop's last cowpath is also about a block west of you. Farmer Willard Jones deeded the property in 1844, but reserved the right in perpetuity to take his cows to and from the barn along a path between Monroe and Madison. Just west of a number "100" in the sidewalk, at 100 W. Monroe you'll see some doors. The path is behind them (air conditioning equipment blocks part of it). No cows have used it for decades, although it is always available to them. It's not much to see.

Chagall Mosaic

Check out the Sharper Image store in the new Xerox Building at Dearborn and Monroe. The merchandise changes all the time. When we were last there, we could have bought (and didn't) gold plated bar bells or a hologram of a woman's hand holding diamonds. Let's cross Monroe, noting the Italian Village, three fine restaurants just to the west of you at 71 W. Monroe, and enter the First National Bank Building Plaza. The building, 60 stories tall, sweeps upward, in a slightly curving shape and resembles an elegantly scripted "A".

In the plaza, by the fountain, is the Chagall. It is a 70-foot-long mosaic called "Les Quatre Saisons," unveiled on September 27, 1974, on a day when Chicago fell in love with Chagall and vice versa.

Norman Ross, veteran Chicago radio personality and vice president of the First National, remembers that when Chagall arrived in Chicago, he discovered that Chicago was stronger and more exciting than he had remembered. So he added darkness and strength to the mosaic, inserting bits of Chicago brick, making some buildings taller, tinkering with it until he almost had to be pulled from his work for fear the unveiling would have to be postponed. Then, Ross recalls, Chagall stepped back, had tears in his eyes, gave Ross a friendly touch on the shoulder and said, "Pas mal (not bad)."

To answer the most-asked question: The mosaic represents the four seasons. On the side facing Dearborn and the Inland Steel Building, the north half is autumn and the south half, the one nearest Monroe, is winter. On the side facing Clark Street to the west, spring

Chagall mosaic at First National Plaza

is on the south and summer is on the northern section.

Chicago Daily News art critic Franz Schulze called the mosaic "the late work of a great artist. It is not a masterpiece, and it is not likely to change the course of art. At the same time, it contains passages of loveliness that could not have been conceived by anyone other than an immensely gifted man."

Throughout the late spring and summer there are free noon concerts here, making this plaza the perfect place for a bag lunch.

There's more. Notice on the northeast corner of Madison and Dearborn an enormous, sensuous sculpture done in 1983 by Henry Moore and titled "External Internal."

Loop Synagogue

Cross the plaza and exit on Clark Street, walking north to the Chicago Loop Synagogue, at 16 S. Clark. There is a metal sculpture above the entrance titled "The Hands of Peace," by Israeli sculptor Henri Azaz. The letters behind the priestly hands say, "The Lord bless thee and keep thee, the Lord make His face to shine upon thee and be gracious to thee; the Lord lift up His countenance upon thee and give thee peace."

"Batcolumn"

When you stand at Madison and Clark, you are only four blocks from the 101-foot-long steel baseball bat, called "Batcolumn," a sculpture by Claes Oldenburg. It stands before the Social Security Administration building at 600 W. Madison, which is out of the way for this walk. When it was unveiled on April 14, 1977, skid row bums living nearby and artistic protestors hooted, "Tear it down," and said it was a "five-story nightstick." Critics were kinder than that, saying that it will look better to us as time passes and may even become "an indelible emblem of 20th Century America in general, 1970s Chicago in particular." Today, it's still a 101-foot-tall, metal bat in a lousy neighborhood and that's why it is only mentioned here, but it is not part of this walk.

"Christ of the Loop"

Cross Madison, and look to the west, at St. Peter's Church and Friary, 110 W. Madison. Its gigantic "Christ of the Loop," an 18-foot-high figure of Christ weighing 26 tons, is the work of Latvian sculptor Arvid Strauss.

If you look to the east, you'll see Madison and Dearborn. Here, on Sept. 7, 1927, Tony Lombardo, a sidekick of Al Capone, was watching an airplane being hoisted up the side of a building. We do not know why the airplane was so engaged and neither are we sure why two bullets suddenly entered Lombardo's head. If it makes any difference at this late date, police at the time suspected that Bugs Moran engineered this execution in revenge for Hymie Weiss' slaying (see Holy Name Cathedral entry on North Michigan Avenue walk).

Miro Sculpture

Continue north along Clark Street to Washington and enter the Chicago Temple Building, 77 W. Washington, where the sounds of organ music softly push aside the angry loop traffic noises. In the

Unveiling the Picasso sculpture in Daley Center Plaza

space of just a few feet, you have seen downtown structures dedicated to the Methodist, Jewish and Catholic religions.

Leave the Chicago Temple Building, but notice the odd sculpture in the plaza just east of the Temple. It is by Miro, dedicated in 1980, and some people believe it represents an abstract woman with a Spanish comb in her hair. Next, cross Washington and walk north on Clark Street along the Chicago Civic Center Plaza (now called Daley Center).

Unity Building

The building to the east, with a restaurant named Mayor's Row in the first floor, was once called the Unity Building. Now it's merely the 127 N. Dearborn Building, and it leans to the south one inch per floor. The tilt is a slight one (no Leaning Tower of Pisa, this) and difficult to see, but the elevator operators there assure passengers that the building does lean. It began its southward tilt when a subway was dug nearby.

Clarence Darrow, the trial lawyer famed for his defenses of labor leaders and the Leopold-Loeb case, once had offices on the seventh floor of this building, built in 1892 by former Illinois Governor John Peter Altgeld.

Picasso Sculpture

The County Building is directly west of you and, behind it, its twin, the Chicago City Hall. Historians love to note that these are virtually identical buildings, yet the County Building cost $1,500,000 more to build than City Hall.

Daley Center is directly to the north. It is made of Cor-Ten steel, which will resist corrosion, allegedly forever. For a long time after the building was completed in 1964, Chicago was blessed with a big, ugly, rusty Civic Center. Now it's oxidized to a nice dark brown and no one laughs at it.

People still sometimes laugh at the controversial, 163-ton, Picasso sculpture, made of the same Cor-Ten steel and sitting in this plaza. Art experts have called it a dog or dodo bird. Sir Roland Penrose (Picasso's friend) said it was the head of a woman with "ample flowing hair"; a local columnist thought it looked like a baboon; and a local underground newspaper believed it was obscene and proved this contention by printing pictures taken of it from behind. One alderman suggested that the Picasso be sent back where it came from and a statue of Ernie Banks, long-time Cubs baseball star and a member of the CTA board in the '70s, be substituted.

Whatever it is, the Picasso sculpture has settled into its site. Chicagoans no longer yell about it or laugh at it. They either ignore it or drive out-of-town friends past it.

History at Clark and Randolph

Continue walking north on Clark to Randolph. The Senate, a gambling den, was located one block to the east of you, at Dearborn and Randolph, in the 1880s. The games were so "high toned" that, when police raided this establishment, Frank Connelly, the owner, took his customers to the police station in carriages, paid their fines and brought them back to continue playing as though nothing had happened.

The Chippewa, Ottawa and Pottawatomie Indians, including 76 of their chiefs, were paid off for their land in 1834 about three blocks west of this spot. Before they left town, local sharpies made sure that nearly everything the Indians received in payment was given to local entrepreneurs for liquor. It has happened to many a tourist since.

If you look to the west, you'll see the Garrick Garage, once the site of the Garrick Building. When it was demolished in 1961, according to a plaque on the garage's west wall, many museums and universities got plaster and terra cotta decorations designed by Adler and Sullivan in 1893. One piece of terra cotta was saved and used to create the design on the front of the garage, which now becomes a sad tribute to the past.

State of Illinois Center

Before you stands either an odd blue space ship or Darth Vader's extra helmet. The State of Illinois Center at 100 W. Randolph was dedicated on May 6, 1985. Ever since, this building designed by Helmut Jahn has been the subject of controversy.

First, there is the overall design. There seems to be no middle ground on this one. People either love it or loathe it. You will either see it as grim, mysterious and forboding or as "the first building of the 21st century," as Governor James R. Thompson said when he dedicated it.

Then, there is the air conditioning. The original plans seemed sound: At night, when electricity rates are lower, eight giant ice cubes were to be frozen. They were to stand in ice banks 40 feet long, 12 feet wide and 14 feet tall in the building's sub-basement. Then, during the day, all that stored cold would be released to cool the building. For some reason, that doesn't really work. Perhaps the 24,600 glass panels conduct too much heat during the day, but in its early months it was a miserable place in which to work.

It is, however, one of those places in Chicago which people must visit, meaning that you will join about 2,500,000 others who stop by each year.

The black and white, friendly, cloudlike sculpture in front of the building is "Monument with Standing Beast" by Jean Dubuffet.

In 1977, a law was passed mandating that one-half of one percent of anything spent on new state buildings must be used to buy art. They have bought well.

On the 16th floor, there are paintings by Gladys Nilsson, Jim Nutt and Karl Wirsum, who were founding members of the Hairy Who, a group of gritty artists who are mentioned in the Su-Hu Gallery walk.

A tour of the building should begin in the atrium, all 7,900,000 cubic feet of it, one of the largest enclosed spaces in the world. It has already been featured in several movies and TV shows, including the big, final shoot-out scene in *Running Scared* with Gregory Hines and Billy Crystal. Remember the bad dope dealer machine gunning the good guys as they went up and down the glass enclosed elevators, while Hines scaled the outside of the building for no reason other than it was both the most difficult way to get inside and the most visually spectacular?

Be sure to visit the State Art Gallery on the second floor, which is devoted exclusively to Illinois artists.

As you go through the building, be sure to notice what isn't there— light switches. They have been eliminated because computers control the lights, making them more energy efficient.

Next go to the 16th floor for a view of the building from the top. A guest book there can be fascinating. In addition to visitors from Istanbul, Korea, Sri Lanka, Finland and Burbank, last time we went there three "Momar Quadaffis" registered.

History and Geography at Lake Street

Let us leave the State of Illinois Center, by walking to Clark Street and proceeding north to Lake Street where the City Saloon would offer a few theatrical attractions as early as 1836. Before radio, television and films, Chicagoans would be entertained by the "Annual Entertainment by the Inmates of the Indiana Deaf and Dumb Asylum" and the Druid Horn Players performing "fascinating numbers played on ox horns." In those days, it was better than staying home and watching the prairie grow.

The Tremont House, once Chicago's most famous hotel, opened one block east of here in 1830s. Sportsmen and tenants would sit in the doorway of the Tremont then and shoot ducks on State St.

The Sauganash Hotel opened for business about four blocks west of here and some 60 people gathered in that hotel in 1833 to vote to incorporate Chicago. There were only 150 people in the village then. Four years later, the first census revealed that there were 4,170 people in Chicago, including Richard Harper, who listed his occupation as "loafer." Today, that man would be either a Chicago alderman or would be otherwise employed by the city.

The Wigwam, a rectangular wooden building, was also built near Lake and Wacker, about four blocks west of you. In 1860, when Abraham Lincoln was nominated there as Republican candidate for president of the United States, one witness recalled "for 10 minutes nothing was heard but the roar of human voices."

If the reader-walker is in a true historical mood, he will want to know he is standing on a former sand bar. Lake Michigan has only gradually receded to its present shoreline. Each time it retreated, it left behind a sand bar. According to *Daily News* reporter Lois Wille, all of suburban Oak Paris is on a former sand bar left there more than 8,000 years ago. Western Avenue, another former sand bar, is 20 feet below Oak Park, and Clark Street, built on yet another sand bar, is 20 feet below Western Avenue.

Lager Beer Riots

Now moving rather quickly forward in time, the corner of Randolph and Clark, just south of you, was the scene of one of the major confrontations of the Lager Beer Riots of 1855, an important moment in Chicago history. Chicago elected a "Know Nothing" mayor, Levi D. Boone. The Mayor belonged to a short-lived political party which hated all foreigners. Boone's first action was to raise liquor licenses 600 per cent and to enforce a half-forgotten law closing saloons on Sundays. Boone applied the Sunday closing law only to bars selling beer. Those selling good old American whiskey were exempt.

This outraged Chicago's Sunday beer-drinking Germans, a group not to be tampered with lightly. Insult our baseball teams or even sneer at our wives' looks, but never, ever take away a Chicagoan's beer.

A mob of over 400 Germans, marching behind fifes and drums, came to Randolph and Clark on April 21, 1855, and told those in the Courthouse there at the time that, if their decision went against the 200 German saloonkeepers arrested for selling beer on Sunday, Chicago would burn. There was a brief battle and the crowd retreated north over the Clark Street bridge, vowing to return with reinforcements.

At 3 p.m., more than 1,000 angry, beer-starved Germans, armed with shotguns, rifles, pistols, clubs and knives, came back to face 200 police and deputies. The Mayor ordered the Clark Street bridge opened when half the crowd was across temporarily splitting the mob. Then the gun battle began. After nearly an hour, 20 men were seriously injured, one German died, and one policeman lost his arm because of a shotgun blast.

The result: The Sunday closing law was no longer enforced, the

Marina City looking down on State Street

voters defeated a state prohibition law a few months later, and the "Know Nothings" were eventually voted out of office.

Eastland Disaster

Walk another block north to the Chicago River and think about July 24, 1915. At 7:32 a.m., 2,500 employees of the Western Electric Co. were on board the steamship *Eastland* ready for an all-day lake excursion. Then the boat tipped on its side, drowning 812 people. One *Chicago Daily News* story said, "A little shoe floated on top of the water, thick with the flotsam and jetsam of the great tragedy . . . the little shoe pleaded with silent eloquence for recognition."

Many theories were advanced as to why the boat tipped over, but none satisfied every authority. Eventually the *Eastland* was righted, and became the *USS Wilmette,* a Naval training ship between World

Wars I and II. In 1921, the *Wilmette* nee *Eastland* became the only American ship ever to sink an enemy submarine in the Great Lakes. It sent a German U-Boat to the bottom in compliance with an arms limitation treaty. The *Wilmette* was sold for scrap in 1946 for $1,937.99.

Marina City

The two circular towers to the east, your right, belong to Marina City, built in 1964. They are 62 stories high and have several restaurants on the ground level, some of which feature a good view of the river, along with mediocre service and food.

This ends the Dearborn sculpture walk. Think of it. Without paying a cent, you have just walked past works by Picasso, Chagall, Calder, Miro, Henry Moore, and Dubuffet. There are times when, mostly inadvertently, man can create beauty in the midst of intense commerce.

7

WACKER DRIVE

RIVER WALK

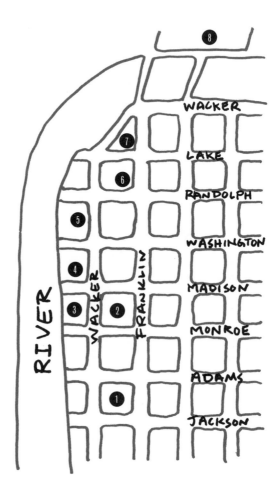

1. Sears Tower
2. 1 S. Wacker
3. Mercantile Exchange
4. Opera House
5. Morton Thiokol
6. Harry's Hot Dogs
7. 333 Wacker
8. Merchandise Mart

Time: About three hours, less if you stride rather than stroll.
To get there: The Sears Tower, at the beginning of this walk, occupies the square block bounded by Franklin, Jackson, Wacker and Adams in the southwest section of Chicago's downtown area. The 1, 7, 126, 151 and 156 CTA buses stop at Wacker and Adams.

An Area of Brand-New Buildings

You will be walking along the south branch of the Chicago River, which is just behind (west) of some of the newest office buildings in Chicago. Because Chicago is justly famous as an architectural museum and because several of these buildings are recent additions to the street, this is a chance to see the latest ideas in commercial construction.

If that doesn't sound very romantic, well, it depends on your definition of romance. A walk down this wide thoroughfare includes a stroll past the world's tallest building, an opera house with a past and one source of the Kennedy wealth.

Sears Tower, World's Tallest Building

The walk begins at N. Wacker and Adams, at the Sears Tower, the world's tallest building, with the world's fastest elevator, and housing, according to the Guinness Book of Records, the headquarters of the world's largest advertiser and general merchandising firm. The Sears Tower is 110 stories tall, 1,454 feet to the top of its tower and 1,707 feet to the very tippy top of its antennas. That elevator to the 103rd floor allegedly zips up to 1,353 feet in 55 seconds, achieving 20.45 miles per hour. It has never gone through the roof.

Sears' literature claims that the Sears Tower "has one of the most complete safety systems ever devised for a high-rise building," thus alleviating fears of the world's biggest "Towering Inferno". This system includes smoke detectors on every floor which will alert a computer, which will then cut off the air flow to the affected arrea.

The Sears Tower, which cost more than $150,000,000 and which took three years to build, features in the Wacker Lobby an animated mural, modestly titled "Universe," by Alexander Calder. The work includes three flowers, a spine, helix, sun and pendulum, each driven by its own motor. With the spine moving at 4 rpm and the helix at 15 rpm, it looks rather happy.

Engineers have determined that during a so-called "Maximum Storm," or one liable to occur in this area only once every 100 years or so, the building would actually sway six to ten inches in the wind. Do not take motion-sickness pills before going to the top—you can't really feel the sway. It is not true that toilets above the 100th floor have waves with whitecaps in them.

After considering the Sears and other towers, *Chicago Tribune* architectural critic Paul Gapp wrote, "There is romance and almost a bit of magic about all this [skyscraper building], but also a touch of madness. Many critics agree that urban gigantism has gone too far in recent years, wiping out any sense of human scale and disfiguring cityscapes . . . Perhaps it is time for a skyscraper embargo."

85

Sears Tower dominates the Loop skyline

There's only one way to see if you agree with Gapp. Visit the Sears Tower and go to its Skydeck, where the admission fee is $3 for adults and $1.50 for children. On a clear day, the view is unsurpassed.

South to the Mercantile Exchange

Leave the Sears Tower on the Wacker Drive side (but do notice the trees growing in the enclosed lobby) and walk two blocks south through a glass, steel and concrete canyon. You will pass Oberweis Securities, the LaSalle National Bank, the Northern Trust Bank and the very white United States Gypsum Building, which isn't square to the street.

Eventually, you will get to 1 S. Wacker, a 40-story building designed by Helmut Jahn, who also created the State of Illinois Center (the Darth Vader helmet on the Dearborn Sculpture Walk). AT & T is in 14 floors of this magnificent, dark glass and steel structure, with a variety of bankers, investment houses, and magazines occupying the rest of the building. Notice the lobby with its marble and its bars of light.

Next, cross Madison Avenue to the Chicago Mercantile Exchange Center, 10 S. Wacker, to visit the world's largest financial futures market.

The visitors gallery is open from 7:30 a. m. to 3:15 p. m. You will look down on a beehive of activity. They're trading futures on live hogs, pork bellies, live cattle and feeder cattle to the left. In the far left corner, the future prices of Canadian dollars, Deutsch marks, Swiss francs, Japanese yen, British pounds and French francs are being determined.

To the right, they're trading interest rate futures for Eurodollars, Certificates of Deposit and Treasury Bills. And to the far right they're trading futures on stocks.

Notice the different jacket colors. Red is for Exchange members, yellow for employees of clearing firms which match purchases and sales, light blue for pit reporters who give the trades to computer operators on the catwalk.

This center communicates with the world through 6,350 phone lines.

If you are hungry, try the Mama Mia Restaurant, which has an outdoor cafe to the west on the concrete banks of the Chicago River.

Civic Opera House

Otherwise proceed north to the Opera House, which is the home of three theaters, including the Lyric Opera and the Civic Theater.

This structure was built by Samuel Insull and it is here that we should reflect on how high human beings can rise and how far they can fall.

87

Insull learned Pittman shorthand at age 14 and that allowed him to become the English representative for the Thomas A. Edison Co. Insull operated the first telephone switchboard in England, with George Bernard Shaw, who would become a famous playwright, as his battery boy.

Insull came to America in 1892, eventually coming to Chicago to buy and operate electrical companies. Later, he expanded by buying railroads.

By 1926, he could look at the city and know that every light in Chicago was shining because of the power he supplied. By 1929, he was the president of 15 corporations, chairman of 56 and a member of the board of 81. The companies he headed were worth between $3 and $4 billion, while his personal fortune was about $150,000,000! He threatened to buy and sell entire political parties!

His empire had 600,000 stockholders; 500,000 bond-holders; 4,000,000 customers and produced an eighth of all the gas and electricity consumed in America.

Because his actress wife felt unhappy and unfulfilled he built the Lyric Opera House, which was also supposed to gain a place for Insull in high society.

The man seemed to be sailing through the Depression with ease and, by 1931, banks were willing to lend money to Insull but not to the City of Chicago.

But then came the day of reckoning. Even Insull's stocks were wilting with the Depression. Then Cyrus Eaton, a mogul, threatened to dump Insull's stocks on the market, further depressing their value, which had to be kept high because the stocks were used as collateral on loans. Insull paid $40,000,000 to Eaton to prevent the dumping, but he could not do that forever.

On July 5, 1932, after the value of his stocks crumbled, the New York bankers were able to force Insull out. When he left his companies, all he had was an $18,000 a year pension. In 1938, Insull collapsed in a French subway station. He had only 35 cents in his pockets. His estate was valued at $1,000; his debts: $14,000,000.

Morton Thiokol Building

Next, cross Washington to 110 N. Wacker, the long, low, four-story Morton Thiokol Building, and think about corporate histories.

The "Morton" in the title comes from the Morton Salt Company, with $370 million worth of salt sales a year and a company with a long and illustrious history. Jay Morton got control of the company in 1886. His father, J. Sterling, was secretary of the Nebraska Territory at age 26 and the founder of Arbor Day. In 1914, the company put a little girl carrying an umbrella and spilling salt on their packages. Originally, the accompanying slogan said, "Even in rainy weather it flows freely," but that was changed to "When it rains, it pours," a phrase which achieved advertising immortality.

As a result of a variety of mergers, the company also made Janitor-in-a-Drum, Spray 'n Wash, Glass Plus and No-Pest strips. Through the years, various Morton relatives have donated a wing to the Art Institute and created the Morton Arboretum in Lisle, Ill.

In 1982, when Morton's sales were approaching a billion dollars a year, the company bought Thiokol Corp. "Thiokol" is from two Greek words meaning sulfur and glue and indicates that the origins of the company were in the discovery of synthetic rubber.

The only problem was in the '30s and even the '40s no one wanted much synthetic rubber. Besides the plants making it smelled like rotten eggs.

Then it was discovered that a liquid polymer made by Thiokol was the best solid propellant fuel binder known to man and Thiokol got in the business of making such rockets as the Pershing, Nike Zeus, Sidewinder, Maverick, and even motors for the space shuttle.

And that is how a salt company got involved in the Challenger Space Shuttle disaster, when one of their rockets exploded, killing seven astronauts on January 28, 1986. Some Thiokol engineers said that it was not safe to launch that day because of the cold weather, other executives pushed for the launch.

Wolf Point

Continue north, cross the Chicago River on the Franklin-Orleans Bridge and then look at the river. Both banks of the river at this point have historic significance. In fact, the city of Chicago was founded both here and to the east at Michigan Avenue and the river, where Fort Dearborn stood. To the east, there are several suitable plaques indicating where the fort was. Here, nothing marks the history which began here, probably because most of it was involved in taverns and boozing.

Chicagoans say that Wolf Point is the spit of land pushing into the river just south and west of the Merchandise Mart where there is a rudimentary park with a few trees, grass and a concrete parking lot. Historically, Wolf Point also referred to the bank of the river on the other side where the 333 Wacker Building stands. No one knows why it is called Wolf Point or who named it.

There are stories that a trading post stood there in 1778 and that it was run by a fellow named "Guarie."

Later, this area achieved historical significance because it was the site of Chicago's first tavern, which started in 1828. Within a year, two more taverns were added to the settlement here and one writer observed ". . . as few as the inhabitants of Chicago were at that time, one of their principal avocations seems to have been that of keeping tavern."

By 1832, the original tavern, under new ownership, was given the name Rat Castle, because of the "regular boarders that infested its premises," and it was generally known as the place where men of character stopped.

The Sauganash Hotel stood on the south bank of the river and it was here that Chicago was incorporated in 1833. Later that same year, Chicago's first election was held there. It was also Chicago's first theater, but it was destroyed by fire in 1851.

A historic tavern should probably occupy both banks of the river here.

Merchandise Mart

The large building to your right is the Merchandise Mart, which with the 25-story Apparel Center to the west of it, constitutes the largest wholesale buying complex in the world. The Mart has been owned by the Joseph P. Kennedy family since 1946 and it is among the enterprises which allow the Kennedy's to be jetsetters and to spend their money elsewhere in the world.

The Apparel Center, a nearly windowless building because that allegedly saves energy (while presumably driving those inside nuts), is not a hit with local critics. Donald M. Schwartz, writing in the *Chicago Sun-Times* in 1977, called it "a vast monotone of largely windowless concrete" with "all the charm of two gigantic cardboard boxes" which "repels your advance, your interest, even a casual glance." Can't win them all.

There is a Holiday Inn on the 14th floor and the rooms circle a huge atrium. Despite the cold concrete there, the staff is friendly. And the place has a great swimming pool for doing laps.

The Merchandise Mart was opened by Marshall Field & Co. in 1930. There is a hall of fame of American merchants in front of the Mart, with the busts of Field, F. W. Woolworth, A. Montgomery Ward, and others.

WMAQ-AM-TV, NBC in Chicago, is on the 19th and 20th floors of this building and that area was also a center for radio broadcasts in the '30s. "The Quiz Kids" began there on June 28, 1940 with this question, "I want you to tell me what I would be carrying home if I brought an antimacassar, a dinghy, a sarong and an apteryx." It went on to become both a popular and loathed show. Every kid in America was compared to Joel Kupperman, who was then the smartest kid in the world. "Curtain Time," "First Nighter" and "Club Matinee" were all broadcast from here, as were the early "Today" Shows, with Dave Garroway closing every broadcast by opening his right hand and saying "Peace."

If you're in a touring mood, Quaker Oats opens its test kitchens on the Mart's second floor from 10 a.m. to noon and from 1:30 to 3 p.m. every working day. Among other things, the kitchens will show you how Cap'n Crunch is made. Large groups should call 222-6809 for reservations.

This ends the Wacker Dr. walk. If you are hungry, I'd suggest walking another three or four blocks north on Wells St., which is one block east of Franklin, to either Carson's for Ribs or Ed Debevics', both of which are mentioned in the Streets of Food Restaurant walk. Both will offer good food at a reasonable price.

8

SUHU

GALLERY WALK

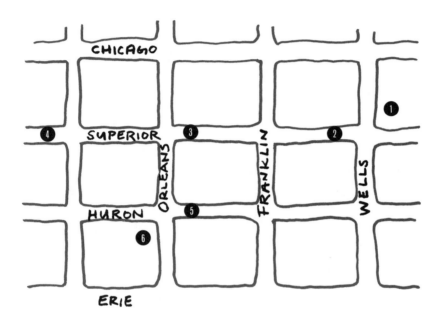

1. Roy Boyd Gallery
2. 200 Block of W. Superior
3. 300 Block of W. Superior
4. 400 Block of W. Superior
5. 300 Block of W. Huron
6. Green Door Tavern

Time: Two hours, less if the art works bore you, more if you become enchanted.

To get there: There is a Chicago Avenue stop on the Ravenswood elevated line. Walk east to Wells Street then take a right to Superior. There is also a LaSalle Street bus which stops at Superior. Wells is one block west.

Chicago's Gallery District

New York has SoHo, San Francisco has SoMa (south of Market St.), but Chicago's SoHo doesn't want to be called SuHu.

The gallery owners here would prefer that their neighborhood have the non-derivative name of "River North." But that applies to more than just the galleries along Superior and Huron Streets.

Once Henry Hanson of Chicago Magazine called the area "SuHu," that's what it became despite the protests of some.

There are dozens of galleries here, along Superior and Huron, between Wells and Franklin Streets. Many of them once had addresses on or near Michigan Ave., but they left that high rent district in favor of SuHu, which also offered more space in converted warehouses. Today, the rents in SuHu are getting higher, but this area will probably be associated with the art world for some time to come.

SuHu comes alive on the second Friday evening of most months, when many of the galleries have the openings of their new exhibits. Starting at about 5 p.m. on that night, art enthusiasts can see the latest paintings at a dozen or more galleries, each of which is also offering a glass or two of free, usually inexpensive wine.

This leads to a festive, energetic, party atmosphere, which is certainly controversial. Imagine, if you will, hundreds of business men and women, art students and visitors going from gallery to gallery, drinking a little wine here and a little wine there, while noticing the exhibits. It is a monthly cocktail-party-happening, and gallery owners wonder, with yuppies meeting yuppettes, struggling artists bumping into futures traders, what is the effect on the serious buyer?

One gallery manager said, "The real purpose of those Friday openings is for young moderns to meet each other over a cheap glass of Italian wine." Another criticized, "Here, the party scene is becoming more lively than the art scene."

Others, such as Esther Saks, whose gallery is at 311 W. Superior, enjoy the openings, "By and large, it's terrific. People from out of town are delighted, but there are times when you stand in front of art objects, protecting them."

If you want an artsy party, go to SuHu on a Friday evening when the place is jumping. Otherwise, visit any other time when the area is quieter and the gallery managers can talk to you at length about the art on display.

We begin our walk near the corner of Wells and Superior. The Roy Boyd Gallery, at 739 N. Wells, is run by Ann Boyd, who was a Chicago elementary school teacher for 20 years. Her husband, Roy, runs their gallery in Los Angeles, which opened in 1981.

200 W. Superior

Moving west on Superior, there are several galleries at 200 W. Superior. Adelyn Hansen, director of the Hansen Galleries, was the furnishings fashion co-ordinator for the Carson, Pirie Scott & Co. department store for 16 years. She would design the show rooms in the furniture department, often buying paintings to decorate them, but that is now her profession.

E. Houk is also at 200 W. Superior and this gallery, which began life in Detroit, specializes in photographs taken before 1950.

The Neal Gallery represents black American artists. Ms. Isobel Neal taught home-bound handicapped children before opening the gallery.

Moving slightly west, to 215 W. Superior, Rhona Hoffman wanted to be a painter as a child. Then, at Vassar, she took her first art class and stopped painting "because it wasn't fun anymore." But she studied art history, opened the store at the Museum of Contemporary Art and finally started her own gallery. Hoffman now has an internationally respected gallery, featuring American and European artists, plus soon-to-be-famous artists.

At the same address, the Neville/Sargent Gallery has Jane and Don Neville as its directors. The "Sargent" refers to Jane's first partner's mother. The partner, and presumably the mother, left more than a decade ago, but the name remains. It is worth the trek up to their seventh floor gallery, not only because of the view, but because they take a chance on young, unknown artists and, as Jane says, "Our prices reflect that fact."

Crossing the street, enter 212 W. Superior, and the Dart Gallery, where you may smell chocolate. Rebecca Donelson, a manager, said that this 100-year-old building was once a candy factory. On hot days, chocolate or caramel can still be seen dripping from the rafters. The huge copper pots near the elevators, which now hold flowers, were once chocolate vats.

The gallery once won a prize as the best renovated loft space. It deals in major contemporary American painters and sculptors.

The Hokin/Kaufman Gallery is a mother/daughter team which specializes in artistic furniture designs. Grace Hokin, the mother, has had galleries for over two decades, but now her daughter, Lori Kaufman, is sole owner. Their January, "Made in Chicago," furniture show annually features one of a kind artist-designed furniture.

Betsy Rosenfield was director of development at the Museum of Contemporary Art before opening her own gallery in 1980 at 212 W. Superior. She features paintings, photography, sculpture, art glass and once had Kenneth Walker as her director. He immolated himself after a controversial trial and his story will be told later in this walk, when we get to the N. A. M. E. gallery.

A Friday night gallery opening in Suhu

J. Rosenthal is owned by Dennis Rosenthal. His middle initial is "J" and he uses it because there was a Dorothy Rosenthal gallery and he wanted to minimize the confusion. Dennis once sold a Braque painting for $400,000, thought he was doing very well in the art world and then changed his mind when, just seven years later, the same painting sold for $3,750,000!

The Bud Holland Gallery, 222 W. Superior, is open by appointment only. Call 664-5000. This gallery specializes in 20th century pictures by Picasso, de Kooning and others. If you are really interested in contemporary art, it is worth making an appointment to see the man described by many critics as one of the "movers and shakers" of the Chicago art world.

Again walking west, the Gilman Gallery, at 226 W. Superior, is owned by Mack Gilman, a former U.S. National Fencing champion and the owner of a 65-acre McHenry County farm, where county champion calves are raised.

Gilman decided that the world should know about Frank Gallo, the sculptor who casts nudes and other figures in epoxy resin. After various established New York galleries refused to show Gallo, Gilman rented two suites in the Sherry Netherland Hotel, held a private exhibition and introduced Gallo to the art world.

Today, Gilman creates videos about the artists he represents, meaning that a TV show about the exhibit may be going on when you enter the gallery. In addition, the videos are available to anyone who buys a painting, making it easier to explain to friends why you got the work in question. Gilman is also founding president of the Chicago Art Dealers Association.

300 W. Superior

Crossing Franklin, enter 300 W. Superior, where the Goldman/Kraft Gallery is owned by Herbert Goldman, who also has a gallery in Haifa, Israel.

Yolanda Saul's Gallery, in the same entranceway, specializes in naive, academically untrained artists, including Grandma Moses.

One of Yolanda's most famous contemporary artists is Lee Godie, described by the Wall Street Journal as "a toothless, smelly shopping-bag lady" with no permanent address who stashes much of her art in public lockers around the city, especially in bus stations.

Miss Godie began selling her art on the steps of the Art Institute in 1968 after her late mother and a red bird told her to start painting.

She is one of a kind, claiming to save $31.50 a month by buying her own tea bags and asking waitresses only for hot water. She sells her art for no more than $75 a canvas.

She is one of several "outsider" artists, including Joseph Yoakum, a former circus roustabout, and Irving Mendes, a retired truck driver and butcher, who have become the darlings of the art community.

Crossing to the south side of Superior, the Richard Gray Gallery, at 301 W. Superior, has sold all the important artists of the late-nineteenth and twentieth centuries, including Degas, Cezanne, Picasso, Braque, Matisse, Arp, Rothko and others.

The Prairie Lee Gallery features Southwest and American Indian art in a space with adobe-like walls.

Walking to the west, the Struve Gallery, at 309 W. Superior, represents many Chicago artists.

Esther Saks, at 311 W. Superior, was an artist who decided she didn't have the passion that profession required. She began collecting after taking a nine-week camping trip, later opened a gallery and now has the largest selection of ceramic sculpture in Chicago.

Phyllis Kind, at 313 W. Superior, has a passion for representing Chicago artists. After nearly getting a doctoral degree in chemistry, after her fourth child was born, Phyllis began representing a group of artists known as the Hairy Who in the late 1960s. These were young, gritty, often humorous artists who banded together while at the Art Institute to declare that there was important and different Chicago art being created. That group included Jim Nutt, Karl Wirsum, Gladys Nilsson and others, all of whom now have important reputations.

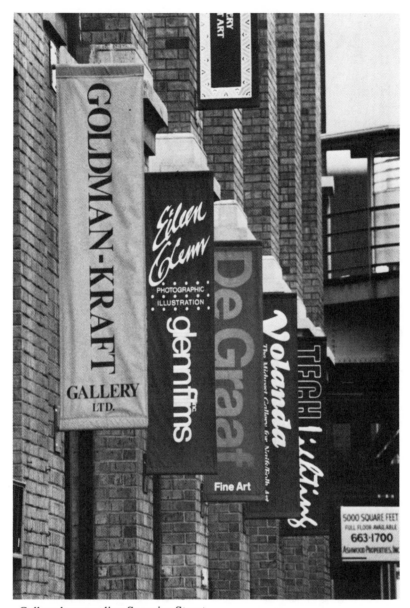

Gallery banners line Superior Street

Phyllis Kind has also opened a gallery in New York so Chicago artists can gain national exposure. And she continues to discover new artists.

Continuing westward after crossing Orleans St., we find Artemesia, at 341 W. Superior, which was begun in 1973 as a cooperative to promote women's art. These days, it also includes men, but it also reverts back to its roots. In 1985, Artemesia had an exhibit featuring pictures of men as sex objects.

The Douglas Dawson gallery, also at 341 W. Superior, features textiles. It began in McGregor, Iowa, as the Casa Del Rio. Dawson sold that shop and moved to Chicago, where he features things woven, including shawls, scarves, and kimonos.

Objects, at the same address, is directed by Ann Nathan, who was in personnel for 27 years until "in a moment of insanity" she quit and became a gallery owner. Objects specializes in (what else) objects, including jewelry, furniture and ceramics. Each Halloween, the gallery holds its Day of the Dead Show, when an altar made of skulls is set up.

Ann Nathan believes she may be the only art dealer in America to take both Visa and American Express. She is certainly a rare gallery owner because art here is priced as high as $20,000 but as low as $20. She is a warm, enthusiastic woman who, despite the Day of the Dead Show, makes art come alive.

The School of the Art Institute maintains a gallery space at 341 W. Superior, allowing students to present paintings, sculpture, mixed media and performance art.

At 361 W. Superior, Exhibit A features ceramics as art. The director, Alice Westphal, was a graduate student in science when World War II ended and she was asked to leave school to make room for returning veterans. For a while she typed transcripts of translations of German aeronautical documents, then she raised a family and took pottery-making lessons. Now she has a famed gallery, and she says, "It is difficult for potters to be received at the same level of aesthetic achievement as painters are."

The N.A.M.E. Gallery, also at 361 W. Superior, began in 1973 when eight artists decided to create a gallery run by artists. The gallery continues to do unusual things, including displaying art by people who live in welfare housing.

At one time, Kenneth Walker was the president of the board of directors of N.A.M.E. Walker was arrested for stealing about $225,000 worth of art from the late artist Miyoko Ito, with whom he had a nine-year relationship. They met when she was 55 and he was a student named Hodorowski, age 21.

Walker, who changed his name in 1984, got a Picasso etching, other etchings and an astoundingly ugly wooden African fetish dog from Ito's collection. After her death in 1983, her husband realized the works were missing and Walker was arrested.

Walker was acquitted, but was facing more criminal charges. Then, on September 21, 1986, his charred body was found near Belmont Harbor. A can of gasoline was nearby and death was ruled a suicide.

Walker was 33, he had been dancing with a man who was not his roommate of nine years on a night before his body was found, and he had been fascinated by the life of Japanese writer Yukio Mishima who also committed suicide.

After his death, police found several stolen works of art in his safe deposit boxes.

Toni Schlesinger, writing in the Chicago Tribune, recalled one New York artist who threw his bride out of a 34th-floor window and a New York art dealer who was charged with kidnapping, sodomizing and killing a young Norwegian man. She wrote, "That was in New York. For Chicago's quickly growing art business, the Walker affair may be a first in the realm of the bizarre."

300 W. Huron

Next, walk one block to your left, going south to Huron. Take another left, walking east to 356 W. Huron. Down a few stairs, you'll find ARC, Artists Residents of Chicago, a co-operative gallery representing 23 female artists.

Another gallery owner, Paul Klein, came to this address in 1981 after owning a gallery near San Francisco. The Chicago International Art Exposition at Navy Pier convinced this former philosophy major from Colorado College to come to Chicago.

The Zolla/Lieberman Gallery is on the first floor of this address and, if she is there, you've got to meet Roberta Lieberman. She will proudly show you around her gallery, which was formerly a Brunswick warehouse where pool tables were stored. Zolla is Bob Zolla, a lawyer who has been Roberta's partner for 20 years.

This was the first gallery in SuHu and, in 1976, that meant that Zolla/Lieberman had pioneering spirit. (It also meant that they would pay $1.80 per square foot for space which can now rent for $20 per square foot).

But Roberta is a woman who enjoys taking chances. For instance, she found Deborah Butterfield of Bozeman, Montana, a woman who made life-sized horse-sculptures out of mud and sticks, certainly not the sort of art one would put in a garden, where rain would ruin it. As Roberta said, "Everyone thought I was mishugah" (crazy in Yiddish). But Zolla/Lieberman represented Ms. Butterfield and sold her early works for $1800. A Butterfield muddy horse now costs $34,000.

In 1981, Roberta learned of a Spanish artist named Chema Cobo. She flew to meet him in Pittsburgh, invited the artist and his wife to stay with her and only later informed her husband that a Spanish artist and his family would be living with them for a while. Zolla/Lieberman underwrote the artist's stay in America and later sold out two shows of his work. Looking back on it, Roberta says, "It was just a gamble that paid off."

Continuing east, at 340 W. Huron, guitar-playing Peter Miller, whose gallery is down a few stairs, is a former stock broker. However, he combines his present and former life because he believes in "art as investment."

Marianne Deson, at the same address, went to Italy with her mathematician-husband when he was studying there. They brought back art works they collected, but quickly either sold or gave them away to friends. After a second trip to Italy, they brought back seven crates of art works and repeated the process. It then became obvious that Marianne, who majored in Sociology and Philosophy in college, should open a gallery.

Over the years Marianne Deson had demonstrated political awareness, something rather rare in the art community. After the 1968 Democratic convention, when Chicago police beat protestors, she had a show of works of art responding to that. Chicago police investigated the exhibit, but no arrests were made.

Feature (and we were warned not to add the word "Gallery") is down a long hallway at this address. Hudson (no other name), the director, is an iconoclastic guy who has a national reputation for finding new, exciting, young artists. He adds, "I beat the bushes a lot for them," but then he complains, "If they make it, they leave you and if they don't, they blame you."

The Walter Bischoff Gallery, which is owned by an architect who lives in Germany, specializes in European art, especially from Berlin. The Paper Press is a not-for-profit gallery which holds classes in paper making and which has an annual Paper Plate Benefit, when artists donate one of a kind paper plates for a silent auction.

Continuing slightly to the east, the Donald Young Gallery, at 325 W. Huron, is owned by a man who was a dealer in London and Paris before coming to Chicago a decade ago. This gallery is internationally respected and, with its high 14½-foot ceilings, it often houses large-scale sculpture shows.

This concludes the gallery walk, although you are only two blocks from the Peace Museum, at 430 W. Erie (Erie is one block south of Huron), the only museum in the country devoted entirely to art that promotes world peace.

And a Bite to Eat

By this time, you are probably hungry and thirsty. The Green Door Tavern, at 678 N. Orleans, on the south side of Huron, has good food, good liquor and a strange history. It was built in 1872, one year after the 1871 fire. It is one of the last frame buildings built in this area before it became against the law to put up wooden structures here.

Something happened to this tavern over the years. It leaned. Enter the bar and look at the door leading to the basement. The door is

100

Green Door Tavern

square, but the frame is at a most rakish angle. Don't worry—the Green Door has listed this way for over 100 years.

Incidentally, a back room in this bar, with its walls filled with Chicago memorabilia, was once a cottage where the original owner lived.

Or visit Scoozi, at 410 W. Huron, a new restaurant which was supposed to recreate a 15th century Italian Artist's studio. You'll know it from the huge tomato above the door.

During this walk, our eyes have been educated as we have looked at all manner of images. And, no matter what you think of the art, by the end of the walk we know that Chicago has a strong, viable and energetic art community.

9 GOLD COAST WALK

ASTOR AND STATE

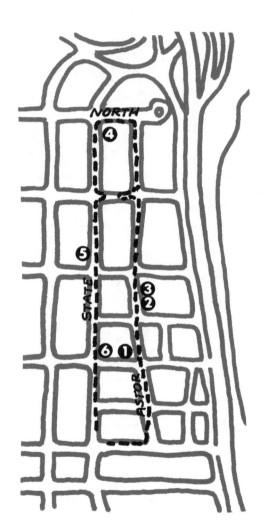

1. 1308–1312 Astor
2. Court of the Golden Hands
   (1349 Astor)
3. James Charnley House (1364
   Astor)
4. Archbishop's Residence
5. Playboy Mansion (1340 N. State
   Parkway)
6. Ambassador East Hotel

Time: Less than two hours
To get there: The number 36 CTA bus stops at Division and
State, one block west of Astor St.

The Lap of Luxury

Chicago's Gold Coast has been home to the city's richest citizens since the 1890s. Modern apartments with faceless lobbies have risen among the old mansions in the past two decades, but today that process has slowed nearly to a stop. That's fine because it preserves a beautiful neighborhood where the top strata of society lived life to the hilt before the stock market crash of 1929.

Early in Chicago's history, Astor St. was named after John Jacob Astor, a pioneer fur trader. The area languished until 1882, when Potter Palmer built the "mansion to end all mansions" at 1350–1560 Lake Shore Dr. Within 20 years, rich folks began forsaking the South Side to join Palmer, even though there was a servant problem. The old lakefront graveyards were nearby. Everytime a foundation was dug new bones were discovered and servants thought the big houses were haunted.

By 1928, the Gold Coast was the Lap of Luxury. A real estate listing for that year described the apartments at nearby 1200 N. Lake Shore Dr. This 13-story building devoted its first two floors to quarters for butlers, chauffeurs and laundresses. The 13th floor had playrooms and extra maids quarters. Each apartment, with 18 large rooms and six bathrooms, had four rooms for "domestiques." The description almost makes one want to study to become a robber baron.

The 1929 stock market crash virtually ended home construction in the area. The Gold Coast began to be ringed by modern high-rises in the '50s, as the wealthy died, moved to the suburbs or sold to developers.

A stroll through Chicago's Gold Coast today recalls life as it was 80 years ago, with occasional jarring modern intrusions in the form of huge signs advertising condominiums.

This walk begins at State and Division St. As you head east on Division, note the sandstone townhouses at 45–47 E. Division. They were built around 1885. Take a left on Astor and walk north.

One of Astor Street's oldest structures is the 2½-story red-brick Queen Anne style building at 1207 N. Astor, which was built around 1881. You'll see a lot of Queen Anne-style homes in this area. In 1891, Industrial Chicago reported that that style "has met with great favor from the barbaric tastes of modern Chicago." Oh well, one man's barbarism is another man's charming city home.

The Art Moderne apartment buildings, at 1260 and 1301 Astor, were built by Philip B. Maher in the 1930s. The Potter Palmers once lived on the top three floors of 1301. According to one critic, both buildings show the influences of Gothic Revival, Cubism, Art Deco, Eero Saarinen, Louis Sullivan and the 1916 New York Building Code.

Astor Tower Hotel

The Astor Tower Hotel, on the northwest corner of Goethe and Astor, has been the temporary home of the Hollywood Squares panelists, The Monkees and other famous acts. According to C. Paul Luongo, who searches the world to find the best of everything from mouse traps to hot dogs, Maxim's Restaurant in the basement of the Astor Tower qualifies as one of the best anywhere because he was "deluged with hospitality" while eating there. The restaurant is romantic if you don't mind sitting fairly close to the couple next to you, has an excellent wine list and is expensive. Hopefully, Luongo was with a wealthy friend on whom to deluge the bill.

Harriet Monroe and Poetry Magazine

Continuing north on Astor St., the 3½-story row houses at 1308–12 were designed in 1887 by John Root, who was Daniel Burnham's partner. Root, who lived at 1310, died in 1891 at the age of 41. Root's sister-in-law, Harriet Monroe, founder of *Poetry Magazine,* also lived at 1310, and died in 1936 at the age of 77 while trying to climb a mountain in Peru.

Ms. Monroe's magazine first published Vachel Lindsay's "General William Booth Enters Into Heaven" in 1913, Lindsay's "The Congo" in 1914, T. S. Eliot's "The Love Song of J. Alfred Prufrock" in 1915 and Carl Sandburg's "Chicago" in 1914.

Poetry Magazine's efforts were not universally appreciated. *The Dial,* another Chicago poetry magazine, wrote of Sandburg's poem (which begins "Hog butcher for the world . . ."), that it was "nothing less than an impudent affront to the poetry-loving public." "Prufrock" wasn't much appreciated either, with Louis Untermeyer writing Ms. Monroe that the poem was "the muse in a psychopathic ward drinking the stale dregs of revolt."

The blocky limestone buildings at 1316–22 Astor were built by Potter Palmer as a speculative venture in 1889.

The high-rise apartment building at 1325 Astor, designed by Andrew N. Rebori in 1928, was advertised as having 11 rooms, four baths and two wood-burning fireplaces in each apartment. Ideal for a family which enjoys being clean.

Irna Phillips, Queen of the Soaps

Irna Phillips, creator of the soap opera, lived in 1335 Astor until her death on Dec. 23, 1973. The Queen of the Soaps, Ms. Phillips was responsible for "The Guiding Light," "As the World Turns," "Young Dr. Malone" and others. Irna's favorite story concerned the selling of "Another World" to Proctor & Gamble. Not wanting to travel to Ivorydale, Ohio, she insisted that the company executives come to

1308-12 Astor—architect John Root and editor Harriet Monroe lived at 1310

her. When they arrived in her apartment, they saw stacks of scripts and dramatic concepts. Before the P&G people could even read this material to see if they liked it, they had to give Irna $5,000. The diminutive lady was playing poker with the P&G board of directors, and the opening bid was $5,000. Miss Phillips got her money.

If you look through the entranceway at 1349–53 Astor, you'll see why it is called the Court of the Golden Hands. Vandals have been at work, and the door knockers on the entranceway with the graceful hands carefully holding an apple have been removed. But they are still on the doors back in the courtyard beyond the gate.

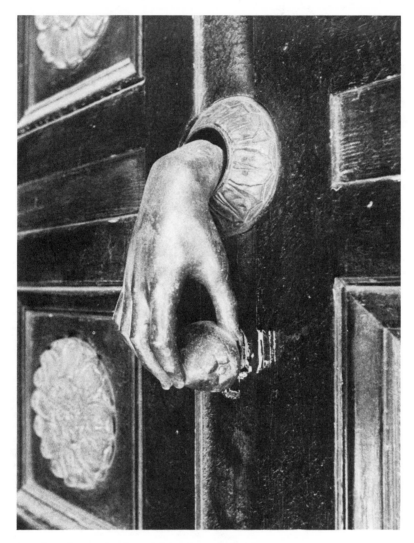

Door knocker at the Court of the Golden Hands

The huge home at 1353 Astor was designed for the William O. Goodman family, who donated Chicago's famed Goodman Theater as a memorial to their son, Kenneth, a Naval Lieutenant who died in World War I. The keystones above the third-floor windows are decorated by bovine skulls.

James Charnley House

We now arrive at a landmark—the 11-room, three-story, single-family residence at 1364 Astor, the James Charnley House, designed

by Louis Sullivan and Frank Lloyd Wright in 1891. To understand why this home is historically significant all one has to do is look at the homes around it, designed at the same time, but decorated with Queen Anne, Romanesque and Georgian revival facades. Charnley looks, and is, modern, a forerunner of the ranch house, the first statement by the then 23-year-old Wright that a city home could be constructed of simple shapes. One critic said that "there was no duplicate of the Charnley House anywhere in the world in 1891," and Wright said, "It is the first modern building."

Wright was an apprentice to Sullivan when he designed this home for a lumber executive, with Sullivan contributing the fireplace and the leaded-glass windows.

For a couple of years in the 1980s, you could have bought this landmark from Lowell Wohlfeil, the owner, for a mere $1,250,000, provided you agreed to preserve the building. Most buyers were happy with the 30-foot-tall atrium and the unadorned wood panelling, but some people wanted to add his and her bathrooms to change the home.

It was bought by the Skidmore Owings & Merrill Foundation, thus both saving and restoring it.

More Astor Street Houses

Cross Schiller, noting the townhouses from 36–48 East Schiller, and notice the Joseph T. Ryerson House, at 1406 Astor. It was built in 1921–22 and patterned after pre-World War I Parisian hotels. Ryerson's grandfather founded Ryerson & Son, now a subsidiary of Inland Steel.

The William McCormick Blair residence at 1416 Astor had its moment in history. Gov. Adlai Stevenson stayed there in 1952. Around midnight on July 26, Stevenson got official word from the Democratic Convention that he would be the new Presidential candidate. He then went to the Bowen House, at 1430 Astor (since demolished) and told 2,000 supporters and newsmen, "The party has reached its decision openly. It has asked me nothing except that I give such poor talents as I have to my country. That I will do gladly. I have no feeling of exultation, nor sense of triumph." A sense of triumph also evaded Stevenson that fall when, although beloved in Illinois, he was defeated by Dwight David Eisenhower.

Across the street, the building at 1425 Astor, built in 1895, was originally the residence of William D. Kerfoot, a city controller and a hero, of sorts, after the 1871 fire. On Oct. 10, one day after the fire burned all he owned, Kerfoot, then a realtor, built a shanty near Washington and Dearborn, the first structure to be erected after the holocaust. He had to construct it back from the pavement and the nearby ruined walls because they were still hot from the fire. Kerfoot

Charnley House

put up a sign which is still on display at the Chicago Historical Society. It said, "W. D. Kerfoot. Everything gone but wife, children and energy."

A large, curved bay marks the G. W. Meeker residence at 1431 Astor, while 1435 Astor is a facsimile of a Georgian mansion. The H. N. May House, at 1443 Astor, was designed in 1891 by Joseph Lyman Silsbee, who employed both Frank Lloyd Wright and George W. Maher as apprentices early in their careers.

The Art Deco home at 1444 Astor was built in 1929, with the limestone for its facade imported from Lens, France. One critic called it "very probably the finest residential Art Deco design in Chicago." Everything collects its honors where it may.

The nearly flat front building at 1447 Astor, built around 1903, was originally the home of Charles Daniel Peacock, who was born in Chicago in 1838, went to a little school house at State and Madison (now the world's busiest corner), and became a wealthy Chicago jeweler, selling shirts studs to gentlemen and brooches to ladies.

The modern high-rise at 1450 Astor, soundly hated by old-line neighborhood residents, has been called a "junkyard" because of its open garage along the sidewalk.

Robert Patterson Home

We now cross Burton and see a grand home at 20 E. Burton, which was built in 1882. Joseph Medill, editor of the Chicago Tribune, gave this home to his daughter as a wedding present (what a father-in-law). Cyrus Hall McCormick II, son of the inventor of the reaper, bought the home in 1929 and tripled its size. In fact, the King and Queen of Sweden once stayed on its second floor. It later became the Bateman school, which defaulted on its mortgage and lost the property in 1950. The home rested in sad dilapidation until 1979 when developers bought it. They announced that it would be restored.

In its heyday, it was quite a home, with from 42 to 90 rooms, depending on how one defined the term. The fourth floor allegedly contained one room lined with 50 locked boxes designed to hold Christmas and birthday gifts. A room close by was set aside, naturally, for wrapping presents. That is an interesting bit of extravagance—a room permanently reserved for Christmas present wrappings.

The home at 40 E. Burton Place (alternate address—1501 Astor) originally belonged to John G. Shortall, who built it in 1909. Shortall became another 1871 fire hero when he saved 20 years of real estate records. It might seem curious—risking one's life for a bunch of papers, but Shortall's heroism allowed the city to rebuild quickly and without lengthy legal battles as to whose property ended where.

Patterson-McCormick mansion at 20 E. Burton

Continuing north, we pass the residence at 1505 Astor, built in 1911 in an English Georgian style. The high-rise at 1515 Astor is on the site of the home of George Frances, who once had a wine cellar with 1,300 quarts of scotch, an equal amount of bourbon and 500 quarts of champagne. That man knew what was important in life.

Next consider the modern, cylindrical Charles Haffner III residence, built at 1524 Astor in 1968. It sympathizes well with the existing street facade.

The walk north on Astor ends at North Avenue where a bronze statue of Dr. Greene Vardiman Black looks benignly south. Before his death at age 79 in 1915, Dr. Black was the author of over 500 books and papers, inventor of 104 different dentist's instruments, a chainsmoker of Havana cigars, and a man credited with laying the foundation of modern dentistry. While on vacation in Alaska, he was caught in a blizzard on a mountain, froze one hand, and amputated part of his own finger.

Archbishop's Residence

If you turn left and walk one block west on North Avenue, you will pass The Archbishop's Residence, at 1555 N. State Parkway, the home of the head of Chicago's Roman Catholics since 1885. Don't

110

The Archbishop's Residence

bother to count them—there are 19 chimneys on this Queen Anne style house. It is the oldest structure still standing in the Astor Street district, and was designed by Alfred Pashley, a Protestant.

Rumor has it that there is a beautiful, high-backed, gilded chair in one room of this house. Its velvet seat is perpetually protected by a silken cord, and the chair is reserved for a visit by The Pope.

President Franklin Delano Roosevelt lunched here in 1937, and Eugenio Cardinal Pacelli visited in 1936. He later became Pope Pius XII, but he didn't sit in the reserved chair.

Now turn left on N. State Parkway and head south. The high-rise at 1550 N. State Parkway was once the finest apartment building in the

111

city, with 14-room apartments. Every room had its own French name and the building has an appropriate Parisian-inspired facade.

Madlener House

The Albert F. Madlener House, at 4 W. Burton Place is the home of the Graham Foundation for Advanced Studies in the Fine Arts. It was designed in 1902 by Hugh M. G. Garden for the president of a huge wholesale liquor firm. The home has been compared favorably to a Florentine palace.

As you cross Burton Place, look to the west at Carl Sandburg Village, which replaced a notorious slum. Its towering apartments often prove that someone can live in the midst of hundreds of people and still be quite lonely.

Playboy Mansion

The George S. Isham mansion, at 1340 N. State Parkway, was where people of refinement went for dancing classes after it was built in 1899. Better known as the Playboy mansion after Hugh Hefner bought it in the 1960s, the mansion now belongs to the Art Institute and is used as a dormitory.

Ambassador West and East

Proceeding south, past 1328 N. State Parkway, which was remodeled in 1956 for sculptress Lillian Florsheim, we quickly arrive at the Ambassador West Hotel, on the west side of N. State Parkway. If you enter, you'll see a glass doorway to the right just before the steps to the ornate lobby. Walk down these narrow stairs, bear left, and follow the underground path, past a drug store facade, and walk upstairs. You have crossed N. State Parkway and have entered the Ambassador East.

The Pump Room, a famous restaurant, is directly in front of the elevators. At one time, when the railroads were important to Chicago and the town was a convenient place to stop while going cross-country, being seated in Booth One of the Pump Room meant you had Arrived, had Made It. That tradition began in Oct. 10, 1938, when actress Gertrude Lawrence sat and ate in Booth One for 90 straight days, creating an institution. Salvador Dali doodled on the tablecloth there and it was promptly washed. Margaret O'Brien wore lipstick for the first time in public while sitting there. Elizabeth Taylor ate there with four of her first five husbands (only Eddie Fisher missed the honor). Lassie was refused service, but Morris the Cat ate there in 1974. In 1968, Sonny Bono became the first man to dine there without a jacket.

Today, Booth One is just to the left of the recently remodeled entrance to the dining room. It has a fancy phone, but fewer celebrities than it had in the past. The place went downhill after Morris and Sonny.

Many of the moments are preserved in the pictures of the great and near-great hanging on the walls in the hallway leading to the Pump Room. It's fun to figure out who is who and see how young they all look.

If eating where the famous folk sometimes dined isn't what you want, cross the lobby and find out who is playing at Byfield's, one of Chicago's best comedy clubs. I have spent many evenings doing a mini-walk which included a visit to Byfield's, where I have never seen a bad performance. And the bar leading in to Byfield's is quite elegant.

Incidentally, the area immediately around the Ambassador Hotels is probably the site of many forgotten tunnels. John A. Huck, who holds the unfortunate distinction of owning the last home to be burned in the 1871 Chicago fire, built a brewery here in 1867 and created two miles of tunnels to store his lager beer. They're 20 to 30 feet wide and six feet high. When the foundations for the Ambassador Hotels were dug, old tunnels were found and destroyed, but many more may be down there. Alas, all the beer is gone.

Either stop for a bite to eat or a drink at the Pump Room, or continue south, returning to State and Division. Note the older home at 1241 N. State Parkway, a cottage built in 1875. The townhouses at 1234–52 N. State Parkway were built around 1890. The white brick Art Moderne Frank Fisher apartment building at 1209 N. State Parkway reflects the tastes of the 1933–34 Century of Progress Fair.

This ends the Gold Coast tour, a quiet neighborhood of gentle tree-lined streets recalling an age when people actually needed four rooms for their servants.

10   LINCOLN PARK WALK

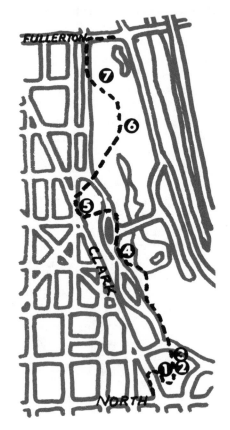

1. Chicago Historical Society
2, 3. Lincoln Statue and Couch Mausoleum
4. Farm in the Zoo
5. Chicago Academy of Sciences
6. Lincoln Park Zoo
7. Lincoln Park Conservatory

Time: Two to four hours, more if you are a slow stroller.

To get there: The Number 22 (Clark) and 36 (Broadway) buses both stop at Clark and North Avenue. If you are driving, take Lake Shore Drive north to North Avenue, go west to Clark Street, turn right and go about a half block to a driveway into a Lincoln Park parking area. City meters there allow you to park for eight hours.

History of Lincoln Park

Lincoln Park, between North Avenue (1600 north) and Fullerton (2400 north), is the most-visited piece of greenery in the city.

It is, if the Park District keeps it clean and if visitors do not throw things in the lagoons, a lovely park, with an historical museum, farm, natural history museum and zoo, plus statues and a botanical garden—a delightful place for a stroll. Here the casual walker can see joggers, bicyclists, catch an inning or two of a softball game or just sit by the lagoon and watch the rowboats. It's a relaxing, expansive place—but walk carefully to avoid what dogs normally leave behind in city parks.

Lincoln Park was a graveyard until Oct. 21, 1864, when it was declared a park. Before that, smallpox and cholera victims from Camp Douglas, a Civil War prison camp, and from other parts of the city, were buried here in shallow graves. If the graves were dug any deeper than three or four feet this close to the lake, the diggers would strike water.

Dr. John H. Rauch, a local physician, complained about the "18,000 to 20,000 bodies undergoing decomposition at this time" in the area. This frightened folks and eventually most of the bodies were moved to other cemeteries. However, some were simply forgotten. When the basement for the Chicago Historical Society building was excavated in 1932, some old bones were unearthed, and many more may still lie beneath this idyllic park.

During the 1871 Chicago Fire, many refugees came to Lincoln Park to sit among the remaining tombstones and open graves, and watch the city burn. By 1879, so many people were using the new-fangled bicycles in Lincoln Park that bikes were banned from the park because they were "foes to the peace of mind and safety of body . . ."

Lincoln Park has also been subject to political corruption. In 1869, the five park commissioners needed five carriages and five chauffeurs just to get to work, where fresh flowers awaited them daily. Later the park superintendent had five buddies on the payroll—and none of them knew a thing about grass, trees or anything botanical, unless you could ferment it and drink it.

In 1904, Lincoln Park was praised as a "sylvan promenade" and an English traveler wrote that after seeing "Lincoln Park in the flush of sunset, you wonder that the dwellers in this street of palaces should trouble their heads about Naples or Venice, when they have before their very windows the innumerable laughter, the ever shifting opalescence of their fascinating inland sea." He meant Lake Michigan looked great!

Chicago Historical Society

Begin the Lincoln Park walk by entering through the modern doorway of the Chicago Historical Society at Clark and North Avenue,
open from 9:30 a.m. to 4:30 p.m., Monday through Saturday; and
noon to 5 p.m. Sunday. Admission is $1.50 for adults, 50 cents for
those under age 18, with children under age six admitted free.
Monday is a free day here.

The Chicago Historical Society has a tradition of hard luck. It was
founded in 1856 and, from all accounts, collected a bunch of junk,
including 2,000 books of sermons. Its entire collection burned (possibly a fortunate occurrence) in 1871, so the Society started finding
more historical stuff only to be burned out again in 1874. Early in its
history, the Chicago Historical Society just couldn't quite learn the
knack of how to preserve things.

Later, there was a stroke of good fortune. When Charles F.
Gunther, a local candy salesman who invented the caramel, died in
1920, the Society bought his collection, which included the entire
Civil War Libby Prison, Lincoln's carriage, Martha Washington's
thimble and the table on which Gens. U. S. Grant and Robert E. Lee
ended the Civil War.

The Society obviously needed a new building to house this collection, so it announced a special members meeting for Oct. 25, 1929, to
raise some money. A bad choice of dates there. The stock market
crashed on Oct. 24.

If you walk straight into the museum from the entrance, you'll see
"the greatest loving cup that ever mortal man possessed," made of
70,000 dimes given by Americans to Commodore George S. Dewey
in appreciation of his victory in Manila Bay on May 1, 1898.

If you are lucky, to your left in the next room volunteers will be
manning the Illinois Pioneer Life Gallery. The rooms show how
people lived in the 1840s, and the volunteers, in costume, do hand-
icrafts and answer questions. The ladies make cloth, hand dip candles and dye fabrics, enlivening one of the dullest exhibits in the
museum.

The Lincoln Gallery on the second floor features a huge bust of
Lincoln by Gutzon Borglum, who created Mt. Rushmore's heads.
This Lincoln has a shiny nose because thousands of people rub it for
luck. Now that this statue is on a new pedestal, far off the ground,
fewer people can reach the lucky nose, but they still try.

The Lincoln dioramas show scenes from Lincoln's life, and the
museum even displays the half-dollars placed on Lincoln's eyes in
death.

Towards the rear of the second floor an entire railroad engine, the
first one to enter Chicago (1848), is on display. The floor needed
special supports to hold it.

116

Couch mausoleum in Lincoln Park

The museum also has dioramas illustrating Chicago's history, a printed copy of the Declaration of Independence, one of the anchors of the *Santa Maria* and, alas, several rooms of furniture, swords and stuff which should have stayed in someone's attic.

The Latin School

Leaving the Chicago Historical Society, turn left (going south), walk to the corner of Clark and North Avenue. The Latin School, designed by Harry Weese, is on the southeast corner. It was founded in 1888 by a group of Chicagoans who wanted to import as Eastern "schoolmarm," Mabel Slade Vickery. Since then, according to one school official, this exclusive establishment has had not "a single breath of scandal." It is also a fine school, with many important graduates, a tradition of teaching both the tough subjects and arts, a faculty liberally sprinkled with advanced degrees. High school tuition is rapidly approaching $7,000 a year. It was mentioned in The Preppy Handbook as THE school in Chicago, but the students are smart, nice creatures and few of them look or talk preppy.

Walk east, following the path around the back of the Chicago Historical Society and past the standing 1887 statue of Abraham Lincoln, one of Augustus Saint-Gaudens' best works which is now lighted at night to prevent trysting near it.

Couch Mausoleum

Continue walking north, past a gray forbidding mausoleum with the word "COUCH" inscribed on it. Ira Couch, who died in Havana in 1857, was part-owner of the Tremont House, then the finest hotel west of New York. No one is sure how many bodies are in the mausoleum with published estimates ranging from one to 13, which might make it a little crowded. The *Chicago Tribune* reported in 1858 that the 100-ton crypt had room for only 11 bodies.

The last crypt was removed from Lincoln Park, when it changed from burial dump to glade, in 1895. Only two tombs are supposed to be there—Couch's and David Kennison's. He was the last known survivor of the Boston Tea Party. Kennison died in 1852 at age 115 and lies undisturbed near the Academy of Sciences.

No one knows why Couch is still in the park. According to one researcher for the Chicago Historical Society, there is no record of anyone going to the Park District or the courts to demand that he stay there. Current theory on the matter indicates that Couch's brother, James, probably had a quiet lunch or drink with city officials and came to a gentlemanly understanding on the matter. That sounds like Chicago.

Walk through the underpass taking you under North Avenue, where there is always plenty of broken glass underfoot, past the Lake Shore Drive exit, and past the 1896 Benjamin Franklin statue, a monument to his signature on the Declaration of Independence. It's been recently resurfaced and looks rather new!

The Lagoon

Walk up the wide, asphalt, tree-lined path towards the Lincoln Park lagoon. To your right was the caped statue of Giuseppe Garibaldi, Italian patriot, which was unveiled in 1901. Only the base remained in 1986. May Giuseppe soon return.

Circle the lagoon to the left and remember the story Herman Kogan and Lloyd Wendt told in their book *Lords of the Levee*. In the 1890s, the Chicago City Council was seriously considering buying six gondolas for the Lincoln Park Lagoon. Alderman "Little Mike" Ryan stopped the debate by shouting, "Why waste th' taxpayers money buyin' six gondolas? Git a pair of 'em, and' let nature take its course."

Farm in the Zoo

Next walk through the Farm in the Zoo, open from 9:45 a.m. to 4:45 p.m. This five-acre farm is designed to show city kids what a cow and a chicken look like. It has a poultry and egg house, (the little chicks born here are fed to the Lincoln Park Zoo snakes after hours because the snakes need the exercise and roughage), a horse stable, a main

The Farm in the Zoo

barn with pigs and sheep, and a dairy barn, under which more skeletons were found when the foundation was dug. Thousands of people each day enter the dairy barn, look at the cows and say, "Moo." The cows do not answer back.

Leave the farm to the right of the Dairy Barn, walk around the lagoon and under the viaduct. Pedal boats can be rented for $4 per half hour and the nearby pizza shack offers tasteless hot dogs and hamburgers for snacks.

Cafe Brauer, built in 1908, was once the home of a great restaurant, where one reviewer noted "all is poetry and romance." There was an attempt to revive the old Cafe Brauer, but in 1969 the later Mayor Richard J. Daley denied the place a liquor license and it has remained a hot dog joint ever since.

Go through the arches just to the left of the rowboat cashier and walk west towards Clark Street, past the statue of Hans Christian Andersen, a plain man with a big nose and a somewhat sad look on his face. The statue, complete with a former ugly duckling, was dedicated in 1896.

Chicago Academy of Sciences

Carefully cross Stockton Drive and walk around the front of the old, but imposing building, variously called the Chicago Academy of Sciences, the Chicago Museum of Natural History and the Chicago Museum of Ecology.

At one time, the Chicago Academy of Sciences was filled with dusty, moldy, stuffed birds, a place to avoid unless one took delight in peering at mournful chickadees. Over the last 20 years, the museum's director, Dr. William J. Beecher, has created a stunning room on the second floor devoted to the Chicago wilderness. Using a practically non-existent budget, Dr. Beecher and his associates gave us a room with animal footprints and the shadows of tree leaves on the grassy floor, plus a cave, a valley, and displays of bears, wolves, owls, shores and sand dunes.

Some cases are rather small, but appear infinitely large. It's done with mirrors! See if you can tell when Beecher's assistants stuffed half a bird or critter and placed it on a mirror so the reflection will create an entire fowl or animal.

After you leave this small gem of a museum, take a right and walk through an underpass lined with stones just north and east of the Academy. If you are hungry, head directly west to R. J. Grunt's, 2056 N. Lincoln Park West, which offers a huge salad bar and gigantic bowls of soup.

Lincoln Park Zoo

If you are not hungry, continue walking north and enter the Lincoln Park Zoo, quickly passing the rotting Viking Ship which sailed from Norway to Chicago in time for the Columbian Exposition of 1893. No one knows why this ship is in the zoo.

Lincoln Park Zoo, which attracts over 4,000,000 visitors a year, began in 1868 when the Central Park Zoo in New York gave Chicago two swans. It is the second oldest zoo in America.

In 1905, when the notorious Alderman "Bathhouse John" Coughlin wanted to build his own zoo near Colorado Springs, Colo., the

Contemplation at the Children's Zoo

Zoo gave him Princess Alice, an elephant with a defective trunk. The Zoo had another elephant anyway. There were no public feedings of the animals in the Zoo during the Depression for fear that it might upset hungry humans. During the late '40s and '50s, then-director Marlin Perkins originated his "Zoo Parade" TV show from here.

Two of the Zoo's most dangerous animals escaped under almost identical circumstances. Bushman, a 470-pound gorilla, wandered into the corridor behind his cage and stayed there for three hours in 1950. Sinbad, a 500-pound gorilla, entered into the same area in 1964. Both Bushman and Sinbad could bend steel bars and only a flimsy screen or two kept Chicago from experiencing its very own King Kongs.

When Bushman got loose, his keeper yelled, "Bushman, get the hell back." Bushman bit his keeper's finger. When Sinbad got loose, his keeper yelled, "Get back in there." Neither gorilla listened, which means that there is a long-term breakdown in man-ape communications.

Both gorillas gave up their short-lived freedom remarkably easily. Bushman was frightened back to his cage by an 18-inch long baby alligator, and Sinbad was tranquilized and carried back. Neither of them even had a chance to pick up a beautiful girl, and gently blow dry her hair as King Kong did.

Petting the animals at the Children's Zoo

The Zoo currently holds a Guinness record for Heine, a chimp who died in 1971 at the age of 50 years and three months, living longer than any other primate on record, excluding humans.

Dr. Lester E. Fisher, the director, says that his Zoo was the first to have a year-round children's zoo, and today it offers visitors a new great ape house, a new sea lion pool, and the ever popular Mike the polar bear and an African dwarf crocodile who has been at the Zoo since 1940.

Zoo hours are 9 a.m. to 5 p.m., with the Children's Zoo opening at 10 a.m. Admission is free.

The Lincoln Park Conservatory

Eugene Field

Near Sinbad the gorilla's home there is a statue to Eugene Field, a *Chicago Daily News* bachelor columnist who became famous for writing such children's poems as "Wynken, Blynken and Nod" and "Little Boy Blue." It is a little-known fact that Field, who died in 1895, "the children's poet laureate," also wrote lascivious verse and had *Daily News* printers make copies for him. He wrote such lines as "Ah that was glorious bangin', good bangin' on the Rhine" and "But when my Julia breaks her wind . . ."

Gardens and Conservatory

Exit just to the north of the Children's Zoo, walking around the 1886 statue of Johann Christoph Schiller, a German poet and dramatist. Just ahead of you is an 1887 fountain titled "Storks at Play," by Augustus Saint-Gaudens and Frederick MacMonnies. It features four boys, two herons and lots of splashing water.

"Storks at Play," also called the Bates Fountain, is in the middle of the colorful Main Garden, which has flowers in spring and summer. Across the street to the west is Grandmother's Garden, so named because at the turn of the century elderly neighborhood women would tend flowers there. There is also a statue of William Shakespeare seated and slightly reclining, surely the least official pose for the Bard of Avon.

The building immediately in front of you is the Lincoln Park Conservatory, built in 1891–2. There is always a jungle climate in the conservatory, which is open from 9 a.m. to 5 p.m. so you can see the flora from India, Sumatra, Brazil, China, Mexico, etc.

This is as far north as you will go on this walk. Either go to Fullerton and Stockton Dr. and take a 151, or 156 bus back to the Loop, or wander across Fullerton and idly watch people practicing in the casting pond, or return by walking east towards the lake and then south.

If you take this route, you'll pass several signs on ridges indicating where the lake left ancient sand bars before it retreated to its present boundaries. You'll also pass an 1891 statue of Ulysses S. Grant, atop a horse atop an arch. When Chicagoans say there is a statue of Lincoln in Grant Park and one of Grant in Lincoln Park, this is one of the figures they're talking about.

If you are hungry, head west on Fullerton to Clark, where you'll find food, drink, and/or pizza.

By the way, if you see someone jogging through Lincoln Park and carrying a bat, do not be frightened. He or she is just ready for the perpetual war between runners and dogs.

11

OAK PARK WALK

FRANK LLOYD WRIGHT

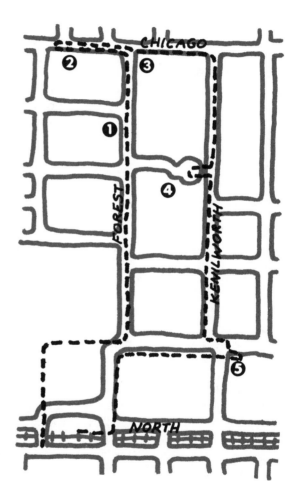

1. Nathan C. Moore House
2. "Bootleg" houses
3. Frank Lloyd Wright Home and Studio
4. Mrs. Thomas H. Gale House
5. Unity Temple

Time: 2½ hours or less, plus 40 minutes roundtrip for transportation.

To get there: By public transportation, take the Lake Street rapid transit from the Loop to the Harlem-Marion stop, about a 15-minute ride past the University of Illinois, on your left, and through the roughest black ghetto in Chicago. At the Harlem/ Marion stop, walk to the east side of the platform (in the direction from which you came) and walk out on Marion. By car, take the Eisenhower Expressway (I-90) west, driving approximately 15 minutes from State Street to the Harlem exit, which is on the left side of the Expressway. Go north (or right) about two miles to North Blvd., which is just beyond a viaduct and before the Wieboldt's store. Take a right on North Blvd. and park in the Oak Park Mall.

Oak Park Mall and Visitors Center

To walk through Oak Park is to touch genius.

Edgar Rice Burroughs wrote his stories about Tarzan in Oak Park. And Ernest Hemingway was born there and left, later scoffing that it was a community of "broad lawns and narrow minds."

But Oak Park, today, reverberates with the ghost of Frank Lloyd Wright, an architectural genius who lived there, revolutionized residential building design and who left in the midst of a scandal after creating twenty-five homes, churches and fountains in the suburb.

(Except for Wright's home and studio and his Unity Temple, this walk will take you past private homes currently housing families. These are not museums and the families request that you respect their privacy.)

When you get off the rapid transit or after you have parked your car, the walk begins at Harlem and Marion Street. Walk under the elevated. Go straight ahead, on Marion, into the Oak Park Mall, as pleasant a city shopping area as you'd ever wish to find.

The first intersection in the Mall, with Barbara's Book Store on the northwest corner, was the site of a pre-Civil War underground railroad stopping place, where slaves recuperated while escaping from the South.

Continue through the Mall, taking a right at the Oak Park Trust and Savings Bank, past the Lake Theater, and out to Forest Avenue. You are at the corner of Forest and Lake Street.

The Visitors Center, attached to the Mall Garage at 128 Forest, has taped tours of Oak Park available in English, German and Japanese. The tours rent for $3, and the Center is open daily from 10 a.m. to 5 p.m.

Proceed north up Forest by making a left when you exit the Mall and going past the Austin Gardens Park, with its bird sanctuary and wild flower garden.

Cross the street and walk past the Oak Park Nineteenth Century Woman's Club, which raises money for scholarships. Frank Lloyd Wright's mother and first wife were among its founders.

126

Thomas House

You'll see your first Frank Lloyd Wright home a little north of the Nineteenth Century Club, the Frank W. Thomas House at 210 Forest, built in 1901, and restored recently at a reported cost of $50,000. (All Frank Lloyd Wright homes are named after their original owners.) Note its distinctive white and green leaded glass windows and its strong horizontal lines. By the end of this walk, you'll be able to recognize a Frank Lloyd Wright home in a crowd of others. If not, merely enter them—when you bump your head on his low doorways, you'll know you've discovered a Wright house.

Continuing north on Forest, you'll see many Victorian homes. Each unique. Each beautifully kept up.

Beachy House

The Peter A. Beachy House, another Frank Lloyd Wright, is at 238 Forest Avenue. The home sits at right angles to the street so Wright could use the foundation of a Gothic cottage, which formerly stood on the site. The home is on the extreme edge of its lot, something unheard of when it was built in 1906. This gave its owner a huge yard, and more grass to cut.

Edward R. Hills House

Moving along, and continuing to walk north, the Edward R. Hills House, at 313 Forest, was moved from 333 Forest in 1906. It was then shifted 90 degrees so that it faced north, and was remodeled by Wright. The new owner, Thomas DeCarro, took almost eighteen months off work to oversee restoration of the home at a cost rumored to be three times its purchase price.

Then the Hills home was almost completely destroyed by fire in 1976. With the help of neighbors, money was raised, and the home rebuilt almost to original specifications. In fact, older pictures show two bay windows on the second floor, instead of the single bay you see today.

Arthur Huertley House

Another Wright home, at 318 Forest, is the Arthur Huertley House, built for a banker in 1902. Note the odd point in front of the arch— Frank Lloyd Wright often included ship prows in his homes, perhaps so they could sail the prairie.

The home is built on wooden piers so that it would settle evenly into the ground. After seventy years, I am told, there is not a single crack in the plaster anywhere in the home. Other interesting facts about this home: The main living area is on the second floor and the

Nathan G. Moore House—ah, the wonders of compromise

arch is Wright's way of paying homage to his mentor, Louis Sullivan, who was famous for his use of arches.

Nathan G. Moore House

Continuing north, we find the Nathan G. Moore House, at 333 Forest Avenue, the corner of Forest and Superior. My guide, Mrs. Vernette Schultz, said, "This home always brings a smile to my face." The reason is fairly obvious—the home is the result of a tussle between architect and client.

Built by Wright in 1895 and rebuilt by him in 1923, the home is a compromise between Moore's demands for Tudor styling and Wright's interest in Japanese designs. The result is a Tudor home, with Japanese-style lower levels, or maybe a Gothic home in Oriental drag. When he first designed it, Wright needed money because of his growing family. This house proves that sometimes in his life Wright could actually design something that satisfied the client.

Copeland House

Farther north, at 400 Forest Avenue, is the Dr. William H. Copeland House, which doesn't look like a Wright home at all. Wright built the garage in 1898, remodeled the home in 1909 giving it a typical Wright, flat-roofed dormer on the third floor and putting most of his distinctive touches on the inside of the home.

You are now at the corner of Forest and Chicago Avenue. If you turn left and walk slightly less than a block to the west, you'll see three homes at 1019, 1027 and 1031 Chicago. These Wright Homes are small, nearly identical and were inexpensive. However, they proved costly in a personal way to Wright.

Bootleg Homes

These are called Wright's "bootleg" homes, although their official names are the Thomas H. Gale, Robert P. Parker and Walter H. Gale Houses. Wright designed these homes in violation of the exclusive contract he signed with Louis Sullivan, the one man on earth Wright loved as one would a father. Wright needed money so he could experiment with the barrel-roofed playroom in his nearby home, but Sullivan learned about Wright's "bootleg" homes. There was an argument in Wright's drafting room, after which Wright did not speak to Sullivan until Sullivan was on his death bed in 1925.

Return to Forest and Chicago, and you'll be standing in front of the Frank Lloyd Wright home and studio, a national landmark, on the northeast side of the street. It was a home of experimentation, joy and intense emotional pain.

It was also a home which was never quite finished, as Wright continued to experiment on his own domicile by constantly rebuilding it. His first wife, Catherine, and his six children lived amid dust and workmen, and Catherine was not a very happy woman.

The Mamad Cheney Affair

She was destinied to be even unhappier because of a 1903 scandal which still shocks the people of Oak Park. Frank Lloyd Wright, husband and father of six children, fell in love with Mrs. Mamad Cheney, wife, mother of two and a "new" woman in 1903. She had an open marriage. Frank Lloyd Wright did not.

So Frank remained friendly with Edwin Cheney, but had problems with Mrs. Wright. Wright finally moved out of his home, adding a floor above his studio to create an apartment which could be rented to increase the family income. The MacArthurs moved in and their son, Charles, eventually married Helen Hayes and was the co-writer of "The Front Page."

View from the playroom balcony in Frank Lloyd Wright's home

Wright's love story had a tragic ending. He built Taliesin, a home near Madison, Wisconsin, for Mamad, who was killed in 1914, when a servant got religion or became insane, set fire to the home which had only a single entrance and exit and hacked with an axe anybody who stepped outside. Within two minutes, seven people, including Mamad, were murdered. The folks in Oak Park now say that Wright, who was in his 40s during the Mamad Cheney affair, was having a mid-life crisis. What a crisis!

Frank Lloyd Wright Home and Studio

After reflecting on the triumphs and tragedies of a genius, walk towards the home, entering on the Chicago Avenue side. Note the columns on the front porch, with secretary birds symbolizing wisdom (and architects), a tree of life and a book of specifications.

Hallway leading to Wright's barrel-roofed playroom

The humorous message of these columns is, "Good friend, if you want to live fully of the tree of life go to a wise bird who knows his specifications to have your plans drawn up."

The home is open for public tours for $4 a person from 11 to 3 p.m. Monday through Friday and from 11 a.m. to 4 p.m. Saturdays and Sundays. The staff is energetic and helpful, but if you are lucky, perhaps you'll be guided by Lyman Shepard, who also performs his impressions of Wright at various gatherings. There are 375 other enthusiastic volunteers to help keep the Wright memory alive.

The Frank Lloyd Wright Home and Studio Foundation dramatically bought this property before it was torn apart and possibly shipped to museums room by room. Do notice how the woodwork has been lovingly restored, how the stained glass windows glow with the sunlight and reflect on how many hours must have been spent by people who enjoy Wright's memory to bring the home and studio to the place it is today.

Mrs. Dawn Goshorn, founder of the Foundation, said that Wright, during a visit to his home, said that "if nothing else remains of mine in Oak Park, my home and the Unity Temple will be enough for people to understand what I was doing."

Finally, after 12 years of difficult work, after finding and spending over $2 million, the restored home and studio was completed in the summer of 1986. It now looks like Wright's home in 1909, Wright's last year in the house, just before he left to go to Germany to create a book of his drawings which would make him an international celebrity. Mamad joined him on that trip, fueling the scandal.

Enter through the living room and notice the words above the hearth, "Truth is Life," which is an adaptation of Wright's mother's family motto "Truth Against the World." As far as Wright was concerned, the hearth was the soul of the family, the place where all should come together, thus the additional words there, "Good friends, around these hearth stones speak no evil word of any creature." I could never understand, if this place was so important, why are the benches there so uncomfortable?

Proceed to the dining room, built in 1895, which was the first room to be restored. Notice the distinctive Frank Lloyd Wright furniture designs.

Next, go up to the barrel roofed second floor playroom, where Catherine Wright once set up a Montessori-type school. You enter the playroom through a narrow corridor, in keeping with Wright's notions of recreating womb and birth experiences within the home.

On the balcony above the hallway there is a statue. Frank Lloyd Wright has several of these winged tributes to victory and he carried them with him when he moved about the world.

Notice the stairway to the balcony. There wasn't enough space in any room for a grand piano, which Wright needed because he required that classical music be played when he did his architectural drawings. Wright stuffed a piano under the playroom stairway and installed hooks so the landing could open up as a normal piano sounding board would. Only the keyboard stuck out from the wall.

Follow your guides and leave the playroom. In the area between the home and the studio, you'll see a honey locust tree growing out of the wall. This is as close as the restoration could get to the original tree, which was a willow, but which died around 1940. Wright believed that nature was a part of man and he became justly famous for homes which did not disturb nature. It is said that he built his studio passageway around this tree.

Frank Lloyd Wright's drafting table

Then go to the octagonal drafting room, where you will notice the chains around the top of the room. In 1909, those chains held up a balcony from which the Wright children would sometimes water-bomb daddy and his apprentices. Now, because of zoning laws, they are more decorative than functional (something about which Wright might be less than enthusiastic). Here, sometimes, the children would learn almost too much about life in 1909, as they would watch Richard Bach sculpt from live nude models.

Now leave the home, turn right and go east on Chicago. The brown and orange house at 931–929 E. Chicago, next door to Wright's home and studio, was his mother's house. We leave it to marriage counselors amongst you to determine the effect of mother's proximity on Wright's relationship with his wife.

Take a right on Kenilworth and proceed south, past immaculate Victorian, Queen Anne and Italianate homes. The white and gray H. P. Young House, at 334 N. Kenilworth, was a farm house remodeled by Wright in 1895.

Mrs. Thomas H. Gale House

You'll see the end of a cul de sac to your right or to the west, called Elizabeth Court a little farther up the street. The Mrs. Thomas H. Gale House is about 100 yards up this cul de sac. This five-bedroom home, designed by Wright in 1909, is supposed to be a series of planes floating in space. It is one of Wright's most unusual Oak Park homes and is seen as a forerunner of the homes he later designed in California.

Unity Temple

Now walk another 2½ blocks, down a pleasant, quiet, well-kept street, past the gothic United Church to the Unity Temple at Lake and Kenilworth, Wright's first public building. This reinforced concrete masterpiece, which established Wright's renown the world over, was built amid great controversy between 1905 and 1908.

Parishioners called the design a "blasphemy to God" or a "fortress." But Wright insisted that no one could understand his design until they worshipped in the finished church, with its acoustically perfect chancery. Wright stayed home that first Sunday, but a trustee of the church quickly called and said, "You're right, Frank, it works."

Walk east on Lake until you reach the Unity Temple easternmost entrance, with its words, "For the Worship of God and the Service of Man." The chancery is upstairs, to the right. Notice that you enter and exist past the pulpit, because Wright wanted parishioners to leave by walking towards the minister, rather than away from him. The church is open to the public Monday through Friday 2–4 p.m. for $3 a person, with an additional tour Saturday and Sunday at 2 p.m. In 1985, the sanctuary was completely restored to its original colors and condition at a cost of $250,000.

The chancery is a nearly indescribable space of light, of rectangles and squares, art glass, balconies and passageways. One atheist said, "It is the one place on Earth I feel close to God."

For the sake of accuracy, we should note that this structure is now called the Unitarian Universalist Church. It was the Unity Church until 1961, but there was another church with the same name in Oak Park—this church changed its name to avoid mix-ups in the mail.

The Unity Temple also concludes this tour. Return to Lake Street. If you turn right, you will pass the concrete Horse Show Fountain, at Lake and Oak Park, built by Wright in 1909. There is a CTA stop at Oak Park. If you turn left, you can walk west on Lake, stop by Scotty's or Murphy's for some food and then return to the Loop via the CTA Harlem/Marion stop. Or you can get your car.

134

Ernest Hemingway's Home

If you wish to see it, Ernest Hemingway's home is at 339 N. Oak Park, and Edgar Rice Burroughs wrote "Tarzan" at 700 N. Linden. The Cheney House is at 520 N. East Avenue, about five blocks east of the Unity Temple. East Avenue and Fair Oaks, which is one block east of East Avenue, are two more streets with many Wright homes.

An excellent book, "Guide to Frank Lloyd Wright and Prairie School Architecture in Oak Park," by Paul E. Sprague, is available from Oak Park book stores for $3.50. This fine guide book is filled with pictures from Oak Park Wright homes and has many walking tours of the suburb.

Frank Lloyd Wright was perhaps the first man with sex appeal in Oak Park. Ancient ladies today remember rushing out to stop him as he rode by on horseback, offer him some gingerbread cookies. When he arrived in Oak Park the prairie grass was as high as a horseman's thigh. When he left, the prairie was dotted with his masterpieces.

12

UNIVERSITY OF CHICAGO WALK

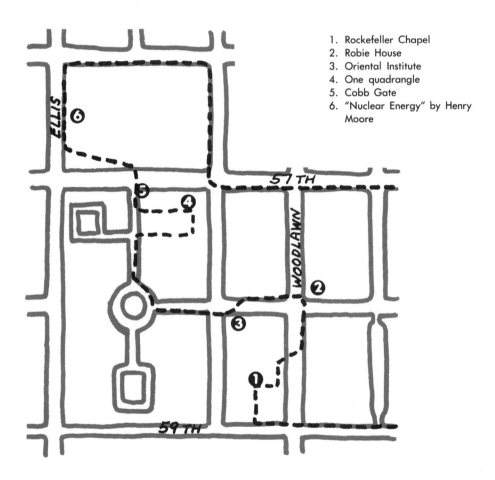

1. Rockefeller Chapel
2. Robie House
3. Oriental Institute
4. One quadrangle
5. Cobb Gate
6. "Nuclear Energy" by Henry Moore

Time: About two hours.
To get there: The Illinois Central stops at 59th St., a short run from its Randolph and Michigan station. Call for schedule information. It is also possible to sometimes find parking close to the 59th St. station.

The Hebrew Professor and the Tycoon

The University of Chicago is a miracle. It is the result of a meeting between a dumpy Hebrew professor and a rich oil tycoon, who never realized that some day he would give more than $80,000,000 to create one of the great universities in the world.

William Rainey Harper, the Hebrew professor, was an educational dynamo—finished high school at age 10, completed college while in short pants at age 14, became a college teacher when he was 16, was in charge of a college at age 19, and could sell anybody anything.

The man never slept. He taught much of the nation Hebrew by correspondence, wrote textbooks, started scholarly journals, created summer schools and conducted five of them at once in 1885, and lectured throughout the country. He would nap whenever anything got dull.

Then Harper began seducing John D. Rockefeller, tycoon. Slowly, without revealing all of his plans, Harper appealed to Rockefeller's thoughts of immortality, the need for a great university and to their joint Baptist leanings. He demanded—and eventually got—as much money as he wanted from one of the tightest-fisted American millionaires.

Harper's task of creating a university where none existed before wasn't easy. The child of one Latin professor, who had been spirited away from Cornell by Harper, was heard praying, "Good-bye, God, we are going to Chicago."

Harper even stole nearly the entire faculty of one school, Clark University. When the University of Chicago opened on Oct. 1, 1892, its faculty included eight former college presidents, the country's first Dean of Women, the first Jewish theologian in a Christian university, and the first professional football coach, Amos Alonzo Stagg. There were 594 students that first day. Harper had created a university.

The University of Chicago today teaches more than 8,500 students, and tuition is more than $12,100 per year. There is one faculty member for every eight students and 55 winners of the Nobel Prize have been associated with the school as students, teachers or researchers.

The U. of C. is the largest, richest and most prestigious private institution in the Midwest. Its professors have helped develop sociology as an academic discipline, discovered the various stages of sleep, created the first self-sustaining nuclear chain reaction, and discovered the jet stream, the solar wind, and Uranium 235. Its alumni include director Mike Nichols, novelists Saul Bellow and Kurt Vonnegut, and Sen. Charles H. Percy (R.-Ill.).

Hyde Park

Its campus is in Hyde Park, bastion of Chicago liberalism, an integrated community of thinkers and protestors. Shortly after the village of Hyde Park was chartered in 1861 (it wasn't annexed to Chicago until 1889), the village protested the foul odors resulting from a company which hauled "offal, dead animals, and other offensive or unwholesome matter" through the village streets to a nearby plant. When the U.S. Supreme Court decided that the company must move, Hyde Park breathed a sigh of relief.

The Midway

The walk begins by going west on 59th St. The Midway, created for the 1893 World's Columbian Exposition, is on your left. In the Midway, you'll see a statue honoring Thomas Masaryk, Czechoslovakia's first president (1850–1937). The steps to the statue are rotting and the whole area is old and ugly. Masaryk is honored because, after being a professor at the school, he returned to Czechoslovakia to become its president. Across the midway, the first building west of Dorchester is the Sonia Shankman Orthogenic School, where Bruno Bettleheim pioneered treatment of autistic children.

International House, at 1414 East 59th Street, was dedicated in 1932 "That brotherhood may prevail." Two of the university's Nobel prize winners, Saul Bellow and economist Milton Friedman, lived in the apartment building just north of International House.

Continue walking west, past the tennis courts, and notice Emmons Blaine Hall, at 59th and Kimbark, part of the University of Chicago Laboratory Schools, where John Dewey gave birth to progressive education. Dewey founded the school in 1894 and demanded that the school encourage the child's curiosity without rote learning, that the child have self-set tasks and that the child, not the subject matter, was the primary concern of all teaching.

One block west, at 59th and Woodlawn, is Ida Noyes Hall, a three-story building resembling a Tudor English manor house and the center of both women's physical education and student activities. Do walk inside and notice the Gothic staircase, windows and columns. This is university Gothic at the ultimate.

Ida's Cafe, on the main floor, owned by a Hyde Park favorite, the Medici, is a friendly place for a bite to eat. The Pub in the basement, serves spirits, has eight "great" beers on tap, costs $2 per year to join, but you have to be a student, faculty or one of their friends to go there.

There are two unfounded campus rumors as to why the Noyes family gave this hall. One alleges that Ida Noyes committed suicide after being rejected by a sorority and the family wanted to bribe the

Rockefeller Chapel

school to forever banish such women's associations (there are none at the university). The other version is that the Noyes family gave a windmill to an Iowa college, whose students promptly rolled it down a hill, causing the family to transfer its support to the U. of C. Such fictions are the stuff of campus legends.

Rockefeller Chapel

Walk diagonally across the foyer and exit, taking a right and walking through the picturesque cloisters section of Ida Noyes. Then cross Woodlawn and enter Rockefeller Chapel. There are so many things to notice and so many facts to enjoy about this place that it's hard to know where to begin.

Taking the facts in a somewhat haphazard order:

• The chapel, donated by a rich Baptist oilman, is amazingly nonsectarian with Old Testament figures to the right of the entrance and pagan philosophers to the left. The outside is also decorated with the seals of private and state universities, and, over the east door, figures of Teddy Roosevelt and Woodrow Wilson holding the seals of Harvard and Princeton, their respective alma maters.

• This is a true Gothic structure, with the arches and buttresses actually sustaining a 32,000 ton load.

• If you go to the rear of the chapel and find the wall, you'll see plaques behind which are the ashes of four U. of C. presidents and five of their wives. People tend to stay at the university for a long, long time.

• The tower rises 207 feet, and it takes 235 steps to the carillon's clavier room and 45 more to the bell tower. The carillon has a six octave range, less one half tone, with bells ranging from 10½ pounds to the 36,926-pounder named Great Bourdon which sounds C-sharp. Great Bourdon is the second largest tuned bell in the world.

• From 1928 to 1961, the bells marked every quarter hour from 9 a.m. to 10:45 p.m. by playing Wagner's "Parsifal Tune." When the four bells playing this tune began to wear out, Easley Blackwood wrote "Chicago Tune," which has been played since 1961. There are carillon recitals Wednesday at about 12:15 during the school year; at 7:30 p.m. Thursdays and 4 p.m. Sundays during June and July; and at 4 p.m. Sundays in August.

• A death knell is signaled by six peals for a woman and nine peals for a man. When President John F. Kennedy was assassinated, there were nine peals, plus 46 more on Great Bourdon, the largest bell weighing 36, 926 pounds, for the years of his life.

• The liturgical banners inside the chapel are from the 1964 New York World's Fair Vatican Pavillion.

• The chapel doors are allegedly locked in the evening because then-President Harper stopped by one night and saw "more souls being conceived than saved."

• The chapel was designed by Bertram Goodhue, who also created the Empire State Building.

Robie House

Exit on Woodlawn, to your right if you entered Rockefeller from the 59th St. side, take a left and walk north past "Modular Aluminum Sculpture: Untitled" by Buky Schwartz, 1976, to 58th St. You will see Robie House before you, at 5757 Woodlawn. This Frank Lloyd Wright masterpiece was designed in 1906. According to architectural critic Bill Newman, it is not true that he demanded that Mrs. Robie wear horizontally striped dresses so as not to clash with the home.

Frederick C. Robie, whose firm eventually became the Schwinn Bicycle Co., spent $35,000 on the house, plus $10,000 on Wright-designed furnishings. The home included several innovations, such as a three-car garage attached to the house and zinc-lined pockets under the bedroom windows, designed for plants and equipped with their own watering pipe. The wine cellar was under the front porch, and the Robie children could enter their recreation room and get to a toilet without passing through other rooms of the house. Robie appreciated that.

In 1957, a panel of architectural experts named Robie House as one of the two outstanding houses built in America in this century. The other house was "Falling Water," also by Wright. A plaque in front of Robie House calls it "one of the most significant buildings in the history of architecture." It was narrowly saved from destruction in 1957, and now houses the university's Alumni Affairs office.

Walk west on 58th St. The Chicago Theological Seminary, at 1150 E. 58th St., has a small chapel to the right of the entrance and various stones in its cloister area, including rocks from Solomon's quarries and a fragment of Plymouth Rock.

Oriental Institute

Cross the street and enter the Oriental Institute, 1155 W. 58th St. (open Tuesday through Saturday from 10 a.m. to 4 p.m.; Sunday, noon to 4 p.m.). Since it was founded in 1919, the Institute has conducted over 100 expeditions. It has helped date the Dead Sea scrolls, saved Egyptian monuments threatened by the Aswan Dam and has been working on an Assyrian Dictionary since 1921. Its collection, open free to the public, includes a copy of the Rosetta Stone; a 40-ton winged bull which once guarded the throne room of an Assyrian king named Sargon II (727-705- B.C.); a colossal Persian stone bull which once flanked the entrance to the throne room of Xerxes; very small fragments of the Dead Sea Scrolls; a collection of the rarest, finest quality Assyrian metal art dating from the Ninth Century B. C.; Persian gold treasure in amazing shape; and one of the finest collections of Sumerian statues (2900 to 2330 B. C.). They are the ones with the really silly looking eyes. One sincerely hopes that the Sumerians didn't look that way in real life.

Notice the 18-foot tall, 18-ton statue of Tutankhamun, which has no name on it because it was erased and replaced with King Harmhab.

Towards the back of the huge first hall there are several mummies and skeletons, which gave me nightmares when I first visited the Oriental Institute. To this day, I am proud to say that, as a 10-year-old, I was brave enough to look at them without closing my eyes.

Incidentally, the Oriental Institute has been the subject of rapt attention by cranks over the years, such as callers who admit they once went to Egypt and discovered that they were God, folks who warn that if a certain Turkish tomb is not immediately closed all who tampered with it would die and a fellow who sometimes performs a ritual dance in front of the King Tut statue.

Last time I toured the Oriental Institute, I met Klaus Baer, a most energetic professor of Egyptology who took me on a whirlwind, in-depth tour, and Gretel Braidwood, assistant to the director of the Institute, who laughingly said that she could be Indiana Jones' girlfriend. Her father, Robert Braidwood, an archeologist for the Oriental Institute, found the tops of 50 human skulls while excavating a 10,000-year-old building in Turkey in 1985. All the skulls had been burned. It's the sort of mysterious find which leads to notoriety. In addition, when Indiana Jones was a meek college professor in the movies, he taught at a school like the University of Chicago (according to Ms. Braidwood) where his professor was named "Ravenswood." Furthermore, Ms. Braidwood is charming and pretty enough so that she might have been his girlfriend. Farfetched? Not if you get a chance to meet her.

As you leave the Oriental Institute and cross University, you can see the modern Albert Pick Hall for International Studies. "Dialogo" a modern sculpture by Virginia Ferrari, is in front of this building.

The Renaissance Society

Continue west, entering an area surrounded by university buildings. While standing near the circle in its midst, the Administration Building is directly before you. To its left (south) is Cobb Hall, the first building built on campus and completed in 1892. On the fourth floor of this building is The Renaissance Society, one of the strangest art galleries in Chicago.

Since 1915, The Ren has been devoted to showing the most avant garde art. It exhibited Picasso and Matisse in the 1920s, Leger and Calder in the 1930s, and Magritte and Henry Moore in later years.

Susanne Ghez, the director, said the gallery, which does not sell its art and which is free, is "the best-kept secret in town."

It is also abidingly weird. During a recent visit, I saw huge sinks or boxes of detergent on shelves on display. There were also wet/dry vacuum cleaners resting on beds of neon lights encased in see-through plastic boxes and the artist claimed that the sculptures were sexually symbolic.

Scientific Breakthroughs

The G. H. Jones Laboratory is to the right (north) of the Administration Building, and Room 405 of this lab is a National Historic Landmark. Here Glenn T. Seaborg and associates first isolated and weighed plutonium in 1942.

In room 110 of this same building, Stanley Miller, then a young graduate student working with Nobel Prize winning chemist Harold C. Urey, sent some sparks through a test tube of gases in 1953. The gases reproduced the atmosphere of the earth billions of years ago and, when the miniature lightning display ended, Miller discovered that amino acids, the building blocks of life, had been created. Room 110 is now a mail room.

Walk to your right, heading north, then take another right just before the ornate gate; and enter a beautiful quadrangle, done in American collegiate Gothic style.

Look up and you'll see Mitchell Tower, copied from the Magdalen College tower in Oxford University, England, and looming to the northeast. Cross the court area, enter Reynolds Club and take a left. The "C" shop is for a quick bite, while Morry's offers inexpensive food in a huge beautiful, ornate paneled room. Observe portraits of University presidents and faculty members as you eat.

Retrace your steps, skirt the north edge of the octagon in the middle of the quad, walk up the six stairs slightly to your right and through the low-arched cloisters and exit past the Botany Pond, former swamp land which remains at the level the land was before the university arrived. Gold fish swim here in the summer.

Take a right and go through the Cobb Gate, built in 1897 by the first campus architect, Henry Ives Cobb. Tradition has it that the ugly gargoyles at the bottom of the arch are admissions counselors, with freshmen, sophomores and juniors as figures up the sides, and seniors as the ugly, but triumphant, winged griffon at the top.

Regenstein Library

Cross 57th St. and note the Joseph Regenstein Library, a $20,750,000

Nuclear Energy by Henry Moore looms where man first harnessed nuclear energy

building housing more than 13 million pieces. Regenstein invented the cellophane window on envelopes and was smart enough to patent his idea.

The library is on the site of the original Stagg Field, home of the "monsters of the Midway," when the U. of C. played Big Ten football. In 1905, one All-American player, Walter Eckersall, could boast that the season resulted in "University of Chicago 245, opponents 5." Big Ten football was sacrificed for "the life of the mind" in 1939. When asked about athletics, former university president Robert Maynard Hutchins said, "I, sir, am a scholar. Every now and then I feel like physical exercise. I then lie down until the feeling passes."

Moore's "Nuclear Energy"

Cut across the grass in front of the Regenstein Library (everyone else does), go left (west) around the building and take a right on Ellis Avenue, heading north. Stop when you reach an unmistakeable, 12-ton sculpture, "Nuclear Energy," by Henry Moore, and nicknamed "The Skull."

This site brings on odd feelings of dread without hope, of silent, pervasive desperation. The plaques proclaim that here on Dec. 2, 1942, man achieved the first self sustained nuclear chain reaction.

At 3:25 p.m. on that day, in a former squash court under the Stagg Field grandstands; "Zip", the last control bar, was withdrawn and, for 28 minutes, Enrico Fermi's so-called "suicide squad" (because no one knew what risks were involved) watched the counters record the chain reaction. Zip was then slid into the pile, physicist Eugen Wigner brought out a bottle of Chianti and everyone drank from paper cups.

It was an event which changed civilization, the equal to the invention of the steam engine or the introduction of the automobile or airplane. For the first time man was not using energy drawn either directly or indirectly from the sun. He had created his own sun, something only God could do before 1942.

Court Theater

Walk past 56th and go straight ahead to the Court Theater, 5535 S. Ellis. Once this theater offered a summer of delights outdoors near the Reynolds Club, where Richard III's battles were helped by real horses galloping through the quadrangle. It is now housed in a modern, 250-seat indoor theater, which means we no longer have to fight mosquitoes to see theater.

David and Alfred Smart Gallery

Walk through the iron gate, east into the Cochrane-Woods arts center and the David and Alfred Smart Gallery, 5550 S. Greenwood (Tuesday through Saturday, 10-4; Sunday, noon-4). This free gallery is quite eclectic, with displays of the most modern and most ancient arts. Notice the Frank Lloyd Wright furniture and windows; Auguste Rodin's "The Cathedral," a statue featuring two hands praying; and George Segal's sensual sculpture in plaster titled "The Lovers."

Walk east again, out the other iron gate to Greenwood. Take a right (south) and go one half block to 56th, take a left to University and then go right one block to Barlett Gymnasium, one of the few gyms in the world with a mural extrolling medieval physical culture in a scene from Ivanhoe and a huge stained glass window. I'm sure people have been worried for years about basketballs and that window.

You are now standing at 57th and University. You can walk about six blocks to the I.C. stop at 57th, passing such restaurants as the Agora, Edwardo's, and the Medici, a coffee house which serves either the best or worst pizza in Hyde Park, depending on which student you ask. You can also return to 59th and retrace your steps to the I.C. or your car.

Writer John Gunther has called the University of Chicago "a peculiar, miniature principality." It survived the red-baiting hysteria of the '50s, did not call police when SDS-inspired students staged a sit-in in the administration building in 1969 (some folks liked that idea, others wanted the hippies beaten to a pulp), and remembers President Harper's 1887 prediction that the university "would in ten years have more students, if rightly conducted, than Yale or Harvard has today." The University of Chicago is still chasing Yale or Harvard in other areas, but many folks think it has already passed them.

13 MUSEUM WALK

FIELD MUSEUM, SHEDD AQUARIUM, ADLER PLANETARIUM

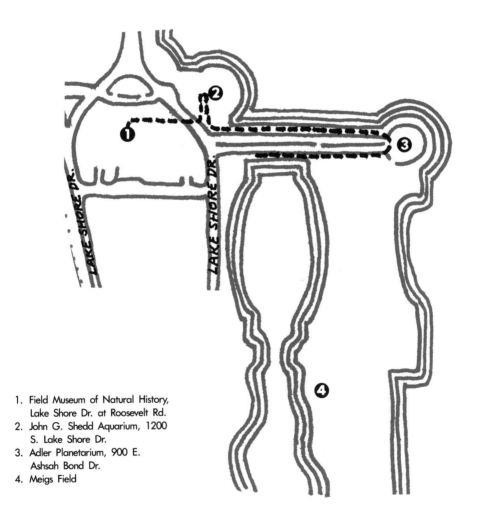

1. Field Museum of Natural History, Lake Shore Dr. at Roosevelt Rd.
2. John G. Shedd Aquarium, 1200 S. Lake Shore Dr.
3. Adler Planetarium, 900 E. Ashsah Bond Dr.
4. Meigs Field

Time: A minimum of one hour per museum. The Adler Planetarium program takes an hour, the Shedd Aquarium can be seen in slightly less than an hour and the Field Museum deserves a two to four-hour stay. Any of the museums can be the subject of a separate walk and probably should be—they are that spectacular.

To get there: By car, go south on Lake Shore Drive and park in the lots either in front of or directly behind the Field Museum. The Soldier Field lot is just south of the Field Museum. Or you can drive around the Field Museum, enter the Lake Shore Drive heading north and take a quick right on Achsach Bond Drive, which goes toward the Planetarium. Parking is often available there. Or, take the 146 Marine/Michigan CTA bus, which runs along the State Street Mall.

Lakefront Explorations

There are three museums, each devoted to different specialties, within a mile of each other on Chicago's lakefront. A day spent with them brings the visitor in touch with man's natural history, aquatic life and the stars, plus offering vistas of Lake Michigan and a chance to see private planes landing and taking off at nearby Meigs Field.

All three were founded by Chicago merchants who wanted posterity to remember them for more than just being dry goods salesmen. All three have had a grand past and are modernizing to prepare for the future.

Field Museum

Begin with the Field Museum, a large, imposing edifice, dominating a curve on Lake Shore Drive. It was located in the Palace of Fine Arts (now the Museum of Science and Industry) when it opened in 1894. It was the outgrowth of the anthropological collections created for the 1893 World's Columbian Exposition in Chicago.

Edward E. Ayer raised the money for the museum from Marshall Field I, who said no, at first. Then, one evening, Ayer demanded to see Field, who asked how much time Ayer needed.

Ayer's memorable, and incredibly confident, reply was, "If I can't talk you out of a million dollars in 15 minutes, I'm no good, nor you either."

Ayer mentioned the name A. T. Stewart, a forgotten merchant, and told Field, "You can sell dry goods until hell freezes over; you can sell it on the ice until that melts; and in 25 years you will be just the figure A. T. Stewart is—absolutely forgotten." The next day, Field gave $1,000,000 and the Museum got started.

148

Two stuffed fighting bull elephants dominate the Field Museum's main floor

From the beginning, this Museum has had a history of unparalleled adventure, discovery and excitement, all with good business sense.

Consider Berthold Laufer, stiff-necked, proud, formal, Germanic and notorius for his attempts to seduce the Museum's female staff. Laufer went to China and Tibet for the Museum in 1908–10 and brought back invaluable artifacts. To get them, he suffered the indignities of being bitten by Tibetan mastiff dogs, having stones thrown at him because he was a foreigner, being beaten in front of the royal palace "for no other reason (but) because I politely expressed the wish to see the king and held presents for him in my hands." The Tibetans even refused to sell him food or fodder for his horses.

There was William Jones, born on the Saulk and Fox Indian reservation, worked as a cowboy, and became the first American Indian to earn a Ph.D. in anthropology. Eventually, the Field Museum sent him to the Philippines where he had difficulty adjusting to tribal near-nudity. He wanted to get home to see the fiancee he left in America 16 months earlier. The tribes weren't cooperating with him to help him get his collection home, and he made a big mistake—he yelled at Takadan, an elder of the Ilongots, a tribe of head-hunters. He quickly learned never to yell at a head-hunter. It was only because of great good luck that his body was recovered with his head still in place.

Elmer S. Riggs poked around Riggs Hill, Colorado, in 1900, and found a leg bone. It was the upper foreleg of an unknown creature. And the bone was six-feet eight-inches long (2.04 meters). Paleontologists thought about that one for a long time and finally decided that the brachiosaurus, as the creature was called, was the largest land animal ever, weighing 85.63 tons, with, of all things, a small mouth and weak teeth. How did it ever feed itself?

Dr. Henry W. Nichols, former head of the geology department, was called Foozleduck behind his back because of his neatly trimmed full beard. He lost half of it while investigating a gold mine near Porcupine, Ontario, in 1919. He avoided a forest fire by jumping into a nearby stream, saved his life, but lost half a beard.

Sharat K. Roy was another museum adventurer who studied in Calcutta, became on expert on the Arctic and succeeded Dr. Nichols as head of the geology department. He set off from Chicago to collect fossils in upper New York State and didn't notice he was heading in the wrong direction until he found himself on a bridge crossing the Mississippi.

Unfortunately, much of the romance and excitement of the Museum is not available to the casual visitor. It's hidden in the archives and stored in the Museum's attics (the brachiosaurus bones are not even on display).

Again and again, the Museum's publications proudly state that it owns over 13,000,000 specimens and artifacts, and "less than one half of one per cent of these are exhibited at any given time." And some of its halls are unlit, dusty and uninviting. But others, especially the newer displays, can be both educational and awe-inspiring.

If you wish to do a little searching, what is exhibited can be fascinating.

Starting with the Main Floor, you'll see:

• The fighting bull elephants, stuffed by Carl Akeley, who created a new, complex taxidermy process while involved in this world-famous exhibit. The job got so difficult that Akeley said, "Only a fool would attempt to mount an elephant."

• The only free-standing (without visible supports) gorgosaurus skeleton in America.

• In Hall 35, the Benld Meteorite, which fell on Benld, Illinois on Sept. 29, 1938, and went through the roof and seat of a 1928 Pontiac coupe. The seat is also on display.

• Su-Lin, the first panda in captivity, sits stuffed in Hall 15, in a case with some raccoons. This is rather sad. The late D. Dwight Davis, Field's curator of vertebrate animals, spent his life studying Su-Lin's body. After 25 years of work, in 1964, he wrote that "pandas are nothing more than highly specialized bears." Experts then thought that the panda was a strange raccoon because the two species have similar chromosome counts. Davis said not so, but the Museum hasn't gotten around to moving Su-Lin closer to her relatives.

• Hall 17 features the giant pandas shot by Theodore and Kermit Roosevelt, the first white men to kill these rare animals.

• Hall 18 has "Man in His Environment," a multi-media maze which swiftly teaches about our effect on Earth. A fine modern exhibit.

• Pullman Hall has a 45-foot whale skeleton suspended from the ceiling. It's awesome.

• The Pawnee Earth Lodge—The only life-size replica of a native American dwelling. You can enter and sit on a buffalo robe here.

• Maritime Peoples of the Arctic and Northwest Coast, with beautiful models of life in that area of the world.

• Plants of the World, the world's largest exhibit of three dimensional, hand-crafted plants. This is not only a beautiful exhibit, it takes botany and transforms it from a namby-pamby field of learning into a vital, fascinating science.

On the second floor:

• One of two copies of John James Audubon's "The Birds of America" book.

• The Hall of Jade, representing 6,000 years of Oriental history.

• The Hall of Gems, including the 5,890-carat Chalmers blue topaz and the four-pound solid gold Philippine Agusan image.

• Hall 38 is the spot which gives this museum the nickname of "the bones place." The 72-foot long brontosaurus excelsus skeleton was actually found in two parts, with the rear collected in 1901 in Colorado and the forequarters in Utah in 1941.

• The portraits of man by Malvina Hoffman. After visiting the attractive, dynamic sculptress, a museum official agreed to have her sculptures cast in bronze. They are supposed to portray typical folks from various races, but Malvina liked sculpting beautiful people. The busts and statues have been criticized as embodying the white man's ideal of beauty rather than, say, the pigmy's. The Museum doesn't tell visitors that they are interesting statues, rather than accurate depictions.

On the Ground Floor:

• The Egyptian mummy collection has no romantic stories attached to it. A rich Museum trustee went to Egypt and, instead of digging in the sand, bought a few carloads of stuff. A guard once claimed the mummies move at night.

• A Place for Wonder is where visitors are encouraged to touch, listen to, try on or examine rocks, skulls, shells, pelts and to rummage through drawers.

The Field Museum, once the repository of what was old and dusty, now even has a McDonald's (a modern food stand, not a prehistoric one!) The old museum is moving with a sprightly step into tomorrow.

The Field Museum is open every day but Christmas and New Year's, from 9 a.m. to 5 p.m. Each Thursday is a free admission day. Otherwise it costs $2 for adults and $1 for those ages six through 17; and $4 for families, which are defined as two adults with unlimited numbers of children.

Shedd Aquarium

Leaving the Field Museum's north exit, turn right and walk under Lake Shore Dr., using the pedestrian tunnel. You will emerge facing the Shedd Aquarium, the largest of its kind in the world.

The joy of the Aquarium is that no child can ever be lost there. It is shaped like a daisy, with tanks in each of the petals. If a child gets lost, eventually he or she will wander into the central area and be found. This allows individual adults to bring groups of five, 10 and 15 children there for excursions without constantly yelling, "Where's Johnny?"

The major attraction of the Aquarium is the coral reef tank, which occasionally must shut down because the parrot fish are eating the

Feeding time in the Shedd Aquarium Reef Tank

fiberglass and latex coral. It's 40 feet in diameter, has 90,000 gallons of salt water held in place by windows 2½-inches thick. The exhibit features a SCUBA-suited diver feeding the 500 tropical Caribbean fish at 11 a.m. and 2 p.m.

While the diver has been engaged in this humanitarian mission, the moray eel has nipped his leg and the sharks have gone into a feeding frenzy. However, the least friendly resident is the sea turtle. The divers hate the turtles and the turtles do not enjoy the divers. Notice this relationship deteriorate as you watch the feeding.

John Graves Shedd came to Chicago after the 1871 fire and told Marshall Field he could "sell any kind of goods in the store every day." He went to work in the stock and shipping room of the linen department of Marshall Field and Co. for $10 a week, became a partner in the firm in 1893, president in 1906, and chairman of the board in 1921. When he died in 1926, he gave $3,000,000 so the Aquarium could be built.

Today there are 203 exhibit tanks seen by over a million visitors a year. The Aquarium is filled with strange and beautiful fish in tanks with labels sure to tell the average visitor as little as possible about what's inside. That situation is gradually changing.

The Aquarium exhibits, which change frequently because the average life expectancy of a fish after being acclimated to an aquarium is around 18 months, include:

• Chico, the fresh-water dolphin, who has lumps all over his body. This is the result of something called the golf-ball disease, an infection which attacked Chico for two years. Fortunately, he survived.

• Josh, a jewfish which weights 450 pounds and is the largest fish in the aquarium.

• The lionfish, with spines which sent one keeper into intensive care for three days after he touched one of them while cleaning the tank.

• The octopus, which no longer escapes from its aquarium. With eight arms, octopii can get out of anything, which presents a slimy problem for the keepers when they show up for work in the morning. The Shedd Aquarium has devised a foolproof system for keeping octopii in tanks. The tanks are lined with astroturf, which feels yechy to octopii and which doesn't give their suction cups anything to hold on to.

• The penguins, who sit in the Lake Michigan fresh water fish section of the Aquarium. They don't belong there, but they're cute and no one seems to mind.

• The lungfish, which has been at the Aquarium since 1933.

• The balanced aquarium room, which isn't really balanced in that oxygen must be added to the water, but which features tiny fish in small tanks under Chinese pagodas. Who can criticize a room which displays a fish called the peaceful puffer?

• Sea anenomes exhibit, which opened in 1980 and which displays the beautiful (and the deadly to small fish) "flowers" of the sea.

• River otters, a relatively new exhibit complete with a water fall and a pond designed to convince the otters that they are actually cavorting on Fox River sandstone bluffs.

There are usually about 7,000 fish on display in the Shedd Aquarium, representing over 700 species of salt and fresh water fish. A trip to the world's largest indoor Aquarium becomes a way to visit creatures living beneath the sea in two-thirds of the world we seldom see.

Aquarium hours are 9 a.m. to 5 p.m., March through October; and 10 a.m. to 5 p.m., November through February. It costs $2 for adults, $1 for children, 50 cents for senior citizens and Thursdays are free days.

Leaving the Shedd Aquarium, walk to your left and head east towards the Planetarium, which sits a half mile out into the lake on what was once an island, but is now connected to the shore thanks to a man-made peninsula. You will pass the statue of Nicolaus Copernicus, a reproduction of an original in the Polish Academy of Sciences in Warsaw. It was unveiled in 1973 at a time when many people of Polish descent were angry about Polish jokes and wanted others to know about the greatness of Poland. The inscription reads, "By reforming astronomy he initiated modern science."

Meigs Field

Meigs Field is to the south. This was originally Northerly Island, part of the 1933 World's Fair, and was mentioned in earlier plans as a recreational facility. Merrill C. Meigs was a pilot and publisher of two Chicago newspapers. He wanted a place to land an airplane near downtown offices, so ground was broken for Meigs Field in 1947, in violation of the Burnham Plan. Notice that Lake Point Tower is only two miles north of the field. Pilots have said that an airplane going 120 mph could hit that tower in less than a minute after take off.

Adler Planetarium

Enter the Planetarium by walking downstairs just west of the present building.

The show there is about an hour long. During the summer, it can be seen seven days a week at 2 p.m., also Fridays at 8 p.m.; Saturdays, Sundays and holidays at 11 a.m., 1, 3, and 4 p.m. Adults are charged $2.50, children $1.50.

155

Entrance to Adler Planetarium and Astronomical Museum

The show begins in the Kroc Universe Theater, which opened in 1973 as part of the Planetarium's new, underground (so as to avoid ruining the view of the lakefront) Astro-Science Center. The theater introduces the spectator to the universe with a fast-moving, multimedia show, which usually includes several films being shown at once, slides projected on the ceiling, music and narration.

Following this, the spectator goes to the Sky Theater, which is dominated by a contraption which looks like a rejected Jules Verne submarine. It is the Zeiss Projector, which weights 17½ tons, has 40,000 individual parts and can project views of the heavens as they would be seen from any spot on the earth at any hour of the day, today, yesterday or tomorrow.

One of the main, often-unspoken attractions of this presentation are the soft comfortable chairs, arranged around the projector. They allow the visitor to lean back and look at the ceiling. Unfortunately, because the air in the theater is so pure (dust interferes with the illusion) and the seats so comfy, many adults doze during the show.

The programs are loaded with information and change format about four times a year. The Planetarium also displays ancient astronomical instruments, an Earth globe six feet in diameter, photographs of space, a moon mural, symbols of space exploration, a 74-gram, 4-billion-year-old moon rock collected by astronaut David Scott during the Apollo 15 mission, a scale which tells you your weight on other worlds, and the world's largest map of the universe seen on the ceiling of the Universe Theatre, with a fiber optic image that takes the viewer back 3.6 billion light years.

The Planetarium, which opened in 1930, is a gift to Chicago by Max Adler, who retired in 1928 as senior officer of Sears, Roebuck & Co. Adler said, "The popular conception of the universe is too meager; the planets and the stars are too far removed from general knowledge . . ." More than 22,000,000 people have since visited the Planetarium.

Doane Observatory

As you exit the Planetarium, walk or drive around it, looking at the Lake and Chicago's skyline as you do. You'll see the Doane Observatory directly east of the Planetarium. This houses a 20-inch computer-controlled telescope and its views are transmitted to a classroom and exhibition area.

This ends your museum walk. The Field Museum, the Shedd Aquarium and the Planetarium—three museums specializing in different views of man and his universe. Yet they are all somehow complementary. They all essentially say that there is something worth saving—and a lot worth knowing—on this Earth and in this universe.

View of the Chicago skyline from the Planetarium

157

14 MUSEUM OF SCIENCE AND INDUSTRY WALK

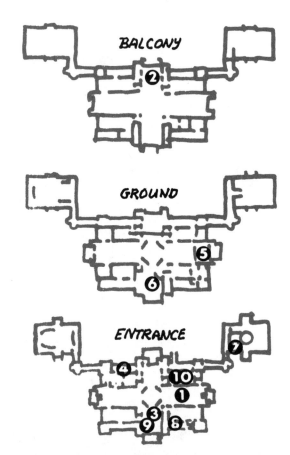

1. Santa Fe Model Railroad
2. Omnimax Theater
3. Coal Mine
4. Omni-Com
5. U-505 Submarine
6. Colleen Moore's Fairy Castle
7. Sears Circus
8. Yesterday's Main Street
9. Petroleum Exhibit
10. Food for Life

Time: Three hours and 36 minutes (the average stay for visitors.)
To get there: The Illinois Central and the Chicago, South Shore and South Bend Railroads regularly leave Randolph and Michigan and stop at 55th/56th/57th Street station, about two blocks west of the museum. This is the safest public transportation. It is not advisable to take the CTA Jackson Park

"B" train to 55th and Garfield and transfer to the Number 1, 6 or 55 buses because the neighborhood there has a high crime rate. If you're driving, take Lake Shore Drive south to 57th Street, where you'll see the Museum and the huge signs directing you there. Now that Chicago has erected a stoplight at 57th Stret and Lake Shore Drive, formerly the most dangerous intersection in town, it's even safe to return home from the Museum of Science and Industry.

Hands On!

The Museum of Science and Industry will defeat you. There is no way you will see everything in this gigantic Museum in a single day.

This Museum is a delightful collection of things which respond when you push a button, lights which glare when you flip a switch or stuff you can operate with a steering wheel or throttle. The Museum's first director, Waldemar B. Kaempffert, enthused in 1928, "We are going to have activity! Buttons to push! Levers and handles to turn! And nowhere any sign reading 'Hands Off'!"

Over 4,000,000 people a year visit this mecca of education by razzamatazz. Where learning is fun. Where science is a multi-media experience. Where knowledge and joy are not separate ideas. In a Greek Temple dedicated to modern technology!

Twice in its history this Museum almost wasn't.

Palace of Fine Arts

It began life as the Palace of Fine Arts for the 1893 Columbian Exposition. What is now the front door, facing the huge parking lot, was actually the rear of a building which faced a lagoon (more about that later) and dozens of other structures.

The 1893 fair is famous for the first Ferris Wheel in America (which took folks 265 feet into the air); for Fahreda Mahzar also known as Little Egypt, a sleek, dark-haired Oriental beauty who entranced visitors with her dance (she married a Chicago restaurant owner and became Mrs. Andrew Spyropoulos); and for giving Chicago the name "Windy City." Chicagoans boasted a lot while trying to get that 1893 fair, and Charles A. Dana in the New York Sun wrote, "Don't pay attention to the nonsensical claims of that windy city." From that point on, Chicagoans became proud of their "wind."

Before the 1893 fair, the Palace of Fine Arts was said to be "unequalled since the Parthenon and the age of Pericles." Because it was supposed to house fine art works by Constable, Monet, Pissarro and others, it was a little more fireproof than its neighbors. It had foundations eight feet thick. But, as marvelous as the place looked,

159

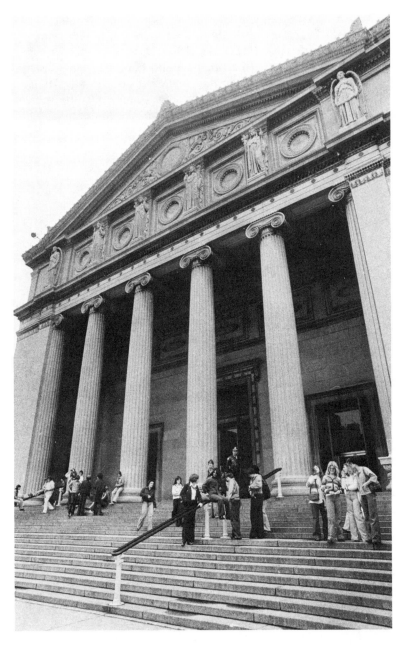

Welcome to the Museum of Science and Industry, or is it a Greco-Roman Temple?

many of its walls were built of "staff," a mixture of plaster and chicken wire, designed to last a year or so.

When the 1893 Fair closed, the Field Museum took over the Palace of Fine Arts, which quickly began to fall apart. By 1905, fences had to be put up around the place to protect guests from falling mortar. By 1921, the Field Museum abandoned the old Palace for newer quarters at Roosevelt and Lake Shore Drive. And the building was said to be "A scaly wormy pile that should be allowed to die!" (See Museum Walk).

That's when the Palace of Fine Arts quickly entered two crises periods. It was narrowly saved from demolition in 1923. After becoming the Museum of Science and Industry, it almost went broke in 1938–40.

On each occasion, a strong champion came along to save it.

Julius Rosenwald, head of Sears, Roebuck & Co., remembered a trip to Munich in 1911 with his son William. The boy continually got lost in The German Museum for the Preservation of the Mysterious Past in Natural Science and History of Engineering, known as the Deutsches Museum. Rosenwald wanted a similar museum of science and technology in which visitors could push buttons and learn. He backed his dream with $7,000,000 in cash gifts and stocks, a fine way to turn dreams into reality.

The staff walls were torn down and a permanent structure was erected. The Museum opened in time for the 1933 Century of Progress Fair, with the coal mine available for youthful Chicagoans who wanted to briefly neck in the dark cars on the way to the mine.

But the Museum was well on its way to becoming a smashing failure, a stodgy place, old before its time. By 1940, it was spending $200,000 a year more than it was earning.

That's when Lennox Lohr became the Museum's president. He had already been a success in three other careers—as editor of a military magazine, as general manager of the 1933 Century of Progress, and as president of the National Broadcasting Co. He should also be a hero to everyone who hates to wake up in the morning. Lennox Lohr never got to the office before 10 a.m.

Lohr fired part of the staff, began to woo both industry and visitors, and turned the museum into the vital, energetic, show biz, educational extravaganza it is today.

Lohr died in 1968, but by that time the Santa Fe Railroad put in its train models (1940), International Harvester created its farm (1946), actress Colleen Moore's fairy castle opened (1949), the walk-through heart was first seen (1952), and the U-505 submarine came to the Museum (1954).

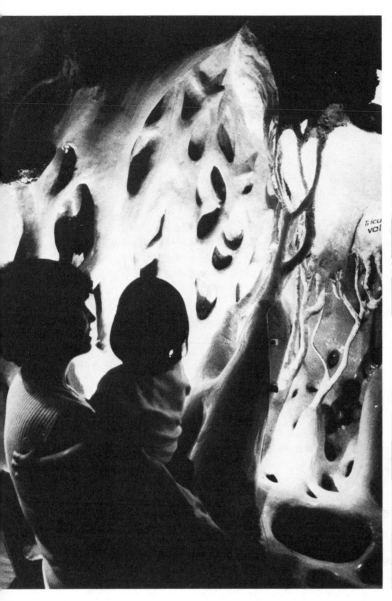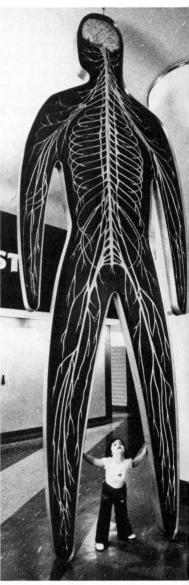

Inside a human heart and marveling at a model of the circulatory system

Open Every Day With Free Admission

Today, the Museum is Chicago's number one tourist attraction with more than 3,000,000 visitors a year. It is open every day of the year, except Christmas. It sets attendance records in December, when it mounts "Christmas Around the World" exhibits. On December 12, 1976, a one-day record of 68,251 visitors was set for a Polish Christmas program. Over 91 million people have visited the Museum since it opened in 1933.

Admission is free because the Museum has figured out clever ways to find cash. Its funds come about equally from:

(1) Industries, which are charged a slightly padded annual maintenance fee for their exhibits.

(2) Guests. The U-505 and coal mine and Omni Max Theater each bring in more than $500,000 a year.

(3) The Chicago Park District

(4) Julius Rosenwald, who left some Sears stock to the Museum.

The Museum is open from Memorial Day through Labor Day from 9:30 a.m. to 5:30 p.m. The rest of the year it's open from 9:30 a.m. to 4 p.m. weekdays, and from 9:30 a.m. to 5:30 p.m. Saturdays, Sundays and holidays.

The best way to see the Museum is to follow a child through it. He or she may not be organized in his or her explorations, but after a few hours many of the Museum's 14 acres will be covered.

If you need a starting point, you might try the Omni-Com, the renewed telephone company exhibit, directly to the right of the entrance. Invariably, there are so many fascinating displays that this single hall takes a full hour to explore while everyone tests his hearing and listens to himself on the telephone. Be sure to check out the whispering gallery. You can hear friends across the hall while facing the other way.

Several of the exhibits are well worth seeking out. Either Museum personnel will direct you to them or free maps are available at the information booth directly in front of the entrance. The book store to the left of the entrance behind the information booth sells printed guides, and the slightly more expensive, three-color "Exhibit Guide" is excellent.

• The U-505, which is just beyond the sea power exhibit on the ground floor, is an actual German submarine captured by Americans during World War II. It was the first enemy ship seized on the high seas since the USS Peacock took possession of the British Nautilus in 1815.

Its capture, on June 4, 1944, is faithfully recorded in a film shown to visitors. Its trek to the Museum involved an almost as difficult, but lesser-known, undertaking. Before it was brought from Lake Michigan to the Museum, motorists on Lake Shore Dr. saw astounding signs saying, "SUBMARINE CROSSING. DRIVE CAREFULLY."

The boat was carefully moved on rollers and then placed in three reinforced concrete cradles, but only the middle one is attached to the U-505. Two-thirds of the boat's 840-ton weight rests on the 20 pairs of eight-inch steel rollers on tracks set up in the front and back cradles. The rollers allow the U-505 to move up to 2-½ inches a year, to compensate for the contraction and expansion of the boat's steel hull in Chicago's heat and cold.

• Colleen Moore's Fairy Castle, which is near the coal mine exit on the ground floor, is a $500,000 doll house which took 700 artists nine years to create. There's a painting of Miss Moore, a film star, in the Great Hall; King Arthur's Dining Room features solid gold dining service; the royal bed chamber has a bearskin rug with teeth taken from a mouse; and the chapel has the world's smallest Bible, printed in 1840 and containing the entire New Testament.

Colleen Moore, whose bobbed hair was a symbol of the flappers of the '20s, later became Mrs. Homer Hargrave, wife of a wealthy Chicago stockbroker. Lohr convinced her to give the fairy castle to the Museum (after she asked, "What on earth would a dollhouse do there with all those gadgets and big machines?") when he said he wanted a few displays purely for joy and entertainment. There is another doll house with quite a different story in the museum, but you'll learn about that one in the Architecture and the City exhibit.

• The Sears' Circus display, which is in the east pavillion of the main floor, features 22,000 miniature carvings bought or created by Chicagoan Ronald J. Weber; a porthole through which a visitor can stick his head and see how he'd look with clown make up; and an eight-minute, multi-media circus film of the Clyde Beatty-Cole Bros. Circus. The film won awards in 1973 and is a "must see" feature of the Museum.

• Yesterday's Main Street, near the entrance to the coal mine on the main floor, perpetually waits for the Hon. J. J. Hone to talk about "Shall Women Vote" and features a 10-cent nickelodeon (a contradiction in terms there, but who cares?).

• Finnigan's Ice Cream Parlor, near Main Street, uses the furnishings of an old pharmacy which began business about a mile from the Museum in 1911.

• The Petroleum Exhibit, to the rear of the entrance floor, puts each visitor in his own bubble for a ride on a 650-foot-long articulated slat conveyor, longest in the world, for a 10-minute trip past 23 exhibit sections about energy. The exhibit cost $1,200,000 to build.

• The Food For Life section, to the left of the information booth, includes a computer which will tell visitors how much nutrition they get out of their favorite meals. The last time we were there, my son, who enjoys meals of tacos, pizza, French fries, potato chips and milk shakes, learned that he was getting lots of vitamins and minerals. It didn't help matters at home.

• Architecture and the City, which has fragments of the world's first skyscraper, the Home Insurance Building, which stood at

Colleen Moore's Fairy Castle

LaSalle and Adams from 1885 to 1931, plus six computer games, two of which will allow you to design your own dream house; an architect's office without an angry client's wife complaining about lack of closet space; and a 16-foot-long scale model of a Georgian style house. The real-life home of Ralph and Janet Falk cost around $6,000,000, but the model, which took eight years to make, cost $200,000. Ralph is the Baxter Travenol Laboratories heir. The same week the model was finally delivered by Maine modelmaker Jay Hanna, Ralph moved out of the real home "for another woman," said Janet. She added that she's glad the model is on display in the museum "where somebody can enjoy it."

• Calculating and Computing, which teaches the history and technology of computing while giving everyone lots of terminals with which to play, including programs to teach sailing, inform us about our car and mortgage payments, a computer which speaks Spanish and English, another which teaches us how to throw a ball from an elevator into a box and Beano, a mathematical bingo game which sometimes lets us beat the computer.

• The Money Center, which teaches us about supply, demand, what is the nature of money and good old fashioned capitalism. It's fun to get an account number from the nearest computer when you start through the exhibit and then see how much (or how little) money you make as you proceed to own a doughnut shop, and do other tasks.

• The Santa Fe Railroad model trains, which has been a favorite at the museum for years. This 3,000 square foot display has 35 diesel locomotives, 85 freight trains, passenger trains looking like the old Superchief and El Captain. A wonder for model train lovers, which is probably every man over the age of two and many women.

• The Henry Crown Space Center and Omni Max Theater, which opened in 1986 and was the first addition ever to the Museum. No one ever figured they would need additional space. This is a must see, a don't miss and an absolutely knock out museum event. The Lunar landing module is there with the legs intact, a rarity since the original left the legs on the moon. This module was used at Cape Kennedy to train the astronauts before they went to the moon, but it stayed on earth. The burned and blackened Apollo 8, which carried three astronauts around the moon, is here also.

There is an amazingly realistic space shuttle ride, which includes a 3-D movie which you see while wearing goggles and gives the spectators the feeling of being on the space shuttle. The secret is that the entire theater moves and shifts, sort of a huge Link trainer which was used to acclimate pilots to flying.

But it is the Omni Max Theater which should draw the curious, the brave, and those who yearn to know what space flight feels like.

As you go inside, be sure to watch the gigantic camera rising and lowering into the theater. The huge hoses attached to it cool the specially built unit.

Once inside, you will be awestruck. Once the film starts, some of you may actually need Dramamine or anti-airsickness pills—it will be that realistic.

The film screen wraps around the audience, which can watch film through 180 degrees of arc. The screen is so large and takes up so much space that it had to be porous to allow air into the theater. About 25 per cent of the screen is really small holes, yet it is one of the most highly reflective movie screens ever built.

The first film (and they will change in the future) is "The Dream is Alive," a movie taken by the astronauts during the three Space Shuttle missions before the Challenger disaster in 1985. It is fascinat-

Santa Fe Railroad exhibit

ing to watch the astronauts sleeping with their hands floating above their chests, and it is tragic that some of the people we see on this film died in the accident.

A bit of final advice: Do stop frequently to see the various theaters, movies and multi-media presentations in the museum. It's a fine way to learn while resting.

Museum Grounds

Before leaving the museum area, stroll to the south of the museum. Take a right as you exit, then another right to go around behind the U-505, the locomotives and the Henry Crown Space Center to the bridge over the lagoon behind the Museum.

Besides offering a stunning, often-ignored view of the Museum, this Bridge is historically significant. In 1938, the ashes of attorney Clarence Darrow, who won the Scopes Monkey Trial, were scattered from this bridge. Each year, on March 13, the anniversary of Dar-

167

row's death, his devotees return to this bridge to attempt to make contact with his spirit.

Don't worry if Darrow's spirit doesn't do much. It never has—and it's not supposed to. Darrow, magician Harry Thurston and Detroit businessman Claude Noble promised each other in a Detroit hotel in 1937 that, if there was life after death, Darrow would attempt to make contact with the living here on the anniversary of his death. Darrow, who believed there was no soul, made the pact in an effort to debunk mediums and the spirit world.

For years, Noble would stand on this bridge, a hymn book in his hand, and say, "Clarence Darrow, if you can manifest your spirit to me, do it now." Darrow never did.

These days, the ceremony still takes place, a wreath is usually thrown into the lagoon (later retrieved to prevent pollution), and speeches about basic freedoms are given. Because it is often cold and miserable in Chicago on March 13, the ceremony is brief, to the point, and sometimes a spectator or two slips on the mud and falls into the lagoon.

Now I know you are tired by this time, but if you will walk just a little further south (probably away from your car and some rest for your weary legs), you will see something quite charming and special for the city of big shoulders, hog butcher to the world.

Beyond the bridge, enter the Paul H. Douglas Nature Sanctuary. Follow the winding path to an exquisite Japanese garden which is on the site of Chicago's first Japanese Garden created for the 1893 Columbian Exposition. This is a peaceful, serene place which is especially beautiful when the mock orange is in bloom.

When I last visited this garden, the moon bridge linking the two isthmuses was gone. Let us hope that the bridge is quickly restored and those who would desecrate an almost secret place of harmony in the city would find other outlets for their energies.

15

BROOKFIELD ZOO WALK

1. Ibex Mountain
2. Lion House
3. Seven Seas Panorama
4. Baboon Island
5. Children's Zoo
6. Tropic World
7. Discovery Center

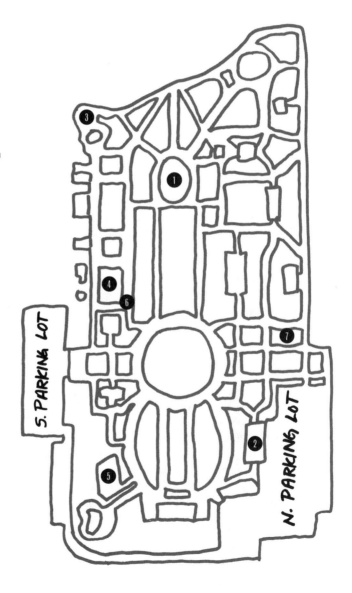

Time: Three to four hours for the zoo, plus an hour roundtrip to get there.

How to get there: Brookfield Zoo is about 14 miles west of Chicago's loop, at First Avenue and 31st Street in Brookfield, Illinois. If you lose the zoo (it's got 200 acres so it's not easy to lose), call 321-485-0263.

By automobile, take the Eisenhower I-290 west to First Avenue or the Stevenson I-55 west also to First Avenue.

By bus, you can take the Regional Transit Authority's Number 304, 331 or the special 333 Brookfield Zoo bus. In Chicago, call 836-7000 for RTA information or 1-800-972-7000 for suburban RTA info. By train, the Burlington Railroad goes from Union Station in the Loop to the new Zoo Stop at the Hollywood Station, three blocks from the South Gate.

Hours: The zoo is open every day. 9:30 a.m. to 6 p.m. Memorial Day through Labor Day. 10 a.m. to 5 p.m. Labor Day to Memorial Day.

No Cages or Bars

A trip to Brookfield Zoo is a declaration that animals are important to humans. Once you are there, you will see humans looking at animals and animals looking at humans, and that's about it. There isn't much else to do.

But that's enough.

Brookfield was one of the first, large-scale American zoos to attempt to present its denizens outdoors without bars between them and the spectators. Monkeys, lions, tigers, sheep, elephants, and many others loll about in the sun, with only a moat between the human and the animals.

Adults ages 12 to 65 pay $2.25, children 6 to 11 and adults over 65 pay 75 cents. It costs $2 to park your car.

The first thing to do, upon arriving at the zoo, no matter what gate you enter, is to take the Safari Train, a 40-minute guided tour of the entire park. Adults, $1.50; children three to 11, 75 cents.

This will allow you to see the entire 200-acre zoo and to begin to understand where the animals you want to see are located. Otherwise, you'll tend to wander about and get quickly tired.

Brookfield opened on June 30, 1934, after eight years of construction, which covered the beginning of the Depression.

The country, and the world, didn't begin to know about Brookfield Zoo until August 22, 1937, when Su-Lin, an adorable panda who cooed, gurgled and burped her way into America's heart, arrived. Su Lin was the first panda in captivity, and how she got to Brookfield Zoo is shrouded in mystery, romance, chicanery, and legend.

170

Brookfield Zoo is famed for its collection of hooved animals

When William Harvest Harkness, Jr. died in 1936, while attempting to capture a panda, his young wife Ruth, a New York dress designer, vowed to complete her husband's mission. Hunters had been attempting to grab the fuzzy adorables for six decades. The former Ruth Elizabeth McCombs accomplished the task only eight days after she entered the Chinese jungles.

We'll never know for sure how she did it. Floyd "Tangier" Smith, a renowned hunter, had announced that he had captured three of the tykes. Did Smith sell his panda to Mrs. Harness? Did she really find the panda just sitting by an old dead tree? Was there hanky-panky in Tibet? Was "Tangier" Smith really the mysterious "Ajax" Smith, allegedly an associate of Mrs. Harkness? Who cares?

Anyhow, Su-Lin, a cuddly little girl, they said, was soon joined by another Harkness panda named Mei-Mei, who was as vicious as Su-Lin was playful. Su-Lin died at the age of 18 months (see Field Museum entry in Museum Walk to learn where she is now), and an autopsy revealed she was a boy. The same thing happened to Mei-

Mei, also a male, and Mei-Lan, who arrived at Brookfield in 1939. Mei-Lan, meaning Pretty Flower, died of old age in 1953, and was revealed to be a male. Brookfield was never too good about sexing its pandas, but then the pandas didn't care much about that sort of thing either.

Mei-Lan bit everything in sight—newspaper photographers, radio microphones, the hand off one keeper and the heel off another. Mei-Lan wasn't cuddly.

Brookfield's other star attraction was Ziggy, the oldest rogue elephant in any zoo, who died in 1975. Ziggy might have killed two men during his life (no one is very sure and Ziggy wasn't talking), and one of them might have been a midget. Ziggy was mean.

Showman Florenz Ziegfeld bought Ziggy (short for Ziegfeld) as a gift for his daughter in 1920. But Ziggy tromped through the Ziegfeld greenhouse and that ended his career as a house pet.

Later, while starring in a midget circus, he kicked through a barn wall and uncovered $50,000 worth of bootleg booze. Still later, he got angry and allegedly threw a trombone player, possibly a midget musician, to his death.

Eventually, Brookfield bought him for $500. Then came April 26, 1941, the day which caused Ziggy to be sentenced to solitary confinement for almost 30 years.

George "Slim" Lewis, his keeper, thinks it happened because the zoo wanted Ziggy mated and Ziggy wanted, well, privacy, a cow of his own choosing, romance. Who can blame him?

He attacked Lewis, all four tons of Ziggy, pinning Lewis between his tusks, which were buried three feet into the ground. Somehow Lewis survived those ivory pitchforks and the keeper managed to gouge Ziggy's eye (the fight did not observe the Marquis of Queensbury rules) and escaped.

Ziggy was chained to the wall of his indoor pen (you can still see the pen in the Pachyderm House) from that day until Sept. 23, 1970, when Lewis came out of retirement to take him for a little walk. It was part of a "Free Ziggy" campaign and eventually enough Chicagoans donated money so a $50,000 outdoor enclosure could be built for Ziggy in 1971.

Moving from Ziggy and Su-Lin, two animals who are no longer at the zoo, to those who are there, recall July 17, 1969 as you pass the polar bears. On that day, five inches of rain fell in about a half hour, clogging the drains on the polar bears' moat. This allowed four of the polar bears to swim to freedom.

Dr. George Rabb, director of the zoo since 1976, recalls that the polar bears immediately rambled across the road in front of their enclosures and raided the concession stand, eating an unknown quantity of marshmallows, plus ice cream. Two of the polar bears then visited the grizzlies in the next door enclosure, but the grizzlies hadn't invited them and chased them away.

The polars bears could not be tranquilized for fear they'd head for the moat, dive in, become unconscious and drown. So Rabb and three others herded the polar bears with zoo vehicles until they went back to their homes. It all happened before noon on a rainy day and no spectators were in danger.

Today, in a very general way, the Zoo is roughly oval-shaped around the Theodore Roosevelt Memorial Fountain and the Ibex Mountain.

In making their way around the zoo, visitors should be aware of some special areas:

Zoo Highlights

• Walking west from the North Gate, the Australian House features a brilliantly conceived "walkabout," taking you through Australian terrain in which brush tailed bettongs, Tasmanian devils, and hairy-nosed wombats move in natural surroundings.

• Brookfield Zoo has an enviable record for breeding (and thus preserving) such hoofed animals as Father David's deer and the addax. Brookfield was the first zoo to breed the okapi, in 1959, and several other births of this animal, which wasn't even known until 1901, have occurred.

• This zoo has the only herd of Dall sheep in America.

• Wild ducks actually use the waterfowl lake called Indian Lake, at the extreme west end of the zoo, meaning that it's emptier in summer when they're farther north. Canada geese, mallards, and wood ducks nest there.

• Olga the Walrus, near the Seven Seas Panorama, a dignified mound of blubber, has been at the zoo since 1962. Because it costs $6,000 a year to feed the 40 to 60 pounds of mackerel, herring, squid, smelt, and clams she eats a day, the zoo has cut back—no more clams for Olga. When looking at Olga, be alert. She spits. By the way, her birthday is celebrated on June 20.

• Seven Seas Panorama offers dolphin shows three times daily in the winter, four times daily in summer and five shows a day on Sundays and holidays. Admission for the shows, which feature leaping, trick-playing dolphins is $1.75 for adults, $1 for children. The summer schedule is 11:30, 1, 2:30 and 3:45 p.m. weekdays and Saturdays, with an additional show at 5 p.m. Saturdays, Sundays and holidays.

• The kiwi, a native of New Zealand, is in the aquatic bird house in the best kiwi display in America. That isn't difficult because only zoos in Washington, D.C., San Diego and Chicago have kiwis, who only eat earthworms. The kiwi is an expensive animal to display and

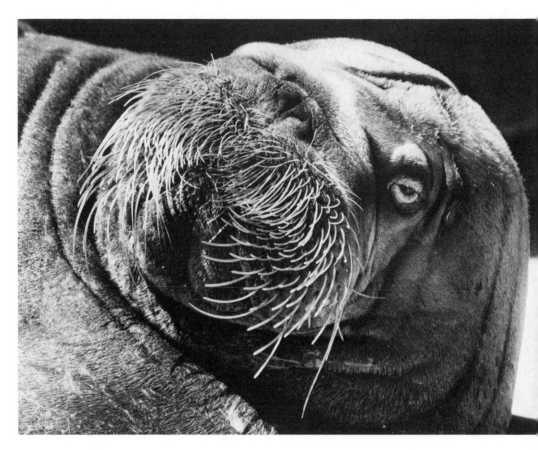

A regal portrait of Olga the Walrus

most of the time it would just stick its head in the burrow "so all the spectator saw was a kiwi butt," according to Dr. Rabb.

• The Reptile House features dangerous snakes; the zoo's oldest resident, an alligator snapping turtle who has been there looking like a mossy rock since 1933; and an entire aquarium filled to a disgusting point with Brazilian giant cockroaches. The zoo has an adopt-an-animal program, which allows patrons to pay for the feeding of zoo critters. The giant Brazilian cockroaches (blaberus giganteus) are often left as orphans in this program, although I adopted one as did a woman in California who, when learning that they were three inches long said that they would be perfect for her ex-husband.

• Excellent signs throughout the zoo explain animal behavior. They are particularly informative around the wolf woods and baboon island.

Tropic World

Tropic World. A must. What an exhibit. What brilliant planning. What pure fun for the spectator and for the animals.

Built at a cost of $10.8 million and opened in stages in 1982 (Africa), 1983 (Asia) and 1984 (South America), Tropic World costs $1 for adults, 50 cents for children and senior citizens. It is the largest indoor zoo exhibit in the world.

You enter by walking between two 45 foot waterfalls and you are in a South American jungle. Birds are flying free, monkeys are casually flipping from tree branch to tree branch, even the sloths are moving about.

Now please do not walk quickly through this masterful exhibit. Stand there. Just look without searching and you will see more animals hidden in the grottoes and among the trees.

Also wait for the thunder and the rain. You will be sprayed a bit, although stepping back a few feet along the path should protect you. The animals and the birds will scamper for shelter, although we saw the sloth come out of a tree trunk for a lazy drink of water squirting on it from the ceiling.

Next move to the Asian exhibit and notice that without bars animals of different species are getting along quite well together. You'll see the siamangs and the black macaques, who normally do not occupy the same islands, grooming each other.

Notice that there is a distinct lack of animals odors in these exhibits. The secret is that the animals do not stay in Tropic World on display overnight. There are holding areas behind the rocks where the animals go at night. Through something called operant conditioning, each group of animals is called in order at the end of the day to return to their assigned areas. The siamangs hear their own bell, the macaques have their particular whistle, and so on.

Of course, there were problems. Many of the animals were unaccustomed to any freedom and, at first, did not want to leave their cages. Later, once they tasted the heady air of Tropic World, some refused to return to their holding areas at night. Sampson the gorilla, who you will see in the next area, was one of those who didn't want to come out of his cage for days and later didn't want to return. Now it can be difficult reasoning with a 475 pound gorilla, but Sampson was convinved to return to his own area at night through the magical introduction of yogurt, which he loves.

Because the animals are fed and sleep in areas separate from the Tropic World on display for visitors, certain bodily functions are more likely to be performed away from the paying guests' eyes and noses. Only the birds, who are fed in Tropic World because they eat throughout the day, perform all their functions there. Consider keeping your hats on in Tropic World.

Carol Sodaro, assistant lead keeper in charge of the Asian exhibit, pointed out that little is as it seems in Tropic World. The leaves on the bushes are all hand painted and the branches are actually 16-guage reinforced steel. The trees and the rocks are made of gunnite, but it is the vines which are a miracle of ingenuity.

Real vines or rope would have been torn to pieces by the hard usage they would get. Furthermore, orang-utans are brilliant animals who can undo, unravel and unlock many of man's devices.

The vines are steel threads covered in an epoxy compound and rubbed with silica. At one time the vines were hooked to the ground with bolts, but the orangs unhooked anything that was so fastened. Notice that the vines are free now at their bases. As Deborah E. Cullen, manager of marketing for the zoo, said, "They won, we lost."

Next move into the African exhibit and notice the tire tracks on the floor of your walkway. A jeep was actually driven through this exhibit when the concrete was wet.

Here you'll see black-and-white colobus monkeys, Sassy the pygmy hippopotamus and gorillas, who so often merely lounge about. Notice Jake the dominant mandrill, surveying his flock from behind a bush. Look for Sampson's footprints in the walkway with the rope handholds above the apes. Listen and find the 48 different species of birds.

In addition to Sampson, the silver back gorilla, if you look closely, you'll probably also see two mature females, Alpha and Babs, who weigh 175 pounds. The less mature gorillas are named Jabari, Aqualina and Beck.

More Exhibits

The Discovery Center, which is very near the North Gate, has a 12-minute, free, multi-media presentation showing the zoo's many faces. There are 28 projectors offering slides on a 12-foot by 50-foot screen and the show is easily worth the time because you'll see close-ups of animals you might miss as you wander through the zoo.

• In the Animals of the African Night exhibit, just across from the Giraffe Yard, you can see the Aardvark and springhaas exhibit, which opened in 1986. The Brookfield Zoo teamed up with the lighting designer for Chicago's Lyric Opera to create a scene of a moonlit night on the African savannah. The lighting along with the thin pane of glass separating the exhibit from the spectator is very effective. Some people are startled to note how close they are to actual wild aardvarks eating their 90,000 ants for dinner inches from the human visitors. You can even see below ground to watch the aardvarks in their burrows.

Children's Zoo

The small, excellent Children's Zoo, where admission is currently $1 for adults and 50 cents for children, allows kids to pet the animals. Afterwards they excitedly tell nearby adults, "I got to feed a bottle of milk to a goat . . . I got to hold a rabbit." Riverside Farm, a barn within this zoo, usually has particularly cuddly animals.

Hint: It is probably better to pack your lunch, if possible, before going to Brookfield, where the commissaries offer your basic hot dogs and hamburger, but no salads.

Zoo birth control

Brookfield, in recent years, has been operating on a deficit. Fewer people are visiting the zoo and the costs of operating it have gone up. To cut expenses, the numbers of animals have been reduced from 2,500 to about 2,000, and the more prolific ones, such as lions, tigers and leopard cats, have been enrolled in a birth control program.

Because of Chicago's climate, Brookfield draws small crowds in winter. Therefore the zoo is starting a long-range building program, which will eventually allows visitors to walk from exhibit to exhibit while indoors. The huge Tropic World, a model, walk-through indoor jungle was the first phase of this program. Brookfield is also constantly updating its exhibits. The zoo spent $12 million to completely replace the marine mammals complex, including the Seven Seas Panorama, which was 25 years old. The new home for the dolphins, which opened in the spring of 1987, is four times larger than the old structure.

Brookfield Zoo allows a visitor to look face to face with a giraffe, lion, bear, tiger, rhino, baboon, Galapagos turtle, wolf, antelope or camel. Nonverbal communication occurs while seeing animals in nearly natural settings, looking majestic. It is a world-class zoo which should not be missed when you visit Chicago.

16 LAKE FRONT BIKE TOUR

SOUTH OR NORTH FROM FULLERTON

FULLERTON

north ride
1. Diversey Driving range
2. Totem Pole
3. Waveland Golf Course
4. Graffiti north of Foster beach

south ride
1. Chess Pavilion
2. Lake Point Tower
3. Navy Pier
4. Balbo Column
5. McCormick Place

Time: About four hours—longer if you love looking at Lake Michigan, shorter if you enjoy the wind streaming by your face as you pedal at full speed.

To get there: The lake front bike path can be reached from several north side areas, some of which have bicycle rental stores and can be found by taking either the Number 36 (Broadway) or 22 (Clark St.) bus.

Bike Rentals

In the springtime, a few weeks after the first frost (actually, I'm being poetic—it starts at Memorial Day) until the leaves begin to turn their multi-colored hues (actually until Labor Day, except that they open on weekends when the weather is nice), Spokes for Folks operates a bike rental near the Fullerton exit of Lincoln Park Zoo just east of the zoo rookery and just west of the Fullerton Outer Drive bridge.

They also rent roller skates and even cross country skis in the winter. They are nice people, although some of their equipment suffers for overuse. Do try out the bike or skate you rent and, if it is not up to your standards (say, with one working wheel instead of two), tell the Spokes for Folks folks and they will gladly exchange your difficult equipment for something slightly better.

You could also look up bike rentals in the Yellow Pages or bring your own bike. Park, if you are lucky, just to the east of the Lincoln Park Zoo.

Whatever the trouble to actually get a bike on the path through Lincoln Park, it is worth it.

The Bike Path

Bicycling along Lake Michigan is just right. It takes too long to walk the Lincoln Park paths and a car zips by too fast. With a bicycle, one can feel the wind, the sun and the lake. There is something infinitely restful about the experience.

Unfortunately, getting to the lake front bike paths can be a bit of an adventure. The city of Chicago has challenged the average bike rider by putting up signs, indicating bike paths, on dangerously lumpy streets with far too much traffic. Many Chicago bicyclists look at the city signs and immediately take them as a signal to avoid those streets.

After renting or bringing your bike, go east on Fullerton. Do not bike on Fullerton itself because the street hasn't been repaired since the lake receded 10,000 years ago.

After going through the Lake Shore Drive underpass at Fullerton, stop and test the wind. Experienced Chicago bicyclists will head into

179

the wind at the beginning of a trip, so hopefully it will be at their backs when they are tired and heading for home. Knowing Chicago, just as they turn around, the wind shifts.

You now have two choices: take the shorter bike path by going north to Bryn Mawr (5600 north) or set off on the longer tour to McCormick Place (2200 south).

Let's head south, towards the downtown skyline, by taking a right along the lake. The wide walks along the Fullerton Beach are often filled with children and riders and sometimes sand or even waves waft over the path. Be careful in this area, but be sure to note the muscled males, the sleek ladies in their bikinis and, usually, a naked child being chased by his or her mother, who is insisting that the tyke wear a suit.

This beach almost wasn't. Over 26 different methods of shoreline protection were tried beginning in the 1870s, including willow wands made into bundles and sunk as a breakwater (they drifted away), piers (washed over), oak pilings (destroyed by waves) and even transplanting sea grass from Massachusetts. During a storm, the water beats this beach with a pressure of 250 pounds per square inch and the 100-year fight continues today.

Go to the right of the boat house at about 1700 north (the double yellow lines on the path indicate that bicycles aren't allowed in front of the North Avenue boat house) and come to a fork in the path. The right hand fork takes you along a narrow sidewalk near parked cars, the left hand fork goes towards the lake, but both forks eventually take you by the Chess Pavilion, where serious, perpetual discussions about the game continue and where there is never a shortage of players. It is an idyllic place to pursue the royal game.

Oak Street Beach and Olive Park

Continuing south, you will pass the Oak Street Beach, Chicago's Capri, where both sexes wear the smallest of string bikinis. The ladies are not yet topless—the last woman to try that in a Rudi Guernich suit was arrested immediately after every newspaper photographer snapped several rolls of pictures which were never seen in Chicago's newspapers.

Follow the curve of the lake at the south end of the beach and bicycle along the lake if that area is dry. If not, there is a narrow and rutted sidewalk at the top of the embankment all too close to Lake Shore Drive traffic.

You will see a refreshment stand, four faded chess tables with chairs and a water fountain just before Olive Park. The Central District Filtration Plant is to the east. It is one of the world's largest, capable of pumping 1,700,000,000 gallons on a busy, dry day. Olive

Chess Pavilion

Park, by the way, is the site of many summer ethnic festivals. The curving, 70-story Lake Point Tower, which was influenced by a Mies Van Der Rohe building designed by the master in 1921 but never built, is ahead of you. This is another building which suddenly popped up on Chicago's lake front with too little controversy over its placement.

Continue uphill, shifting to lower gears to make the ride easier and stop for a moment to look at the lake, Navy Pier, and Mayor Daley's Youth Foundation and the Chicago Fire Department Gymnasium, an indoor joggers' favorite because six times around the huge gym equals a mile run.

Navy Pier

Navy Pier, designed to handle passenger and freight ships, was built as part of a deal with the federal government, which had to approve the city's plans for new parks in 1912. By the time Navy Pier was constructed in 1914, Calumet Harbor got the cargo ships, the railroads were getting popular, cars were sending passenger ships to the junk yards and few people wanted to use the theater, dance hall and restaurant at its east end. Navy Pier stands today as a monument to planning for yesterday's transportation innovation. After spending $8 million to restore it. Navy Pier is the home of the finest art show in the world, trade fairs, a wooden boat show, concerts and even a dinner for the then premiere of Israel and 900 guests in May, 1978. After languishing, after being filthy and rusty for decades, parts of the Pier are still filthy and rusty, but much of it is glorious today. Toast the sunset from one of the boats anchored by the Pier. Or, if a show is going on, visit the Pier, walk to the very end and turn back to see one of the world's great skylines at sunset. Life may not offer a better chance for romance than this!

Continuing south along the Lake Shore Drive almost "S" curve, site of major traffic jams for decades until it was remodeled and straightened in the 1980s (oh, thank you, Chicago politicos for *finally* recognizing that need!), cycle past the Outer Drive East. The geodisic dome squatting near the building is a swimming pool and private athletic club.

After you cross Randolph Street, you will cycle down a long hill, effortlessly going by Harbor Point Condominiums, the Naval Armory, Columbia Yacht Club, the Chicago Yacht Club and Monroe Harbor, a placid body of water which stretches from the Armory to the Shedd Aquarium. Although the Lake Shore Drive traffic growls insistently, the view to the east is serene, as sailboats rock near the buoys and lovers sprawl on the grass.

Meigs Field

Biking past the Shedd Aquarium, continue south along Lake Shore Drive. Burnham Harbor and Meigs Airport are on your left (to the east). The airport, which should be a city park, was built in 1947 so businessmen could land their light planes close to the Loop. Unfortunately, the fog and winds make Meigs less than an ideal airport. Lake Point Tower is less than a minute away by airplane, a fact which makes flying in and out of Meigs an exciting adventure.

Balbo Column

Note the Balbo Column, on a white pedestal just east of Soldier Field. The column came from Ostia, the port of Imperial Rome in 1934 and, according to the inscription, is a gift to Chicago from "fascist Italy with the sponsorship of Benito Mussolini." This tribute to fascism is melancholy testimony to the fact that Chicago does not choose its friends well.

Bikes and boats at Belmont Harbor

The column commemorates July 16, 1933, when 24 seaplanes, led by Gen. Italo Balbo, landed near Navy Pier after a 16-day journey from Italy. There were six stops along the way and one crash in Amsterdam. Gen. Balbo was a hero and wherever he went in Chicago, men in black shirts and ties raised their arms in a fascist salute.

Gen. Balbo continued to be a hero until June 28, 1940, when he was shot down over Tobruk, Libya. The Italians said the British did it, but the British denied that they had any fighters in the area at the time. It was revealed, in 1948, that Gen. Balbo was shot down by Italian fire, indicating that either the Italians were abysmal gunners or that Mussolini didn't approve of his Air Marshall's popularity.

After following Lake Shore Dr., bear left at the end of the McCormick Place parking lot so you can go around this huge exhibition hall and see the little-used area to the east of it. Rest, enjoy the calm beauty of the scenery, and then return to Fullerton, having completed a 12-mile bike tour.

North from Fullerton

If you chose to bike north from Fullerton:

This shorter bike path is reached by turning left before the Fullerton Avenue viaduct, where a curving path takes you by a small water fountain.

You will then bicycle past Diversey Harbor, the Diversey Miniature Golf Course and Driving Range (open from 8 a.m. to 10:30 p.m.), and by a long greensward. When you see a large tree in the middle of the now lumpy bike path, bear right and go under another viaduct, then follow the path to the left as it goes by Belmont Harbor. It is well worth pausing here becuase the still waters and the handsome boats often combine to make a memorable, relaxing picture.

Incidentally, Diversey is named after Michael Diversey, a Chicago brewer. According to one historian, in 1862 the Lill & Diversey brewery sold beer "from the frozen regions of the north—the rock girt shores of Lake Superior—to New Orleans, the Naples of the South—from the Falls of Niagara to the newly discovered gold regions of Pike's Peak." It would probably make a better story if we could write that Diversey was honored for his brew, but he got streets named after him because of his many donations of land and money to local German Catholic churches. When he died in 1869, his monument in St. Boniface Cemetery bore the name "Diversy," although he never spelled his name without an "e" while he lived. No one knows why his name was mis-spelled in death.

I think some of the most colorful boats in Chicago stay at Belmont Harbor, although I am told that Jackson Park rivals its north side cousin. Whichever side is right, Belmont Harbor is well worth a rest, a sigh and a quiet look. Also notice the Belmont Yacht Club at the south end of the harbor. The gun shots you hear come from the private gun club to the south. They are shooting at clay birds, with their pellets landing in the lake.

Heading north, you will find the Totem Pole at Addison and Lincoln Park. This was the "Kwa Ma Rolas" pole of the Haidan Indians of British Columbia. Legend has it that it was not carved by the hand of man, but that it came floating down the Nimpkish River one day to tell the Indians the story of their tribe. It's a complicated story. Briefly, the low man on the totem pole represented a warrior whose wife was stolen by a killer whale. Now look to the top of the pole, where the Kolus, the Thunderbird's sister, sits. Under the Kolus is the steel-headed man, who was formerly a trout, who became a man, who saved the wife, who founded the tribe and who helped everyone live happily ever after.

The steel-headed man has been troubled of late. Since J. L. Kraft, founder of Kraft Cheese Co., donated the pole to Chicago in 1929,

Totem pole at Addison

the steel-headed man's hands have moved at least four times. Yes, Chicago possesses a totem pole infected with spirits. At one time, the steel-headed man's left hand even covered his eyes, possibly to avoid looking at accidents on Lake Shore Dr. He has held his spear directly in front of him with both hands, grasped it lightly with his right hand, and now appears to be holding a shortened pole over his right shoulder, as if he's batting for the Chicago Cubs. The movements are unexplained, although some spirit-world scoffers believe thay are caused by Park District workers who regularly repaint the pole.

More than five decades after it arrived, the original pole was sent back because it was learned that it had religious significance. The Indians then carved a new pole, which was dedicated in 1986. It has not been there long enough for workers to notice that parts of the pole do or do not move.

Golf course

The bike path now passes tennis courts and goes uphill by the Waveland Golf Course. Legend has it that each hole was modeled after one of the most difficult holes in various courses throughout the country. There are 48 sand traps here and it is actually claimed that they represent the 48 contiguous states of the Union, something I am sure local golfers appreciate.

You will now approach several forks in the path. Do not panic. Go to the left and you will skirt Lake Shore Dr. Go right and you will approach the lake. Either way, you will bicycle in a large half circle and will eventually link up with the other half of the path. You won't get lost.

At the north end of Belmont Harbor, towards the lake, you'll see the fenced Bird Sanctuary where up to 125 species can be seen (binoculars and a bird book do help).

Graffiti

After going by Foster Beach, note the graffiti on "the rocks," the concrete blocks leading to the lake. Generations of high school and college students have painted here, leaving wisdom and whimsy.

In 1975, someone named Diana painted the poignant, "Albert, I may be a little screwy, but I love you." In 1972, Sue painted, "Dear Steve, when I first met you (7/17/67) my greatest dream was to some day marry you and have a family of our own. We have our family, but when our [sic] we going to marry?"

Return to Fullerton. The restaurant at 2450 Clark offers hamburgers and beer, which can be eaten while sitting at outdoor tables shaded by umbrellas. There is a bike rack to the north of Jerome's.

186

If you do stop to eat and park your bike in a bike rack, it is advisable to securely lock it. If possible, unfasten your front wheel and take it in the restaurant with you. You are in a big city where bicycles often disappear.

Here's hoping you enjoyed one of the most beautiful bike paths in the world. The benediction to this tour is: May the sun warm you today and may you be able to sit down tomorrow.

17 NORTH SIDE DRIVE

MILWAUKEE AVENUE TO MONTROSE

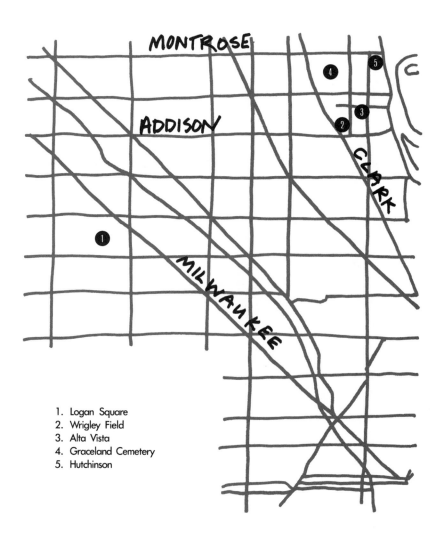

1. Logan Square
2. Wrigley Field
3. Alta Vista
4. Graceland Cemetery
5. Hutchinson

Time: About two hours.

To Get There: Chicago has a simple grid pattern to its streets, with State and Madison being zero and the numbers going higher as you go north, south, east or west from there. This drive starts at Chicago Avenue, which is 800 north of Madison, and Milwaukee, which is one of Chicago's rare diagonal streets. At this point, it is about 1100 west of State Street. This drive originally started where Milwaukee Avenue began, but a bridge was being repaired at the far south end of Milwaukee Avenue preventing us from going there without very confusing detours.

Milwaukee Avenue

This meander through the north side of Chicago will follow a traditional Chicago migration route. For decades, immigrants have lived at first near the city, moving farther north or south as they grew richer.

Later, their sons or daughters or grandchildren would move to the suburbs. Then, after their children were grown, they'd return to the center of the city, buy a condominium and tell everyone how convenient life has suddenly become for them.

The North Side Drive begins at Milwaukee Avenue and Chicago Avenue, in an industrial district. Milwaukee Avenue began as an Indian trail, became a planked road in 1849 and quickly became rutted and in disrepair.

According to *Chicago Daily News* columnist Mike Royko, "In time Milwaukee Avenue became probably the most colorful street in Chicago. Its south end became a haven for immigrants and a streetcar ride was a short tour of Europe. The street sliced through Little Italy, Little Poland, Germany and Scandinavia. A person who walked the length of the street could hear the words 'stick 'em up' in half a dozen languages."

Strange Stuff at Randolph Street Gallery

Just south of Milwaukee and Chicago there is the Randolph Street Gallery, at 756 N. Milwaukee, home of some mighty strange exhibits. Each fall they feature the most modern of art in outdoor sculpture installation. One "artist", after drinking lots of beer, created "art for dogs" by indicating with his own bodily fluids specific areas near the gallery where dogs should urinate.

Perhaps the most interesting exhibit occurred here in 1984, when the Ronco Show took place. There was an exhibit which made art objects of Veg-o-matics (over 9 million sold), the Seal-a-Meal, Steam-a-Way, the Smokeless Ashtray, the Sit-on Trash Compactor "which really works," the Buttoneer (because "everyone knows the problems with buttons is that they always fall off"), the Splatter Screen, the In-the-Shell Egg Scrambler which solved the "French toast problem," Mr. Microphone, an electric whisk which doubled as a flashlight, a spray gun which both fertilized grass and waxed cars, Rat Away rodent repellent, Mr. Dentist "the plaque attacker," the Record Vacuum, the Hula Hoe called "the weeder with a wiggle," and the ever-popular Pocket Fisherman.

The exhibit came just after Ronco Teleproducts Inc. filed for Chapter 11 bankruptcy proceedings, meaning it was the first Christmas without pocket fisherman ads on TV in years.

Two brothers, Sam and Raymond Popeil, founded Popeil Bros. Inc. in 1939 and became millionaires. Then, Sam's son, Ron, founded Ronco, became one of the all-time great TV pitchmen and is father's business rival.

Things got even worse in that family when, in 1974, Sam's estranged wife, Newport Beach (Calif.) socialite Eloise Popeil and her boyfriend were found guilty of offering two guys $25,000 each to kill Sam in his Drake Towers apartment on Chicago's Gold Coast. The prosecutors called Mrs. Popeil a "practiced adulteress," but she insisted that she was only stringing along with the murderers-for-hire because she thought that the two men were sent by her husband to frame her. Then Sam showed up as a surprise witness, testifying that his wife was having an affair with her boyfriend in the $700,000 Newport Beach house he bought for her as a vacation home. It took the jury 38 hours of deliberation over eight days to find Mrs. Popeil guilty. She served 19 months of a one- to five-year sentence.

According to Sam's obituary in the Chicago Sun-Times in 1984, Sam and Eloise "were divorced, but later remarried." Any way you slice or dice their relationship, it "really worked" for them, when it did.

Legendary Machine Gun McGurn

Just beyond Chicago Avenue, at 805 N. Milwaukee, meaning you have turned 135° on to the diagonal street, where an office furniture store now stands, was the spot where Machine Gun McGurn was killed in a bowling alley. McGurn is generally given credit (or blame, depending on your attitude about such things) for the St. Valentine's Day Massacre. Seven years later, on Feb. 15, 1936, three men surrounded McGurn as he was about to bowl. After they shot him, they left a comic valentine saying:

"You've lost your job, you've lost your dough,
Your jewels and cars and handsome houses!
Things could be worse, you know—
At least you haven't lost your trousas!"

McGurn, who said he didn't want to be in the rackets because "you fear death every moment," didn't laugh at the Valentine.

When he died, the Chicago Daily News said that McGurn was "reputed to have killed two dozen men." His obituary continued, "Not since the Medieval days of the Italian city states has there been a hired killer as gracious, debonair and deadly. What their velvet-clad and plumed young men with Florentine daggers were to the Sforzas or the Medici, McGurn was to no less a buccaneer than 'Scarface Al' Capone, who revered him for his deadliness and his loyalty."

You will shortly pass the intersection of the Kennedy Expressway and Milwaukee, where, according to Mike Royko, Elijah Wentworth opened an inn in 1830. Whiskey was sold for nine cents a pint, a factor which helped Milwaukee Avenue be born, grow and prosper. A man could spend 18 cents then, and not be able to see Milwaukee Avenue at all.

You will continue driving northwest on Milwaukee Avenue for about 20 minutes. It is advisable to have a companion read about the various sites as you pass them rather than driving and reading at the same time.

Haymarket Martyrs

You will next pass a site which should be remembered and isn't. Albert Parsons and his black wife, Lucy, lived at 1129 Milwaukee in 1887, and it was here that Parson's body was brought after his hanging.

Parsons was one of four men executed for allegedly conspiring to throw a bomb at police on May 4, 1886, during the Haymarket Riot. Workers had gathered to demand the eight-hour day, when many people were working 15 and 16 hours a day. Someone threw a bomb and, during the melee which followed, four workers and seven policemen were killed.

Eight men were arrested. With a prejudiced judge, a jury list chosen by a man determined to see the so-called conspirators hung, and one juror who was a relative of a policeman who died at Haymarket, the outcome was predictable.

The world protested that the trial was a way for the rich to execute the poor, but the four men were hung anyway. Wealthy folks in Chicago were still a little nervous about the matter so later they bought land north of Chicago, gave it to the Army and eventually it became Fort Sheridan. Federal troops would be close by in case of future civil insurrections.

Ethnic Shopping

Once past Division, 1200 north, you'll enter an intense, four-block shopping area. It is crowded, dirty, boisterous, run-down, with Latinos edging out the European shops which made this street famous.

A storekeeper here was once seen putting shoes on display outside his store. A reporter observed, "You sure trust your neighbor."

The man shouted, "Sure! But I only put the right shoe outside on display. The left shoe stays inside."

"Ever get robbed by a one-legged man?" asked the reporter.

"Sometimes."

Continuing north, pass Dr. Michael's Herbs, at 1223 Milwaukee, a store with a distinct licorice smell and which features over 500 herbs and teas.

This neighborhood has changed rapidly in the last decade. When this book was first written, you would now be passing Wladyslaw Sajewski's Music Store, Vikula's Meat Market and Zlata's Belgrade Restaurant. Now this still seedy area has a Latin pulse and most of the old Serbian-Polish stores have disappeared.

Luxor Baths

When you are at Milwaukee and North Avenue (1600 north), you are at an ethnic crossroads. If you take the "soft" left, the 45 degree angle one, you'll be on North Avenue. Just a few yards west of the elevated tracks is the slightly seedy Luxor Baths, established in 1923, and a place where generations of lawyers, gangsters, newsmen, workers and, on Wednesdays only, women have gone to sweat in the Russian bath (hot water on hotter stones), the Turkish bath (dry heat from radiators), the steam room or to bask in the whirlpool and the swimming pool.

Wicker Park

If you take the "hard" left, the 135 degree turn, you'll be going south on Damen. One block away is a one-way street called Wicker. Take a left, go east on Wicker to Schiller, take a right and return to Damen, where you'll take another right and return to Milwaukee and North Avenue. Milwaukee is the angle street to your left and, if you're heading in the right direction, you'll see the numbers are going up.

With the previous maneuvers, you have gone around Wicker Park, a triangular, heavily used little city park with quite a history. Nelson Algren sat here while dreaming up the plot for "The Man with the Golden Arm." According to columnist Mike Royko, generations of Jews, Russians, Slovaks, Ukranians, Poles and Puerto Ricans have played baseball, chess, cards and drunk wine from brown paper bags in this park. Two generations ago, Mike Todd ran the crap games in this park and he went on to produce "Around the World in 80 Days" and to marry Elizabeth Taylor. Mike Royko played marbles here, but he became a newspaperman. Who knows what he might have accomplished if he ran the crap games.

Logan Square

By the time you reach North Avenue, 1600 north, you leave the congested Polish-Puerto Rican shopping district, and Milwaukee Avenue will seem much tamer until you arrive in Logan Square around 2600 North, named after "Black Jack" Logan, a Civil War hero. His name is given to this square, but there is nothing else about the man—not a single statue or plaque—to tell us why he is so honored. The giant column, topped by an eagle, in the center of the square commemorates the 100th anniversary of the State of Illinois. No one knows why the eagle faces south.

You are at another imaginary, but real city boundary. To the south and east, the neighborhood is Hispanic. To the north and west, it is Polish. Both are inhabited by thousands of people speaking their native languages and neither are overwhelmingly friendly to folks who do not speak their language.

Animal Kingdom, at 2980 N. Milwaukee, features the usual puppies, birds and hamsters, plus an occasional cougar or monkey. The employees seem to genuinely care about the animals they have for sale.

To sample the local food, stop in any of several Polish delis along the way. Czerwone Jabluszko, meaning red apple, at 3127½ N. Milwaukee was founded by Bruno Jaromirski in 1985. He will proudly show you his Polish hams and sausages, Hungarian salami, and Greek halvah.

At Addison, 3600 north, you'll see Carl Schurz High School, named after Lincoln's minister to Spain, a German refugee who became Secretary of the Interior in 1877 and later a New York editor. The school was designed in 1910 by Dwight H. Perkins, and is sometimes called a large-scale masterpiece, a thoroughly functional design.

Take a sharp right on Addison, just past Pigouts, with a huge hot dog and hamburger dancing on the roof. If you're passing the high school, you've gone too far north. Drive east, towards the lake. This will be rather a long drive, perhaps as much as 20 minutes. You will pass the Mirabell Restaurant with an outdoor beer garden and a sign indicating where WGN-TV, Chicago's independent (not network affiliated) station is. Across the Street is Lane Technical High School with a totem pole on the front lawn.

Wrigley Field

After you cross some railroad tracks and Clark St., you'll see Wrigley Field, home of the Chicago Cubs. Let us consider the hapless, hopeless, almost helpless Cubs for a moment. It will be a lesson in humility for us all.

The Chicago Cubs have not been in a World Series since 1945. 1945. They have tried everything—except getting good players. In 1976, the owner, the late Phillip K. Wrigley, publicly said the Cubs were "playing like a bunch of clowns." One wonders what he thought of them from 1945 to 1976.

The Cubs have featured a shortstop with a deformed finger on his throwing hand (Roy Smalley), the most valuable player in the National League while the team was in last place (Hank Sauer), and a relief pitcher who fell off the mound before throwing a single pitch (Jim Brosnan). Once Babe Ruth pointed to center field and then hit a home run exactly where he pointed—and he was playing against the Cubs.

One Cubs outfielder claimed the vines in center field had poison ivy and would not follow fly balls to the wall. Another Cub long-ball hitter had only one weakness—he couuldn't slug any fast ball pitched waist high and over the center of the plate.

In the past, they would have one fine player, a true superstar sentenced to forever play with losers as though for penance for some unmentionable deed. Each spring this player (in years past it would usually be Ernie Banks) told everyone that the Cubs had a chance. Then they wouuld do well during the exhibition season and even win a few games when it was cold in Chicago and no one was looking.

By the time All-Star game time arrived, the Cubs might be in second or third place. Then they would slide, skid, fade, error their way to their rightful place in the universe—somewhere near the bottom. If the league had eight teams, they'd be near eighth place, unless they could convince the St.Louis Browns to stay in business a few more years. If the league was expanded to 10 teams, they'd find 10th place. If the leagues were divided four ways, subdivided, and parceled out (as they are today) so that the new leagues contain eight, six, four or even only two teams each, the Cubs would be in eighty, sixth, fourth or third—never, ever second.

And yet Chicago loves the Cubs, loves the fact that as of now they have never played at night, that their field has such nice vines and grass, and that they provide a little excitement, but not too much.

The Cubs are a lesson for us all. If you had been trying to do something and had consistently failed since 1945, would you still both be popular and in there trying? The Cubs have been doing just that for more than 40 years now, four decades. The Cubs give all of us something to look down upon, and that is a public service.

And yet. And yet. Believe me, as an undying Cubs fan, I write this with hope eternal. They have been showing signs of life of late, since they were bought by the Chicago Tribune. This year, this year for sure, they could go all the way.

194

A home on Alta Vista

Alta Vista

On the east side of Wrigley Field, take a left on Sheffield, go two
blocks north to Grace Street, take a left and go another couple of

blocks to a small, one-way street called Alta Vista, which is 1054 west. Because Alta Vista is one way, you'll have to go around the block by taking the alley-street called Seminary, which is just west of Alta Vista. Enter another age.

Alta Vista, a Chicago landmark built from 1900 to 1904, is a street transplanted from London. A plaque at the south end of the street says that "every townhouse on one side of the street is duplicated with only minor variations at the diagonally opposite end of the block." In other words, with a few differences due to remodeling, the townhouse at 3800 Alta Vista is identical to 3847, 3802 to 3845, etc. In the middle of the street, the pairings are 3822-3825, 3824-3823, 3826-3821, and so on.

Alta Vista is also known as "the block of the 40 doors" and it features 20 different types of facades on each side of the street.

It was built by Samuel Eberly Gross, who billed himself as "the world's greatest real estate promoter" in the 1890s. He achieved some literary fame when he sued Edmund Rostand, author of "Cyrano de Bergerac," claiming that Rostand's play was stolen from his blank verse comedy titled "The Merchant Prince of Cornville." The world laughed when he sued, Rostand cried, "But there are big noses everywhere in the world," but the courts agreed with Gross, awarding him the play's royalties. Actor Richard Mansfield was prevented from performing in the play in America until the 1920s.

According to his obituary, Gross divorced his wife in 1909 and one month later, at age 66, married an 18-year-old lass from Battle Creek, Mich. By the time he died four years later, much of his $5,000,000 fortune was gone. We refrain from assuming that his bankruptcy, death and misfortune are any comment on May-December marriages.

Graceland Cemetery

After driving through (or, better, walking along) Alta Vista's 480-foot long facade of stained-glass transoms, and townhouses with Ionic columns, Georgian feaures, etc., turn right on Grace Street and go west, up that potholed street to Clark Street, where you will turn right (north). Drive just past Irving Park to the Graceland Cemetery and Crematorium, 4001 N. Clark Street. The entrance is virtually on the corner of Irving Park and Clark, between two ancient posts. Stop at the office to the right of the entrance, near the greenhouse, and ask for a free tour map, or just drive slowly through the cemetery, or park near the greenhouse and walk.

Graceland, dedicated on Aug. 30, 1860, is the final resting place for many of the people who made their fortunes in Chicago before and after the turn of the century. A tour past their ornate mausoleums indicates that it doesn't matter whether or not you believe in life after death. For them, it was the death after life that was important.

Getty Tomb in Graceland Cemetery

The most elaborate and expensive tombs are towards the northeast corner of the cemetery, near the Willowmere section, where the wealthy can rest eternally while overlooking a pond.

To get there, drive or walk to the right of the office. When you pass a statue titled "Eternal Silence," but more commonly called "Death," by Lorado Taft, take the second left, proceed past the 10-foot high statue of a crusading knight marking the grave of Victor Lawson (founder of the Chicago Daily News) and veer to the right as you pass the Schoenhofen pyramid. Peter Schoenhofen was a brewer of Edelweiss beer, and his pyramid-shaped tomb is decorated with Egyptian plant forms and guarded by a barefoot angel.

Near the Schoenhofen pyramid is the Corinthian column marking the George Pullman tomb, designed by Solon Beman, who also designed Pullman village.

In Emmett Dedmon's book, *Fabulous Chicago,* he notes that Pullman feared his grave might be desecrated after his death. To create his grave in Chicago's Graceland Cemetery, "A pit as large as an average room had been dug on the family lot and lined across the base and walls with reinforced concrete 18 inches thick. Into this, the lead-lined mahogany casket was lowered, covered with a wrapping of tar paper and covered with a quick-drying coat of asphalt, which would exclude all air from the casket. The balance of the pit was filled to the level of the casket with solid concrete, on top of which a series of heavy steel rails were laid at right angles to each other and bolted together. The steel rails were then embedded in another layer of concrete . . ." After which, the grave was covered so that it looked like all the others in Graceland.

The Bertha and Potter Palmer tomb is a little further down the road and it is an example of going to one's reward as stylishly as one lived. Their sarcophagi are under 16 Ionic columns, a copy of a Greek temple which somehow doesn't look out of place in a cemetery on Chicago's North Side. Nearby, on an island in the middle of the pond, are the granite boulders marking the graves of Daniel H. Burnham, father of the Chicago Plan, and his family. At his request, the island remains in a wild, if slightly littered, state.

Just to the west of the pond is the Getty Tomb, a Chicago landmark created for Carrie and Alice Getty, wife and daughter of a lumber tycoon, by Louis Sullivan. A plaque there states that the tomb "marks the maturity of Sullivan's architectural style and the beginning of modern architecture in America."

The lower half of the square tomb is rather plain, but the upper half, with its small Sullivan arches and detailed ornamentation, makes this a beautiful box with stunning bronze doors.

The praise for this tomb is almost embarrassingly gushing. Frank Lloyd Wright said it was a "piece of sculpture, a statue, a great poem

803 Hutchinson Street, a home with imposing limestone walls

addressed to human sensibilities as such. Outside the realm of music what finer requiem." One historian noted that Sullivan was never "more subtle than when he sketched the lacelike patterns circling the arches. . ." Another writer praised it for "harmony in mass. . ." and yet another writer said the tomb "approaches so closely to perfection that one gasps at his temerity." As you can tell, it's one hell of a tomb.

Lots of other folks—and a few of their pets—are buried in Graceland, including Cyrus Hall McCormick, inventor of the McCormick reaper; packer Philip D. Armour; architect Ludwig Mies van der Rohe; merchant Marshall Field; National Baseball League founder William Hulbert, whose tomb is marked by a large seamed baseball; heavyweight champions Bob Fitzsimmons and Jack Johnson; and detective Allan Pinkerton, whose tomb has a long inscription recalling his many deeds and concluding that Pinkerton was "A friend to honesty—a foe to crime." Many of Pinkerton's employees are buried in the same plot, including Kate Warn, probably America's first woman detective, and Tim Webster, hanged as a Union spy in Richmond, Va., on April 29, 1862.

I once set off on a trek to find lot 300, where Charles Dickens' brother, the brother's mistress and children are allegedly buried in an unmarked grave. Charles Dickens was very angry because Augustus ran off to Chicago and left his wife in England, so the writer never gave the money needed to mark where Augustus lies. We couldn't find Lot 300 or even an indentation where the grave might be.

Leave Graceland by taking a right on Clark Street, going north to Montrose, where you'll take a right and go east to N. Marine Drive, which is just before Lake Shore Drive. Turn right on Marine Drive, go two blocks south and take another right on a westbound one-way street, Hutchinson Street.

Suddenly, after driving along a cemetery, after going by some fairly run down apartments, and after skirting an area favored by Appalachian whites, you enter the 19th Century. You are in what was Lake View, a resort and farming community in the 1850s which was annexed to Chicago in 1889. Wealthy folks had their country homes here and, when land values increased, they began subdividing and building on their own property.

The first house on the block, called the Scales House, is in the Queen Anne style, with a rounded turret and a vaguely English look.

Driving up this quiet street, which is a Chicago landmark, you'll see a modern-looking turn-of-the-century home at 706 Hutchinson; the Ionic columns on the Wiliam F. Monroe House (he founded a cigar store chain) at 716 Hutchinson; another Prairie School of Architecture example at 737 Hutchinson; and identical homes built for two brothers in 1909 at 747 and 757 Hutchinson.

In the 800 block, limestone is used at 803 Hutchinson; the Claude Seymour House at 817 Hutchinson was designed in 1913 by George W. Maher, a respected architect; the W. H. Lake House at 826 Hutchinson is also a Maher built in 1904; and the 839 Hutchinson may have been a Maher.

Turn right on Hazel Street and return to Montrose, where you'll take another right and go to Lake Shore Dr. If you follow the signs leading you south, you will return to the Loop. If you wish to continue driving, turn north to the North Suburban Drive.

Otherwise this ends the North Side Drive.

18 SOUTH SIDE DRIVE

DEARBORN STATION TO MCCORMICK PLACE

1. Dearborn St. Station
2. Chicago Fire Academy, 137 W. DeKoven
3. Hull House and the University of Illinois
4. Coliseum, 14th and Wabash
5. Glessner House, 1800 S. Prairie
6. Illinois Institute of Technology
7. Comiskey Park
8. The late Mayor Richard Daley's home, 3536 S. Lowe
9. Stock Yards Gate, near Halsted and Exchange
10. Chinatown
11. McCormick Place

Time: Less than two hours.
To get there: We begin at Congress and State Street, driving south on State.

The Changing South Side

The South Side of Chicago is where the city was born, grew up and became powerful. It was, for many recent decades, the Irish political heart of Chicago.

During this drive, you will experience the dizzying changes a big city can offer. You will see where the wealthy lived in the late 1800s and where the poor live today.

Every neighborhood in Chicago can be friendly. And every neighborhood has its tough element. So be sensible during this drive and walk where it is so advised, but keep your car doors locked at other times.

The south side is changing but then this has always been true. Originally, the area over which you will be driving was near a huge mud lake. Later, parts of the South Side became the fashionable place to live in Chicago and still later a slum, the port of entry into Chicago for immigrants. Today, some of the slums have reverted to mud lakes, as old buildings have been torn down, to be replaced by empty lots awaiting tomorrow's bright new idea for housing. This could be the urban pattern—mud lake to settlement to wealthy folks to slum to mud lake, and then we start all over again.

Drive south on State, past Congress, past the William Jones Commercial High School and the Pacific Gardens Mission at 646 S. State, founded in 1877 to help the Skid Row drunks. Take a right on Polk and you'll see a red brick railroad station, build in 1885.

Dearborn Street Station

The Dearborn Street Station was once the eastern gateway for the Atchison, Topeka and Santa Fe Railroad and trains such as the Super Chief, El Capitan, Maple Leaf, Phoebe Snow, Blue Bird, The Warbash Cannonball, and Georgian stopped there. Railroads using the station included the Chicago and Eastern Illinois, Erie-Lackawanna, Grand Trunk Western, Monon, and Norfolk & Western.

The station became the focal point of the $1 billion South Loop New Town project, a community of 13,000 homes to be built over the next few years. The abandoned railroad station, now the oldest surviving railroad terminal in Chicago and one of the oldest in America, has a new lease on life. Park nearby (a bit of a feat since spaces are at a premium here) and visit the station, with its new green, peach and tan marble floor, its most modern clock and the variety of shops there.

A 1922 fire destroyed the original clocktower and ornate weather vane which was once part of this station, and the entire structure was almost demolished. But it was saved, meaning that Chicagoans are finally interested in preserving their past.

Walk across Polk on Dearborn to find two delightful small restaurants, Moonraker, with its dark sea-influenced interior, and Deli on Dearborn. Both will put tables and chairs on the adjoining sidewalk when the weather is good.

Printer's Row and River City

You are in the Printer's Row area. Many of the huge buildings here, which once housed presses of all descriptions, have become rental or sales properties and the newest, most desirable area for young professionals, or yuppies, is a loft apartment here.

Return to your car and drive west on Polk to Wells, where you will take a left and park. By all means, go inside River City, 800 S. Wells, to see the atrium of tomorrow. Tell the guard you want a tour and he'll let you go up the elevators to the "RR" level.

River City is 446 apartments, with studios renting for $680 a month and four-bedroom penthouses for $3490 a month in 1986. The penthouses have three levels, 3½ baths, a gym room, sauna and whirlpool bath.

Only a few years ago, people would have thought you were crazy to live immediately south of the loop an area with "vast tracts of unused railroad yards, underused industrial sites and unusable vacant lots," according to Steve Kerch of the *Chicago Sun-Times.*

Then, in 1984, $60 million was spent on the first phase of a gigantic, serpentine construction which includes apartments, 240,000 square feet of commercial space, a 70-slip marina, a health club, jogging track and party rooms.

The architect was Bertrand Goldberg, who also created Marina City in 1963-64 and who obviously likes curves. River City, from either the outside or the inside, has a futuristic, but human look. For Chicagoans who remember how abandoned and dangerous this neighborhood was before River City, it is a miracle.

Return to your car, get back to Polk and retrace your drive, going east to Clark, where you will take a right, going south. Drive up the ramp to Roosevelt Road and take a right, going west two stop lights to Jefferson. You know you have reached the correct corner when you see the Chernin's sign just ahead of you. Chernin's is one of the largest, cut-rate shoe stores in Chicago with salesmen picked for their hyper-activity. Stop here if you want to quickly buy a pair of good, but inexpensive shoes.

Chicago Fire Academy

Otherwise, turn right on Jefferson and drive north to the Chicago Fire Academy, at 147 W. DeKoven. It's hard to miss the Academy—a bronze statue, titled "Flame" by local sculptor Egon Weiner is in front of the building.

The friendly firefighters there will be glad to show you through the academy. They'll point to a plaque on the floor opposite the library which marks the exact spot where the fire in the O'Leary barn started in 1871, frightening Mrs. O'Leary's herd of five cows, burning 300 people to death, making 100,000 people homeless and leveling 2,000 acres, or about a third of the city. The wind was so strong in a northerly direction that the O'Leary home, south of the barn, was untouched by the blaze.

Generally speaking, most Chicagoans accept the story that the 1871 fire started in Mrs. O'Leary's barn when one of her cows kicked over a lantern. However, Mel Waskin, who grew up in Chicago and who is creative director for Coronet Films, wrote the book "Mrs. O'Leary's Comet." He blamed the fire on a comet called Biela II, part of Biela I, which split in two in 1845 and headed for parts unknown. As evidence, he cites the fact that intense fires broke out at the same time in Chicago, Peshtigo, Wisconsin, and Manistee, Michigan. Who knows, the firefighters may be pointing to the spot where arson by comet was committed.

Because of Chicago's severe winters, the Fire Academy has a drill hall with a ceiling sixty-four feet off the ground. New firefighters can slide down poles and jump into nets while indoors.

Hull House

Continue north on Jefferson, while edging into the left-hand lanes, and take a left on Taylor, going west. Cross the expressway and take a right on Halsted, going north. When you notice the distinctive red brick and white columns of Hull House on your left, take a right on Polk (the next street) and park in the city lot there. Walk across the street and enter Hull House, 800 S. Halsted.

This neighborhood had known waves of immigrants before the University of Illinois and expressways ended its existence. The Irish were here in the 1850s, then came the Germans, then the Bohemians in the 1860s. It was a Jewish ghetto in the 1890s, an Italian community in the 1900s and later it was popular with Greeks, Mexicans and blacks.

Jane Addams moved into an abandoned mansion here on Sept. 18, 1889, and changed the world. She created a new form of social service. In 1910, Jane Addams wrote, "We were ready to perform the humblest neighborhood services. We were asked to wash the new-born babies, to prepare the dead for burial, to nurse the sick and to 'mind the children'."

This, in a neighborhood where, according to an 1895 Hull House report, the tenements were filthy sheds, with "foul stables and dilapidated outhouses, broken sewer pipes, piles of garbage fairly alive with diseased odors, and numbers of children filling every nook . . ."

By 1907, there were thirteen buildings associated with Hull House, where the city's first kindergarten was established in 1889, where Benny Goodman played in the boys' band, where Jane Addams tried to solve the social problems of her day. Miss Adams didn't like the way garbage was collected around Hull House, so she got a job as a garbage inspector. She, or her associates, fought for women's suffrage, unions, the National Association for the Advancement of Colored People (which she helped found), and opposed sweat shops and World War I.

In 1931, Jane Addams won the Nobel Peace Prize, which can be seen in the parlor of Hull House.

Jane Addams was a complex modern-day saint—a fussy picture straightener, a woman who needed adoring followers, a so-called "new" woman who projected a sexually pure and innocent image, the epitome of the 19th century heroine, a tough woman who often won her battles with local authorities, an angel of mercy who was also a shrewd business woman, an expert public speaker, a fundraiser who was so shy about her slender body that, even when sharing a hotel room with her long-time friend, Louise DeKoven Bowen, she would dress completely in the closet and emerge with her hair done.

While walking through the restored Hull House, realize that before Jane Addams there was poverty. After Jane Addams, there was poverty and perhaps hope. After a pioneering Hull House survey of the people in the neighborhood revealed that 19,000 humans had no bathing facilities, Jane Addams got angry and the result was the firing of half the city's sanitation inspection bureau. Mrs. Bowen helped get the first factory inspection law, Chicago's first juvenile court, and convinced the police department to hire policewomen.

Through all these battles, all these victories (and even the temporary setback during World War I, when many people objected to Jane Addams' pacifism), there was Jane Addams' humanity. She saw an old German woman being forcibly taken to the County Infirmary as she clutched a small battered chest of drawers. Jane Addams wrote, "To take away from an old woman whose life has been spent in household cares all the foolish little belongings to which her affections cling and to which her very fingers have become accustomed, is to take away her last incentive to activity, almost to life itself. To give an old woman only a chair and bed, to leave her no cupboard in which her treasures may be stowed, not only that she may take them out when she desires occupation, but that her mind may dwell upon them in moments of revery, is to reduce living almost beyond the bounds of human endurance."

University of Illinois Chicago Circle

Leave Hull House after touching the spirit of Jane Addams, take two quick lefts and enter the University of Illinois Chicago Circle Campus by walking into the large building in front of you, past the book store, following the signs to the Lecture Center, between halls D 1 and 2 and C 1 and 6, and into the outdoor amphitheater.

This campus, now populated by over 20,000 students, was opened in 1965. Walter A. Netsch, Jr., of Skidmore, Owings and Merrill, created an instant commuters' campus where buildings are grouped by their functions and by the numbers of people who might use them. Other campuses feature buildings devoted to engineering or biology or English. Circle Campus groups all the lecture halls in its center because they draw the heaviest traffic. The high-rise buildings on the perimeter of the campus are offices and within them, some university officials claim, even the halls gradually dwindle in width away from the central area of heaviest use.

This campus does hold a Guinness Record. While in the campus dream laboratory, Bill Carskadon had the longest recorded dream, lasting two hours and 23 minutes, on February 15, 1967. The brothers Guinness do not report what was the subject of the dream, but it must have been quite a story.

The Coliseums

Now leave the campus and Hull House by driving south on Halsted (to your right as you face the loop) to Roosevelt Road, then take a left and go east to Wabash, and take a right. You may see the Coliseum at 14th Place. The castle-like wall formerly belonged to the Confederacy's Libby Prison. In 1888, a group of Chicago businessmen thought it would be a great idea to bring the prison here, piece by piece, reconstruct it and open a museum. When the museum folded, parts of the prison were torn down and later the Coliseum was built. The last time I passed the Coliseum, everything was torn down but the old Libby Prison walls. Weeds were growing and a sign warned "no defacing stone walls."

If a building has memories, this one could almost vie with the original after which it was named.

Bathhouse John Coughlin and Hinky Dink Kenna, two notorious aldermen, held their First Ward balls here. More than 15,000 people attended their 1908 fling, including every scarlet woman, second-story-man, female impersonator and dope fiend in town.

Bathhouse read a poem saying, "On with the dance, let the orgy be perfectly proper," willing women were stripped, men in women's costumes cavorted, drunks pased out and remained standing because of the density of the crowd, according to Herman Kogan's and Lloyd Wendt's book *Lords of the Levee*.

Despite the fact that 100 extra policemen were on duty, only one person was arrested and convicted for that night's activities—for gate crashing. One brothel madame said of these parties, "Joy reigned unrefined."

Continue south on Wabash to 18th St., take a left and go to Prairie, and park.

If you walk to the northeast corner of 18th and Prairie, you'll see a plaque marking the spot where the Indians attacked the refugees from Fort Dearborn in 1812. The home on the southeast corner, at 1801 Prairie, is the W. W. Kimball House, which belonged to the manufacturer of Kimball pianos and organs. It was designed in 1891 by S. S. Beman, who created the community of Pullman and who modeled the home after the Chateau de Josselin in Brittany.

Glessner House

Now walk across the street and enter the Glessner House, 1800 S. Prairie, a home which changed all residential architecture in America. Glessner house looked startlingly different when it was built in 1887, and does so now.

John Jacob Glessner was Cyrus McCormick's competitor in the farm machinery industry, although he eventually merged with McCormick and others to form International Harvester Co. When Glessner decided to build a new home, he went to Henry Hobson Richardson, a Boston architect who liked to do his drafting while wearing a monk's costume because he weighed 370 pounds.

Glessner's diary states that Glessner asked Richardson if he could design a home and Richardson said, "I'll plan anything a man wants, from a cathedral to a chicken coop. That's the way I make my living."

Richardson said windows were "not to look out of." He added, "You no sooner get them than you shroud them with two thicknesses of window shades and then add double sets of curtains." So he created the first true city house, almost flush to the sidewalk, with few windows facing the street, but many of them looking out on an inner court.

The home was immediately loathed by the neighbors. George Pullman, who tried to get the house torn down said, "I don't like it, and I wish it weren't there. I don't know what I have ever done to have that thing staring me in the face every time I go out of my

Library in Glessner House

door!" One architectural critic inferred "its purpose to be not domestic but penal."

But the Glessners loved the place, bringing over the fire from the hearthstone of their old home, carrying Virginia Creepers for the courtyard and accepting Boston ivy from a friend for the outer walls.

The Glessners enjoyed entertaining, and their diary notes that Theodore Thomas, conductor of the Chicago Symphony, would often bring over a third or more of his musicians, hide them about the house and surprise Mrs. Glessner with music for dinner. The entire symphony was secreted in the house for the Glessners' 25th wedding anniversary. No one knew they were there until they began playing a delightful concert.

Glessner House, which was threatened with demolition in 1966, has been lovingly restored by the Chicago Architectural Foundation. Visit the upstairs bedrooms, which display Glessner antiques, furniture designed by the architect Richardson and period wallpaper.

Widow Clarke House

Next, exit Glessner house and walk south on Prairie Avenue. This is a cul de sac with photo displays of the grand homes which were once there and the Widow Clarke House about halfway up the block. This is Chicago's oldest surviving building, built in 1836 by Caroline and Henry Clarke.

But the house was unfinished when Clarke lost his money in the Panic of 1837. A visitor in 1841 noticed that the rooms were decorated with prairie chickens, plovers, and half a dozen deer carcasses. Clarke was better as a hunter than as an interior decorator and the game was used to feed his family.

Clarke died of cholera in 1849, but his wife continued to live there. The Clarke House escaped the 1871 fire and was moved 30 blocks from its original location in 1872. When it was bought by the City of Chicago in 1977, the entire home was hoisted up and over the elevated tracks and returned to its present site, which is only three blocks from where it was originally.

Today, it has been furnished by the Colonial Dames of America so that it looks as it did between 1836 and 1860.

Tours of the Prairie Avenue District are conducted daily, except for Mondays, from April through October, and daily, except for Mondays and Wednesdays, from November through March.

Having understood what life was like for the wealthy in Chicago in the 1880s and being thankful that parts of this street were preserved, leave Prairie Avenue and drive west to Michigan Avenue. Take a left and go south.

The Second Presbyterian Church is at 1926 S. Michigan. Lightning struck the steeple in 1900, it burned and was never replaced. That's why the tower on the church looks shaved off on top. There are eight stained glass windows in this church from the Tiffany Studios.

At 24th and Michigan, you'll pass the white-brick offices of the *Chicago Defender,* founded in 1905 and Chicago's largest black newspaper. At 26th and Michigan, where you will turn right, you'll notice Mercy Hospital to the southeast. It was the first hospital in Illinois and treated the 1871 fire victims.

At State, take a left and go south, past the St. James Roman Catholic Church built in 1879 at 29th and Wabash; past the Dearborn Homes to the Illinois Institute of Technology from 3100 to 3500 south on State. The present campus epitomizes the philosophy of one of its designers, Ludwig Mies van der Rohe, "Less is more," with its low, simple, glass and steel structures.

Illinois Institute of Technology

IIT had its start in 1890 when the Rev. Frank W. Gunsaulus gave a sermon on philanthropy while meat packer Philip Armour was in the audience. It must be ranked among the world's best sermons because shortly after that Armour began donating money to create the Armour Institute of Technology, forerunner of IIT.

Comiskey Park

Continue south on State to 35th, where you'll take a right and go past the Stateway Gardens housing project. After you cross over the Dan Ryan Expressway, you'll go by Comiskey Park, home of the Chicago White Sox, who won a pennant in 1959. When they did, Chicago's Fire Commissioner, the late Robert J. Quinn ordered the city's air raid sirens to wail. He forgot it was 1959, when people were concerned about Russian bombers, when they still had fully stocked bomb shelters in the back yard. Hundreds of people got frightened, some even panicked, and spent a terror-stricken night in their shelters. Quinn was a bit over-enthusiastic.

But then Quinn was always a character, causing massive traffic jams one morning when he ran his rookies down the middle of an expressway to get them in shape. During an investigation of Fire Dept. ambulance safety, Quinn was asked why when so many people were being injured inside them, the department insisted on having Cadillac-built ambulances. Quinn said that he thought that Chicagoans would feel better knowing that, if they were going to die, they would die in a Cadillac!

Perhaps in the fleeting moment as you pass this park, you might remember Gandil, Cicotte, Jackson, Felsch, Weaver, Risberg, Williams and McMullin, who were barred from playing baseball for life because of taking bribes in the 1919 World Series. They say that Jackson, Weaver and Cicotte might be in the Hall of Fame now if that hadn't happened.

The scandal helped the Sox lose the 1920 pennant. They were one game behind Cleveland in September of that year, with three more games to play when Eddie Cicotte talked to a Cook County grand jury and seven of the eight players were immediately suspended. Cleveland won the pennant.

Incidentally, Charles A. Comiskey, then owner of the team, paid the Black Sox, as they came to be called, betwen $5,000 and $12,000 per year for their services. The ballplayers were offered that much per game by the gamblers. Sometimes a good paycheck helps folks be morally straight.

Comiskey Park, built in 1910, is the oldest in the major leagues. It houses a team perennially plagued by weak hitting. Sox Park is a huge, forbidding place with a concrete sidewalk near the walls. But Chicagoans love it and want to keep the Sox there. They get angry at recent suggestions that the team move to the suburbs or another town.

A forbidden picture of Mayor Daley's house

Mayor Daley's Home

Continue up 35th to Lowe. There's the Ninth District Police Station on the corner. In about the middle of the block, at 3536 S. Lowe, is the home of the late Mayor Richard J. Daley. He grew up here in Bridgeport, spent his life here, became Mayor of Chicago in 1955, sent John F. Kennedy to the White House, orchestrated the 1968 convention and died in 1976.

During his term, the face of the city was changed. He helped build expressways, universities, sewer systems, O'Hare Airport, the Civic

Center and other structures. Many of his friends were indicted, the city remained corrupt, the Democratic machine got older but stayed powerful, the schools deteriorated, the streets became a little less safe, the quality of life declined, but new buildings went up, new highways went through and old slums were torn down.

And Bridgeport, a small, predominantly white Catholic community, remained powerful in the city. Kids learn politics in the cradle here and go on to be policemen, lawyers, judges, etc.

If you attempt to take pictures of Daley's home, a policeman, who continually guards the home, will suddenly appear to stop you. Do not argue. Do not protest about your rights under the Constitution. You are in Bridgeport, a half block from a police station. Choose a better place to fight for tourist's rights.

Continuing south on Lowe, turn right on 36th, go one block, take another right on Union and return to 35th St., where you will take a left and go to Halsted, where you will take another left, going south about a mile immediately past Root Street.

In 1865, Halsted stunk. It was so muddy, a man had to vault across it with a pole. Hog's hair left to dry for mortar created a stupifying odor. And the Sunday sport around here was betting who could skin a steer the fastest.

Stock Yards Gate

Take a right on Exchange and you will immediately see the Stock Yards Gate through which more than a billion animals went to their deaths. The stock yards opened in 1865, created Chicago's image as "hog butcher to the world," and entered a decline after World War II. Wilson & Co. left in 1955, Swift discontinued most slaughtering operations in 1958, the Armour plant closed in 1950, and the stockyards themselves closed in 1971.

The stone steer's head near the top of the Gate is supposed to be a likeness of Sherman, the steer who won the grand sweepstakes at the first American Fat Stock Show in 1878.

If you are a vegetarian, this is a place to quickly leave because it is the site of a billion animal deaths. If you are a steak-lover, it is a place to revere. In any case, circle the gate and return to Halsted, taking a right (south).

You will quickly pass the International Ampitheatre, site of the 1968 Democratic Convention, although the "police riot" was northeast of here at the Hilton Hotel.

Chinatown

Go to 43rd. Take a left (east), after you cross the bridge over the Dan Ryan, take a left on LaSalle and head north towards the loop on the Dan Ryan Expressway, following the signs saying "Lake Shore

Street sign in Chinatown

Drive," "22nd Street," and "Chinatown." Take a left on Cermak going west, then take another left on Wentworth, going through Chicago's small Chinatown, with its restaurants, gift shops, and pagodas on its telephone booths.

Turning right on 23rd Place you'll notice that the street signs are also in Chinese. Go to Princeton, take another right and return to Cermak. Turn right and head east.

Everleigh House and the Levee

As you drive east, you will be only a block from the site of the Everleigh House, 2131-33 S. Dearborn, the finest brothel in Chicago history. From February 1, 1900 until October 24, 1911, Minna and Ada Everleigh ran a whore house which featured a $15,000 gold piano, twenty gold-plated spittoons, where the women were the finest in the land. Prices started at $50, but newspapermen were admitted for free.

A home for the elderly now sits where debauchery achieved new heights of sophistication. The ladies wore evening gowns and were encouraged to read. Parlors had such names as the Moorish, gold, silver, copper, red, rose, green, blue, Oriental, Japanese, Egyptian, and Chinese rooms. There were two mahogany staircases, flanked by potted palms and statues of Grecian goddesses.

One girl insisted on having fresh cut red roses everywhere in her room. Another girl had everything in white in her boudoir with an ermine coverlet on her bed.

Money was mentioned only as a guest left. Champagne was $12 a bottle. Few men paid less than $200 for the evening and many left $1,000. The sisters admitted that their personal profits per year were around $120,000.

Bawdy history was made here when Prince Henry of Russia went to the club and, during a party in his honor, one Romeo drank champagne from a lady's slipper for the first time.

The Everleigh Sisters' downfall came because they decided to advertise. A tame pamphlet boasting of the club's many advantages, including steam heat, caused a public outcry and forced the police chief to close it. After drinking all the champagne they could, all the girls left.

This area was part of the notorious Levee, home of madams, panderers, call girls, white slavers and other energetic folk. Emmett Dedmon's book, *Fabulous Chicago*, notes that in this neighborhood the brothel called California had fifty prostitutes; Frankie Wright's brothel had books and was called the Library; the French Elm featured walls covered with mirrors; Black May's girls boasted there was no degeneracy they would not perform, and the Dewey Hotel specialized in Russian Jewish prostitutes broken in to "the life" by profesional rapists working on the top floor.

Al Capone Territory

Continuing east, you will quickly pass through another notorious area, where Al Capone thrived in the '20s. Once past the Raymond Hilliard Center, 2030 S. State, designed by Bertrand Goldberg of Marina Towers fame, you'll be close to 2300 S. Michigan, site of the Metropole Hotel. Capone had fifty rooms in this hotel patrolled by gunmen. It's now an empty lot.

Al Capone also used the Lexington Hotel, at 1825 S. Michigan, as a headquarters from 1928 to 1932, and that is only a few blocks to the south as you cross Michigan.

In 1986, this was the site of one of the great televised scams of all time. Inside this hotel, which was built in 1892, workers found a 7 by 10-foot vault with walls that were 36 inches thick.

This discovery led to "The Mystery of Al Capone's Vaults," a two hour syndicated television show seen on 181 stations in America and by gangster aficionados in Brazil, West Germany, Argentina, Italy, the Netherlands, the Bahamas, the Dominican Republic, Costa Rica and Paraguay.

After five months of publicity hype, after nearly two hours of background material, host Geraldo Rivera looked into the mysterious vault and said, "It seems . . . we've struck out." There had been suggestions that the "bones of (Capone's) criminal rivals might be hidden there." Instead, during the TV program, nothing was found except dust, concrete and a 60-year-old empty gin bottle.

But have no fear. Even if the vault was empty, the program was a success. It had the highest rating ever for a nationally syndicated show on independent stations (34 rating, 48 per cent share of the audience) and it was second to the Super Bowl in ratings in Chicago with 57.3 ratings and a 73 per cent audience share. The Tribune Entertainment Company figured to profit to the tune of $1 million and Rivera, on the strength of the program, was later the subject of plans to develop a daily, hour-long program titled "Geraldo Live." Not bad for finding one old bottle.

Also, in this area, 2222 S. Wabash was the site of the Four Deuces, a saloon where Capone got his start as Johnny Torrio's bodyguard and where a dozen murders were allegedly committed. Colosimo's Cafe was once at 2126 S. Wabash and Big Jim Colosimo ran it until he was shot there on May 11, 1920. Big Jim, who wore diamonds on his fingers, shirt, vest, belt, suspenders and garters, fell in love with Dale Winter, a vaudeville singer. His associates didn't like his marriage to a nice girl like Dale, and so he entered gangster heaven.

If you continue east on Cermak, you'll come to First National Frank of Chicago, 333 E. Cermak Road, a hot dog stand with a bank decor featuring teller's windows, waste baskets for "paper deposits," and a take out area with a sign indicating it is for withdrawals. According to the book *Hot Dog Chicago* (yes, Chicago has an entire book devoted to reviewing hot dog stands), this restaurant is "first rate (or should we say 'AAA'). Try the First National Frank, a huge delicious natural casing Vienna hot dog."

There is a Chicago style hot dog, which is somewhat more spicy than elsewhere in the country. About 80% of the Chicago hot dog stands sell products of the Vienna Sausage Co., which has its headquarters at 2501 N. Damen. The company store there sells terrific hot dogs.

To qualify as a real Chicago hot dog, it must come on a fresh poppy-seed bun, with yellow mustard, a pickle spear, tomato slices, hot short peppers, relish, copped onion and some celery salt. Anything short of a garden-on-a-bun doesn't qualify.

McCormick Place

Continue east, past R. R. Donnelly, the world's largest commercial printer, and veer to the left at McCormick Place. This book contains no walks originating from McCormick Place at the request of a spokesman for the giant exhibition hall. McCormick Place is "totally busines-oriented. There is no lounge area in the lobby. There aren't even any clocks in this place. The reason this place is popular with exhibitors is once a guy is here, he's stuck."

This is the largest exhibition hall in America and the second largest in the world (one in Cologne, Germany, is bigger). In 1967 a previous hall, an ugly concrete slab, was extensively damaged by fire. The place was so hated that many people rejoiced. The new McCormick Place, which still eats up too many acres of lakefront, at least looks better. Throughout the year the hall is host for shows devoted to boats, housewares, cars, flowers, electronics, gourmet food and even the National Gin Rummy Tournament.

Soldier Field

Go north on Lake Shore Dr. past Soldier Field which is perpetually the subject of grandiose plans to remodel it. According to Lois Wille in her book *Forever Open, Clear and Free,* you can't play baseball in Soldier Field; it's only 300 feet wide. And it's difficult to see a football game in this cross between a European soccer field and a Greek theater.

But this place is revered by Chicago football fans because the Chicago Bears play their home games here. They were the Super Bowl champs in 1986, finally bringing sweet victory to a city long on sports enthusiasm and short on winners. It was the most decisive win in Super Bowl history, 46 to 10 over the New England Patriots. And that victory came after the Bears won all but one game in the regular season. Quarterback Jim McMahon ran for two touchdowns and William "The Refrigerator" Perry, who normally plays defense, lumbered for another one in the nationally televised rout.

In addition to Chicago Bears' football games, the two most interesting events in the Field's history occurred in 1927 and 1950.

In 1927, Harold Lloyd, Buster Keaton, Douglas Fairbanks, George M. Cohan, Flo Ziegfeld, Bernard Baruch and 150,000 others saw the famous Jack Dempsey-Gene Tunney "long count" heavyweight championship. Tunney, who was guaranteed $1,000,000, became the first man in history to be a millionaire simply by going through a 30-minute physical drill. In 1950, a park district official was sued for divorce and his wife accused him of maintaining a trysting place under the Soldier Field stands.

With the happy thought that even cold concrete can yield to love, this ends the South Side Drive.

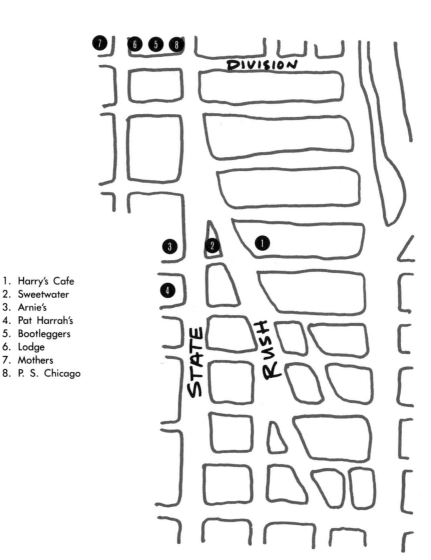

1. Harry's Cafe
2. Sweetwater
3. Arnie's
4. Pat Harrah's
5. Bootleggers
6. Lodge
7. Mothers
8. P. S. Chicago

Time: An entire evening, plus however long it takes to recover from a hangover.

To get there: Either take the CTA subway to Division and walk two blocks east, or take the Number 36 Broadway bus to State and Division. If you drive, it is advisable to park in one of two nearby city lots, at 875 N. Rush or 506 N. Rush. You may have to wait for your car to be delivered to you when you pick it up. There hasn't been a parking place on the streets east of Rush since the day after the fire of 1871.

Infamous Rush Street

Rush Street sits like a gigantic, hard-edged, venus fly trap for conventioneers. The Division St. area, near Rush St., has bars for lonely single folks—or married people pretending to be single.

Between the conventioneers anxious to boast of recent deals and singles yearning for frantic coupling, comfortable and even gracious establishments are to be found in this area.

Just as the ocean tides ebb and flow, the prostitutes traditionally appear on Rush after 2 a.m. They are attracted to the frustrated men leaving the topless bars and they become more obvious because police cars, which normally arrest prostitutes, sometimes go off duty then.

Rush Street is named after Dr. Benjamin Rush, who signed the Declaration of Independence, was a doctor during the Revolution and accepted no pay for his services, and saved 6,000 people during a yellow fever epidemic in 1793. He never visited Chicago.

Rush Street first enters the history books as a cow path. The wealthy people living on the North Side during the 1860s all had cows. They were herded by a man who looked like a Cossack and who rode north on Rush Street each morning, blowing a brass horn and summoning his aristocratic cows. Except for the now-phantom cows, Rush Street has nothing of historic, artistic or architectural merit.

This pub crawl begins on the south east corner of State and Division. It should be noted that, while tracing the steps you are about to take, the author had a drink in only every third bar and then it was half a glass of beer. Despite this wonderful restraint in the pursuit of responsible reporting, he was quite tipsy when he completed only half the crawl. Pace yourself, folks, this is going to be a long night.

We begin by walking south, passing Sammie's and going to Bagel Nosh, 1135 N. State, one of the rare, non-alcoholic stops on this walk. This is a friendly deli, the place to go if you yearn for chicken

218

soup. You know, a scientific study did prove that a little chicken soup is very good for the symptoms of the common cold.

Passing the Kentucky Fried Chicken stand, veer slightly to the left at Cedar St., walking on Rush. You'll know you're on the right street if you pass the Solomon-Cooper Drug Store on the corner.

Guadalaharry's, at 1043 N. Rush, is a Mexican restaurant and singles bar with a souvenir counter selling Guadalaharry t-shirts and headbands. I have never seen one around Chicago, so they must all go to nice folks from Arkansas.

Next door, at the corner of Bellevue and Rush is Harry's Cafe, 1035 N. Rush, which has windows which can be opened so one can eat and drink while sitting on Rush St. and a roof-top garden bar. The owner, Tom DuBois, named his establishment after a famous bar in Paris.

Take a left on Bellevue and go to Kronies, 8 E. Bellevue, "home of the liter." That's what it says on their matchbooks and on signs. It means that you can go here to order a liter of Long Island iced tea for around $8. This near-lethal concoction is vodka, gin, rum, tequilla, triple sec, sour mix and Coca-Cola.

The Long Island iced tea record holder in Kronies is some guy from Tennessee who drank 14 of them. Most folks would find it very difficult to drink 14 liters of water. This visitor not only accomplished this feat, but left under his own power. However, he probably walked home to Long Island, rather than Tennessee.

Eliot's Nesst, a bar which has probably taken the name-pun too far, is at 20 E. Bellevue, nearly next door. It features a disc jockey playing '50s and '60s music, free drinks for a $1 cover charge from 7 to 8 p.m. on Tuesdays and free snacks.

Return to Rush and cross it, going to Sweetwater, at 1028 N. Rush. This place is a frank imitation of Maxwell's Plum, a bar and restaurant in New York. It sits on the former site of Mr. Kelly's, a nightclub which once presented the finest comics and entertainers in town. It was there that I first heard Woody Allen say of his ex-wife that she was once raped "but it wasn't a moving violation."

Sweetwater will put out chairs and tables for sidewalk drinking during the summer. Or the cafe windows can be removed on nice nights.

Inside there is a dark art deco mirror on one wall, a huge painting of a languid nude on another, and chandeliers over the bar. You'll usually find an upscale collection of Rush St. Romeos and high fashion ladies here.

Next walk a very, very short block west, cross State St. and enter Arnie's, in the Newberry Plaza at 1030 N. State. It is to the left of the lobby just beyond the entrance to the garage.

This is an art deco bar and restaurant with vaguely (Aubrey)

Just watching the people go by at Melvin's

Beardsley pictures on the wall. There is also an elegant white baby grand piano at the end of the bar for the pianist or combo. The bar, with its low light and ceiling, is a friendly place usually populated by folks who dress well and can afford the best. The restaurant specializes in a standing rib roast of lamb.

There are actually four restaurants or saloons here owned by Arnie Morton, whose son owns the Hard Rock Cafe. Just north of Arnie's is Arnie's (Outdoor) Cafe, which is where the Gate of Horn nightclub once was. On December 5, 1962, Chicago police arrested comic Lenny Bruce for giving a "lewd and obscene" performance there. He was saying very bad words and performing anti-Catholic jokes in a strongly Catholic town, something not protected by the First Amendment in Chicago at the time. Bruce was sentenced to two years in prison and given a $1,000 fine in March, 1963. The conviction was reversed in 1965, shortly before Bruce died.

The other Arnie Morton restaurants at this location are Morton's Steak House, which once featured 48-ounce porterhouse steaks, and the Maple St. Pier, a mesquite-grilled seafood restaurant.

Walk slightly north (to your left as you leave the lobby) and enter the next revolving door. Morton's Steak House is downstairs, and the Hunan Palace is on the second floor. There are posh red couches at the entrance to this Hunan, Mandarin and Cantonese restaurant, which surrounds an atrium with tropical trees and plants.

It is a place of quiet, of repose. Be sure to order one of the soongs, which is chopped chicken, lobster or shrimp wrapped in lettuce leaves.

Next, leave through the revolving doors, cross Maple and stand outside Pat Harrah's, 12 W. Maple, to read the sign boasting "bad booze, bum food, rotten service, great seating." Here is a bar proud of its funkiness. In fact, the patrons call it "a hole in the wall" or "the saloon Damon Runyan would have wanted to open." Past the funhouse mirror at the entrance, you'll notice that the establishment lists towards the lake, the result of a settling of the building. Call this one the "unsingles" bar for neighborhood types to unwind.

The Waterfront is just to the west at 16 W. Maple in a building built by a cattle baron in 1891. It features two floors of intimate rooms for seafood eaters.

Return to State and take a left, going to Melvin's, at 1116 N. State (a place also mentioned in the Oak Street walk). This is the best spot to sit outdoors and watch the parade of Near North Side crazies. You may see a one-man band, a man in a cheap hula skirt passing out advertising pamphlets, hear a kazoo concert or watch the local bums, hookers and madmen passing by.

Continue walking north, passing the McDonald's, Rose Records and the very busy cash station. Notice that an automatic teller etiquette has developed since these contraptions were created. No one in line stands too close, no one peaks over the shoulder at the transaction taking place and no one shouts, "I'm a winner, look at the cash coming out of this baby."

Ristorante Zio, at 1148 N. State, is in a former ice cream parlor. It remains a bright, well-lit, clean place, which is now an Italian restaurant.

We have now returned to Division and State. By taking a left and heading west, we will plunge into a large collection of singles bars. Look around. Notice how the energy of the area has changed, as young men look at the passing young ladies and both sexes wonder who will get lucky tonight.

Down a flight of stairs at 5 W. Division is P. O. E. T. S. The letters stand for no abbreviation and the place has less to do with Keats and

Yeats than meets (or, some would say, "meat" as in meat-market). Television sets replay the highlights of recent hot buns, bikini, swim suit and hot leg contests. I suppose that means that, after entering such contests, your image would be shown after you marry and become a grandmother. There is a mirrored dance floor, ladies drink free Sunday through Thursday, and actor Tom Cruise once had a drink here.

Gingerman, next door at 7 W. Division, boasts that it has the largest dance floor in this area. Tuesday through Thursday, it offers free beer, although the glass costs $2. It seems to be a place to meet people and the manager, Jeff Senzel, said he would like very much to meet his wife-to-be there. Help him out.

Continuing west, but only going 20 feet or so, Le Petit Cafe, at 11 W. Division, is a chic gourmet carryout place which also seats 15 people.

Bootleggers, a long, dark, heavily wooded singles bar with throbbing music, is at 11 W. Division. The Rob Lowe film, "About Last Night," was filmed in part here, although it was named "Muther's" in the movie and a basketball free-throw cage was constructed (and later torn down).

The Snuggery is a two-story singles bar at 15 W. Division. The managers say that from the second floor a patron can have the best view of Division Street. Fortunes may be made on such slight distinctions.

If you look at the pictures opposite the second floor bar, you will see Al Capone and his cronies enjoying this place when it was called the North Star Inn in the '30s.

According to the July, 1984, issue of Playboy Magazine, the Snuggery is one of the best singles bars in the country. It boasts two dance floors, ladies drink for free from 9 p.m. until closing on Tuesdays and Thursdays, and a variety of sports stars from the San Diego Padres and the Chicago Black Hawks are supposed to visit. The decor makes the patron feel comfortable and the Snuggery has a reputation for being a well-run, even classy singles bar.

The Lodge, at 21 W. Division, caters to an older, singles crowd, over age 30, possibly because it reminds them of the bars around their college campuses. It has, according to Dennis McCarthy's *The Great Chicago Bar & Saloon Guide*, "a drink-that-draft-beer-and-be-rowdy atmosphere." Dennis, who is probably unwise in allowing this sort of thing to happen to his lady friends, once experimented by sending a woman acquaintance alone into the Lodge before he entered. Within two minutes, she was surrounded by eight guys and "their various hustles were as rapid and multiple as you would expect from the street beggars of Calcutta."

The owner, Paul Risolia, once tossed Jonathan Winters out for playing the piano.

222

Leaving The Lodge, take a left and continue west to Dearborn, where you will take another left. O'Leary's, at 1157 N. Dearborn, is an Irish pub with a real dart board (no magnets or Velcro here).

At the corner of Dearborn and Elm, there is Ranalli's a two-story sports bar and grill with outdoor seating on a second floor balcony that's slightly away from the Division St. noise.

Cross Dearborn and enter Biggs, 1150 N. Dearborn, a marvelous continental restaurant in the John DeKoven mansion, built in 1874. Biggs retains the DeKoven's original woodwork, mirrors and charm.

Return to Division, one block to the north, cross the street. Edwardo's Natural Pizza is just to the north of this corner.

Houlihan's Bar and Restaurant, at 1207 N. Dearborn, has a little plaque at one corner of the bar proclaiming that this establishment entered the "Guiness Book of Records" in 1985 for having the world's largest St. Patrick's Day party. Actually, the 205,854 people squeezed into the 40 Houlihan's around America.

Houlihan's appeals to the slower, quieter folks in this area because the music is not loud and the bar area is spacious and relaxed. The restaurant features Cajun chicken, seafood and caramel ice cream desert.

Mothers, at 26 W. Division, is actually a place mom probably would not enjoy. It is a basement, rock 'n roll joint which offers an annual lip sync contest (the owners claim to be the first in the country to create such a contest), the Thursday Fistfull of Dollars contest (a lady can merely grab as much money as she can from a goldfish bowl containing $5,000), and a hot leg contest for the woman with the shortest shorts.

I suppose mom would like the place if she had great legs.

Bato Prostran, the doorman, said that standing on Division checking identification cards is "the purest form of entertainment I have ever seen. Guys come by thinking they are God's gift to women, women think the same thing and everyone is looking for Mr. Right."

Not everyone finds Mr. or Ms. Right. Comic Robin Williams once came here to play pinball by himself all night.

Mother's was seen in the film "Class," with Jacqueline Bisset, Andrew McCarthy and Rob Lowe, the story of a guy who falls in love with his roommate's mother. The moviemakers thought that the audience would believe that "Mother's" was a place for people to pick up mommies, so the bar's name was changed to the Free and Easy in the movie.

She-Nannigans, next door at 16 W. Division, is a sports bar, with 14 TV monitors, trying to look like an Irish pub. The scenes when Tom Hanks' mother, played by Eva Marie Saint, went to a bar to shoot baskets after breaking up with his father, played by Jackie Gleason, in the film "Nothing in Common" were shot in the free-throw cage at She-Nannigans.

Again moving to the east, P. S. Chicago, at 8 W. Division, is a casual singles club for Yuppies. One couple, who met there, returned after their marriage for a reunion. A baby sitter was taking care of their child, indicating that sometimes people can find stable relationships which begin in Division Street bars.

P. S. Chicago features a long, narrow dance floor, a back room which is only a little quieter than the front area and waitresses in short skirts. It also has a yearly best-fitting jeans contest for both sexes plus a Don "Miami Vice" Johnson look-alike contest.

If you go to the corner of State and Division and look North, you will see Yvette, a French restaurant patterned after the century-old P. J. Clarke's in New York. The large windows here open to create a sidewalk cafe, the front area has white paper on top of the tablecloths and crayons so you can decorate or scribble. The walls are covered with turquoise piano keys on a purple background.

Return to Division St., which you will cross, heading east. The Hotsie Totsie Yacht Club and Bait Shop, at 8 E. Division, doesn't sell minnows. Gary DeAngelis, the owner, is friendly, gregarious and will do everything in his power to make the customer feel at home.

The Rookery, at 12 E. Division, is a disco dance bar. It is a place to go to step, move and jump, but not to talk. The music is loud.

This ends the Rush-Division bar crawl. My researcher, Donna Neuwirth, suggests, "If I were a starving student, I would come to Rush St. at 5 p.m., buy a Coca-Cola in three or four bars, free hors d'oeuvres myself silly, and leave quickly before the people who might actually enter a wet t-shirt contest arrive."

A caller to one of my radio shows offered this excellent advice for succeeding in the singles' bar scene in Chicago, "Go ugly early." He meant that the least attractive of people should be singled out early in the evening for special attention.

On the other hand, perhaps the best approach to succeeding in the often wild and cruel Division Street singles scene is to ask a variety of people there for advice on how to succeed. The worst-case scenario for that approach would be that you could turn their responses into a movie, film it on Division and then buy your own singles bar.

20 STREETS OF FOOD

ONTARIO-CHICAGO
RESTAURANT WALK

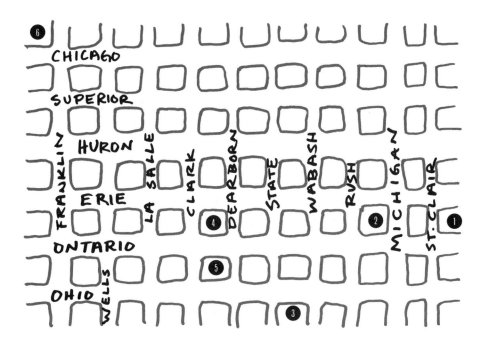

1. Richmont Hotel
2. Lawry's
3. Pizzeria Uno
4. Limelight
5. Hard Rock Cafe
6. Raccoon Club

Time: An evening or a lifetime, depending on how much the walk affects your future.
To get there: The CTA Buses numbered 11 and 151 and the express buses numbered 125, 145, 146 and 147 all stop at Michigan and Ontario.
If you drive: Don't.

Ontario and Michigan

If you drink and eat at each restaurant on this tour, you will have tried as many as 30 establishments, your stomach will have given up all hope of ever digesting anything again and your nose may be numb.

So pace yourself. Look in some bars, drink at others, eat at others, avoid any place with a long line or snooty doormen unless this book says it is worthwhile and then only wait 10 minutes to be seated.

This is one of the rare east-west walks in this book and it is new. The Ontario Street restaurant strip wasn't zoned or planned that way, it just happened, meaning that sometimes there are traffic jams along Ontario for no reason at all.

And yet this is the one walk inside the city where you are guaranteed to meet Young Upwardly-mobile Professionals, Yuppies. Chicago, being a blue collar, gritty kind of town, tends to send its yuppies out to the suburbs, where they congregate in large groups at tennis clubs which encourage them to donate their used balls to the poor. (A practice I thought sure to cause the next urban riot).

However, there are growing enclaves of young engineers, doctors, lawyers, accountants and salesmen in Chicago who earn good salaries and do not want the long commute times to the suburbs. To them, this walk is dedicated.

We begin at Ontario and Michigan. Walk one block east to the Richmont Hotel, with its 191 remodeled rooms, and its Rue Saint Clair "an American bistro." Frankly, I think most drinks and food here are outrageously overpriced ($16.95 for a filet mignon), but the outdoor cafe seems French and charming. Perhaps you feel like watching the passing scene for a few moments while drinking a good American Chardonnay.

Having a quiet moment to contemplate St. Clair Street. (I have often walked down St. Clair and can't find a single reason to sit in an outdoor cafe and contemplate this nondescript street, but you might) let us move resolutely to the west. We walk by Hatsuhana, 160 E. Ontario, (unless we want sushi or Japanese wine) and head on to Charlie Chaing's, 158 E. Ontario.

Charlie Chaing's was previously Maison De Lago, a Spanish resturant. Mr. Chaing is a former chemist from the University of Illinois who has opened a series of Mandarin and Szechwan restaurants around the country.

The major point to remember about this clean restaurant is that the menu, ranging from wok-grilled salmon steak to crispy lemon chicken to Peking duck, excludes monosodium glutamate (MSG), the stuff which causes some folks to have allergic reactions to Chinese food and to get headaches an hour after putting down the chop sticks. Chaing's says it is the first Chinese restaurant in Chicago to completely eliminate MSG from all entrees.

Having tried the excellent steamed dumplings and perhaps a bit of wine, we next walk a few feet to Howard's Knight Tap, 152 E. Ontario. This bar and restaurant is exactly 12 feet wide so you are assured of being close to whomever is there. Howard Jones, the owner, serves only one beer on tap, Leinenkugel, from Chippewa Falls, Wisconsin "because it's so good." Walk through to the back, into the patio, where various media types can often be found unwinding after a tough day. Then look up at the small building there. You can, if you wish, enter that building, walk up one flight of stairs and sit in a room overlooking the patio. This is euphemistically called the "Sky Box."

A few feet to the west is Shuckers, 150 E. Ontario, a quiet seafood restaurant with excellent clam chowder and jumbo shrimps. The second level has one room with fishing trophies on the wall and another with Chicago memorabilia, some of which hints that this was once the home of Robert McCormick.

Continuing to Michigan Avenue, in the lower level of the 625 N. Michigan building there is the Lower East Side, with sophisticated murals and the best appetizer tray to come with a meal.

Lawry's and Chez Paul

Tarry there if you wish (the waitresses are friendly and the service is superb), or continue to the west. Do drop in Lawry's, which was once the Kungsholm, a Danish restaurant and home of a famed puppet opera. Look at the ornate decorations, consider having one of Lawry's famous salad bowls (yes, the restaurant is owned by the spice people) or go all out and have a prime rib in either the English ($17.95), Lawry ($18.95) or Chicago ($20.95) cuts.

If you take a right on Rush St. and walk a very short block, you will arrive at Chez Paul, 660 N. Rush. There were tunnels connecting Lawry's and Chez Paul at one time because both were homes belonging to the McCormick family, whose wealth was created by reapers (farm implements).

The Chez Paul building was built in 1875 as a mansion for Robert Hall McCormick, who was once the ambassador to Italy and who used this stately home as his ambassador's residence to entertain princes, dukes and the elite.

Do walk inside, where the original marble stairs are now carpeted, where two marble pillars have brass bands around them because they were splintered in a fire decades ago and where other marble columns are from the Italian Exhibit of the 1893 Columbian Exposition.

The dining rooms have a sense of quiet elegance and the great stairway to the rear of the entrance demands the presence of ladies in ball gowns.

Bill Contos, the owner, is the oldest son of the founder, Paul, who started his boys on the bottom rungs of food service. Bill, who is one of the friendliest people in town (he's the guy with the distinctive mustache), began as a dish washer. Despite having a grand restaurant, Bill hates "stuffed shirtism," demands to be called Bill and makes everyone feel as if they are members of his comfly club.

Onward on Ontario

Return to Ontario and cross to the south side of the street where Cafe Jasper, at 105 E. Ontario, is a good place for white wine and salad for lunch. Ohba, at the corner of Rush and Ontario, is a fine Japanese restaurant and, around the corner to the south, Moe's Deli has one of the smallest outdoor cafes in town.

Continuing slightly west, the Lenox Restaurant in the Lenox House Hotel, 620 N. Rush, has the second best Reuben sandwich in Chicago according to one newspaper critic.

Once again moving west (but only slightly—we are probably walking less than 100 yards before we stop), you will find Su Casa, one of my favorite Mexican restaurants, at 49 E. Ontario. There is something about the dark interior, the comfortable chairs, the strolling guitarists, the cozy bar and the very good, salty margaritas which welcomes a stranger to this restaurant.

If you walk to the corner, you will see Pizzeria Due. One block to the south, there is Uno's. Both will have waiting lines, although I sometimes like to avoid the lines by dashing into Due's and buying a frozen pizza.

Chicago's thick-crust, oozing in cheese, utterly distinctive pizzas were created here, the city's gift to the world. These pizzas are the best, revered by pizza lovers, blessed by anyone who has been away from Chicago for a long time and has had to suffer through out-of-town imitations. The pizzas weigh between four and five pounds, yet the crust is miraculously crunchy. Frankly, you have not visited Chicago and you do not know this city until you have had an Uno's or Due's Pizza (I do not distinguish between them, both are excellent).

By the way, Due's is in the Saxet Building, which a plaque says is "one of Chicago's finest examples of Victorian architecture."

Next you will see the Moorish, outrageously overdone Medinah Temple just to the west. It has a stage big enough to accommodate elephants and trapeze artists during the Shrine Circus performances each spring.

But continue to walk west, to the rear of the Temple, where you will see the entrance to the Tree Studios Building just east of State Street. It is one of Chicago's secret places, an L-shaped garden in the midst of the hullabaloo of the city, with vines growing on the wall of the temple and artists' studios facing the flowers and trees.

This is private property, but if you are lucky, the doors will be open and you might take a peak past the foyer into the garden.

In the 1920s, this was the center for artists who embraced abstractionism, cubism and post-impressionism against sculptor Lorado Taft and the traditionalists housed in the Fine Arts Building. Their motto was "No Jury Means Freedom," and they gave the No Jury Ball and Exhibit. One dawn, artist Rudolph Weisenborn, president of the group and a man whose painting hangs in Riccardo's today, was routed out of bed by two Chicago detectives. They were rounding up "anarchists" and people who were against juries. Weisenborn was only released after he revealed that the No Jury art group also exhibited in Marshall Field & Co.

When you are at the corner of State and Ontario, you will see Stats across the street. This is one restaurant which deserves the description "eclectic." The menu features a bit of everything and the bar offers a relaxed high-tech atmosphere.

If you want to walk less than a half block, we can interrupt this bar and restaurant tour for a short, quaint shopping excursion.

Taking a left on State St., you'll find the Romano Gallery, at 613 N. State, with Art Deco furniture, and the State Street Collection, at 609 N. State, a small shop specializing in vintage kitchenware. In other words, this is the place to go if you have been looking for Aunt Jemima cookie jars.

Charles Inc., at 607 N. State, sells antiques.

The Medinah Barber Shop, at 605 N. State, is a real anachronism, with three old fashioned barber chairs and $7 haircuts.

But we have many more saloons and dancehalls to visit (and, to paraphrase Robert Frost, pints to drink before we sleep, pints to drink before we sleep). Retrace our steps back to Ontario and walk a block west to the Limelight.

The Limelight

Every time I visit the Limelight, I have the impression that this would be the perfect place to be just before the end of the world because it seems like a vision of what some of us will experience in the hereafter.

To your left, as you walk past the doormen, there is often an exhibit of people in cages, actors behind glass demonstrating various deadly sins or robots having sex.

Inside the Limelight, you are assaulted by the sound, which is just above the painful. There are several cavernous dance rooms. The Limelight has 40,000 square feet of space because it is in a 19th century mansion (called "the Castle") which formerly housed the Chicago Historical Society.

The owner, Peter Gatien, the son of a retired postmaster, studied business administration at Ottawa's Carlton University. He took a $17,000 award he got for losing an eye during a high school hockey game to open the first of two denim stores in Canada. He then turned a country and western bar in Ontario into a successful disco.

Eventually, at the ripe old age of 23, he opened the first Limelight in Hollywood, Florida. A millionaire at age 27, Gatien sold the Florida Limelight and opened a new one in Atlanta. Then in 1983, came the Limelight in New York, where the famous and the drugged-out came to dance. Here, Janet Leigh once re-enacted the notorious shower scene from her 1960 film *Psycho*. Often, fans came to be snubbed at the door because they weren't recognized by the tough doormen.

The Chicago Limelight was opened in July, 1985, and its opening night was a big mistake. Too many people were invited. The doormen didn't recognize some of the guests who believed they were invited just to create an anxious crowd at the door. Once inside, they found bedlam and the Limelight (instantly nicknamed "Slimelight") got bad press.

Since then, the Limelight has been working hard to be a good citizen. It has learned that Chicagoans do not enjoy being treated like cattle (the way New Yorkers obviously do). You will now find that the doormen are polite, but firm as they enforce the dress code (no jeans or sneakers, please).

The art inside the Limelight, which changes frequently, is often huge (in keeping with the space) and very modern. There are also many special events here, such as fashion shows or after-theater parties, and many of them start late (after 11 p.m.) Ask at the door to find out what is happening on the night you are there.

The Chicago Chop House is next door to the Limelight at 60 W. Ontario. According to owner Henry Norton, this restaurant has more historic Chicago pictures than "any place in Chicago, including City Hall." There are pictures of every Mayor, plus Chicago's famous gangsters. The Chicago Chop House sells a 64-ounce t-bone steak "for three or four customers or for William (Refrigerator) Perry by himself," according to Norton.

Hard Rock Cafe

Next, cross the street and try to get into the Hard Rock Cafe, which always has a waiting line. It is the sixth Hard Rock, which had a flawless opening on June 27, 1986, with Robert Palmer singing "Addicted to Love" to hundreds of guests in the restaurant and under a tent placed in the west parking lot. The Hard Rock was going to learn from the Limelight's mistakes the year before.

230

The owner is Peter Morton, son of Arnie Morton, who owns many restaurants in Chicago. Peter is also the grandson of a Chicago bootlegger and the great-grandson of an Iron Mountain, Michigan, saloon keeper. When I asked Arnie, the father, if he was proud of his son on the night the Hard Rock opened, he said, "He's still basically a saloon keeper."

The Chicago Hard Rock cost $3.5 million to build and is supposed to resemble a rich teenaged rock music fan's bedroom, according to Peter.

As you enter, Indiana Jones' leather jacket hangs on one wall (Steven Spielberg is an investor). George Harrison's original Beatles' uniform is also there, with Michael Jackson's platinum records, David Bowie's saxophone and guitars belonging to a variety of rock greats, including Mick Jagger and Keith Richards of the Rolling Stones.

The Los Angeles Hard Rock is famous for its 1959 lime green Cadillac sticking out of its front facade. After it opened in 1982, Peter Morton began telling folks that this restaurant was "where the '50s meet the future," that his chain was "trying to be the MTV of restaurants," and that he was opening "an emporium of junk." All those descriptions fit Chicago's Hard Rock.

There was a line waiting for hamburgers the moment the Chicago Hard Rock opened, a tribute to Morton's ability to get publicity, attract celebrities, create a '50s diner with an '80s high-tech feel, and sell lots of salads, chicken, fish and steaks. Morton is basically a shy, casual guy who readily admits that he'd rather play tennis. He once said that "people are motivated to eat out in Los Angeles by vanity, lust and greed." In Chicago, people are obviously motivated to eat out by a good hamburger and a chance to see Mick Jagger's guitar on the second floor of the Hard Rock.

Leaving the Hard Rock's rock 'n roll museum, head west once again, cross Clark St., and enter the world's most unusual McDonald's. In fact, if you wish to save money, avoid the crowds, and yet see great rock memorabilia, go to McDonald's in this neighborhood.

The tables here are covered in zebra and leopard prints. A perfect 1959 Corvete convertible is parked in the window, there is an old jukebox with '50s and '60s tunes (where else can you go in mid-afternoon to hear Chuck Berry or Dion and the Belmonts?), life-sized statues of the Beatles dressed in Nehru jackets seem to walk in their glass case, and straw dispensers resemble big strawberries or Oreo cookies. There are framed pictures of Elvis and Marilyn Monroe and a Phillips 66 gas pump. This is one of the three highest-volume McDonald's in the world, and it also offers banquet facilities or delivery service in antique cars.

McDonald's with a '50s theme

This McDonald's is owned by Angelo Lencioni, who is president of the River North Assoc., a group of merchants. The Irish came to this area in the 1840s, often living in wooden shacks until the fire of 1871 devastated their homes. Then the Swedes came, followed by the Italians. At one time, when the area was industrialized, it was known as Smokey Hollow.

Now, quite suddenly, it has become the fashionable place to be, with new restaurants being built here and old lofts are becoming expensive condominiums.

Moving to the west, we pass Morrie Mage's, a huge sports store with constant ski and tennis racket sales. You can also get baci balls (the lawn bowling game beloved by Italians) here.

But let's stay in our '50s mood and go to Ed Debevic's, 640 N. Wells. Thousands of dollars were spent to re-create the high school hangout of your youth, if you are in your late 30s to 50s. Ed Debevic is fictional, but the restaurant, designed by Spiros Zakas, is based on a real greasy spoon in Atlanta in the '50s.

There are the quaint slogans on the walls: "If you can find a better diner, eat there." "One at a time. The hostess has only one set of nerves." "Ed's chili dog—the Cadillac of chili dogs."

You will quickly notice the gum chewing, wise-cracking waitresses and waiters, with white uniforms festooned with sloganeering buttons. The waitresses, especially, seem to audition for their roles, and many of them sport black bras under their white uniforms, slips just a tad too long for the skirts and black-rooted blond hair.

The food here is good AND inexpensive. And this is one place where you can ignore your parents' admonitions never to eat meatloaf in a restaurant (my mom and dad always warned that meatloaf was made from leftovers) and enjoy the best meatloaf in town.

Once you get inside (there is often a line), the service is fast and good, the food is excellent and Ed Debevic's own beer is watery, but cold.

Across the street, to the south, there is Carson's for Ribs, which did win a Chicago Magazine contest for the best ribs in town. The ribs here are meaty and the sauce is superb, but I prefer the chicken. Both the ribs and the chicken are served with bibs. Don't be shy; wear the bib. You will need it.

The bar features large-screen television and free chopped liver appetizers. Once inside the comfortable restaurant be sure to try the coleslaw, which I love.

If you wish, continue walking a half block west of Anchini's only because it appears to be a combination fast food restaurant and cemetery monument company. The "fast-a-food" joint is built on part of the Tuscany Studio property, with the statuary squeezed to the east. You can see the fountains, bird baths, lions, angels and imitations of The David just behind the restaurant.

Return to Ontario and Wells. Just to the west is Lino's Ristorante, one of the best Italian restaurants in Chicago. Ditka's and City Lghts is across the street at 223 W. Ontario. Yes, it carries the name of Chicago Bears' coach Mike Ditka. And yes, the man who guided the Bears to the 1986 Super Bowl championship is there sometimes. The place opened August 3, 1986, while the Bears were playing the Dallas Cowboys in a London Exhibition game.

Next, walk north on Wells Street. The Wells Street Deli, at Huron and Wells, claims that it offers "happy food."

The Brehon Pub, at 731 N. Wells, is a true Chicago journalistic landmark, with nothing there to indicate that it was once the sight of a famous investigation.

It was called The Mirage in 1976, when it was owned by the *Chicago Sun-Times*. Pamela Zekman, who has since become an investigative reporter for local television, convinced the newspaper to buy a saloon, open it and hope that local inspectors would ask for bribes.

Within a few months, The Mirage was the subject of systematic shakedowns by building, health, fire, liquor and electrical inspectors. It was offered kickbacks to put in pinball machines and jukeboxes.

If you enter the Brehon today you'll see a strange wooden railing over the bathrooms towards the rear. A structure here once hid the

TV cameras for the 60 Minutes TV show and the newspaper photographers recording the bribes.

During the investigation, many accountants offered advice on double bookkeeping, with one set indicating how much was actually earned and another set of books skimming a third to a half or more off the totals to avoid taxes.

Various licenses were eased through the City Hall hierarchy because city officials were "greased," or bribed.

Inspectors regularly overlooked safety and health code violations either after they were presented with an envelope containing cash or the bribe was added to the contractor's bill as a cost of doing business.

City crews, assigned to other tasks but actually loafing, fixed streets in exchange for a few beers.

Possibly the strangest moment during this investigation of Chicago corruption came when it was suggested that The Mirage become a front for prostitution. One couple, Roger and Angel, wanted to install B-girls, ladies who would neck and pet with customers in exchange for drinks. According to the book *The Mirage*, by Zekman and Zay N. Smith, Roger asked, "You know what we could do in November?"

"What?" Smith asked.

" 'Toys for Tots.' We could tie in with that. Every customer has to bring in a toy before the girls would serve him. We could work it that way."

There were headlines around the world when the stories about The Mirage broke, but there was no Pulitzer prize. From the beginning, the *Sun-Times* staff worked hard to avoid the appearance of "entrapment," of trapping inspectors into offering bribes. But the Pulitzer Prize judges were allegedly wary of encouraging such "entrapment," and denied journalism's ultimate prize to a clever, creative, tough expose.

Continue walking north to Chicago Avenue, and then turn west one block to the Dixie Bar and Grill, 225 W. Chicago, a converted warehouse where Mardi Gras seems to be a permanent celebration.

In recent years, Chicago has embraced Cajun cookery and here is the local headquarters for mudbugs, voodoo chicken, blackened swordfish, and pasta jambalaya. Be brave, because the food is far better than the names of the dishes.

The Dixie also features live jazz and a "happening" atmosphere where bands might begin a parade at the drop of a mudbug. Of course, at actual Mardi Gras time the Dixie jumps, with many patrons in costume, but there is a New Orleans feel to the place year round.

Continue west to the corner of Chicago and Franklin, cross the street and go north on Franklin a few feet to the Raccoon Club, 812 N. Franklin.

Jan Hobson created a group called Jan Hobson and her Bad Review, which sang "The Raccoon Song" throughout Chicago for several years. During the song, the entire audience would imitate raccoons washing their faces and food.

Jan wanted a place where she could perform and created The Raccoon Club, which is now one of the best jazz clubs in Chicago. It is small, intimate and any group playing there is worth the listening. You can stand at the bar, drink and listen to the music without paying a cover charge; or you can eat a light meal and drink at a table while enjoying music that should never die.

Several times a month, usually on Saturday nights, Jan Hobson and her Bad Review entertain. Don't worry about asking because they always sing "The Raccoon Song."

This ends the Ontario-Chicago, east-west, yuppie bar and restaurant crawl. If you have visited and sampled each place on this walk, it is time to go home and rest. You have done enough for one night!

21 GREEK TOWN PUB CRAWL

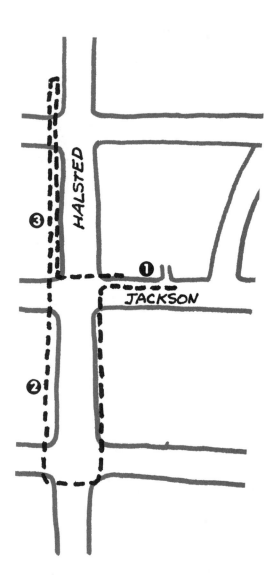

1. Greek Islands Restaurant
2. Parthenon Restaurant
3. Dianna's Opaa Restaurant

Time: All evening. Schedule at least four hours.
To get there: Drive or take a cab to Jackson and Halsted, which is just south and west of the loop. Many of the restaurants have nearby parking lots and, except on Saturday night, it's usually

easy to find a place to park. Via public transportation, the buses to Union Station will take you within two blocks of Greek Town, and these include the 38, 121, 151, 156, 128, 15, 60, 125, and 157 buses. The 126 stops at Jackson and Halsted.

Changing West Side Neighborhood

By the end of this pub crawl, you will talk like Zorba the Greek, walk at a 45-degree angle and maniacally yell, *Opaa* every 30 seconds or so. Don't worry. Such behavior is perfectly normal after a tour of Greek Town.

Greek Town is an attempt to recreate cafe life in Greece within sight of Chicago's Loop. It is one of the city's most popular areas mainly because it features inexpensive food, ethnic restaurants and cheap wine in a friendly atmosphere.

It is a symbol of snatching a partial triumph out of a genuine tragedy.

A true ethnic neighborhood existed for generations just south of where you are now. Then the city put through the Congress St. Expressway, and later renamed it the Eisenhower Expressway. Still later, Chicago decided to plunk the University of Illinois Chicago Circle Campus on top of a neighborhood of Greeks and Italians.

There was a fight. Oh, was there a fight. In 1962, Florence Scala, a neighborhood resident, led a round-the-clock sit-in in the late Mayor Richard J. Daley's office, but it did no good.

She told Studs Terkel, "The bulldozers were there. They were tearing down the houses . . . and Victor Cambio of Conte de Savioa, that wonderful grocery that had foods from everywhere. The fragrance . . . Tearing down the buildings of Hull House. There was a Japanese elm in that courtyard that came up to Miss Binford's window . . ."

Anthony Koclanakis, once president of the local Greek businessmen's association, said, "All businessmen here are newcomers, maybe ten, fifteen years in this area. The whole area got smaller after the university came here. There used to be many residences, many businesses, ten different coffee shops where old men played backgammon." The university came, many of the Greek people went away. Chicago lost a neighborhood, but gained an area with wonderful restaurants.

Shaking off our momentary nostalgia for what was before 1965, let us stand at the corner of Jackson and Halsted. Walk to the south on Halsted one long block to the Courtyards of Plaka, 340 S. Halsted to begin our trek through the Grecian islands of Chicago.

The Plaka refers to an area in the old quarter of Athens, near the Acropolis. When you are inside this restaurant you are supposed to feel as if you are under a tent (made of aluminum) in a courtyard.

It is a fitting place to start a Greek Town tour because this restaurant is quieter and more subdued than most of the street, with a pianist quietly playing Greek songs most nights of the week.

If you are hungry, you might try the Athenian feast, with saganaki (more about that later), shrimp salad, spinach cheese pie, eggplant salad, Greek salad, roast leg of lamb, boned chicken in cream sauce (kotopita), moussaka, rice pilafi, vegetable, creme caramele and coffee for $13.95 per person.

If not, drink a little roditys, observe the relative peace and quiet, and then press onward. The Hellas Coffee Shop, at 334 S. Halsted, is supposed to feature ice cream, but the people there seemed more interested in an endless card game.

Passing the Athens Grocery, at 324 S. Halsted, the Panhellenic Pastry shop, at 322 S. Halsted, features kataefe, a walnut and peanut concoction with honey oozing from it.

The Parthenon

A Greek Town landmark, the Parthenon, is at 314 S. Halsted. Order *saganaki* here. The owner, Chris Liakouras, claims that he invented this flaming cheese pie in 1968 when he put brandy on caseri cheese and discovered that it helped the taste, rather than destroying it. Ask for *saganaki,* yell *Opaa* (hooray) and duck, because the brandy brandished by the waiter does flame.

Liakouras says that today cafes in his homeland are imitating his discovery of flaming saganaki. He adds, "Our customers enter very sober, very nice. When they walk out, after drinking the wine, they are always smiling."

The Parthenon has also ranked among the Top Ten Chicago restaurants in several judgings.

Be sure to notice the picture in the window, titled "We created flaming saganaki (it took some practice)." The waiter's hair is on fire!

Once inside the restaurant, we are supposed to feel as if we are in a Greek home. The pictures on the walls are of various family members, military heroes, weddings and so on, but no one knows whose famiy they are. The photos were bought in an antique store in Greece.

Ex-comedian Dick Gregory broke one of his anti-Vietnam fasts here. Comic-actor Godfrey Cambridge ate here while on his diet and basketball player Bill Walton ate here while his foot was hurt because he needed fresh fruit and vegetables.

According to the co-owner, Gregory Karabis, the saganaki and the gyros (ground beef, lamb and pork) were originally given away for free to introduce them to Chicago. Now that everyone knows what they are, the gyros is $4.95 and the saganaki, which is the lightest and least salty in town, is $2.70, flames included.

Continuing on our way north (we have many glasses of roditys to drink before we sleep), It's Greek to Me, in a former warehouse and pastry shop at 306 S. Halsted, is bright and charming with a variety of dishes which are lightly spiced. When you are inside this restaurant, you are supposed to have the feeling that you are on a Greek island with blue sky overhead. I recommend the stuffed mushrooms with crabmeat and the arni exohiko, the lamb stuffed with artichokes, pine nuts, feta cheese, peas and tomatoes.

Crossing Jackson, the Roditys, at 222 S. Halsted, features a huge mural of a harbor. Look at the stones embedded in the wall near that mural. They are about all that remain of the original decor when the place was redecorated in 1985.

The Roditys, once rather cold and sterile, is a warm friendly place today. The decor tends to make the patrons feel expansive and open. This is a good place to order the family style dinner with soup, saganaki, salad, gyros, a combination plate with moussaka, pastichio, dolmades, lamb and vegetables, wine, dessert and coffee for $9.75 per person.

Dianna's Opaa

Dianna's Opaa, at 212 S. Halsted, is just north of the Roditys. Dianna's is the territory of Petros Kogiones, the owner and a man determined to set a Guinness record for kissing women. At last count, he has kissed over 2,000,000, although one customer claimed it was over 4,000,000 because one kiss with that customer's wife was worth 3,000,000 kisses with anyone else's. It's the sort of discussion one has after a bottle of *Roditys.*

Petros, who is never without his cigar, claims that his is the first restaurant in Greek Town only to serve food and not to feature belly dancers. Dianna's is in a former nightclub, and some customers now eat on the stage. The circle of mirrors on the ceiling is a remnant of the room's more flamboyant days.

The *saganaki* is excellent here, as is the *gyros* and the *taramasalada,* a fish roe salad to be eaten with Greek bread. Order tham all!

If the feeling is right and the evening is particularly happy, Petros will dance with a full glass of wine on his head, put it down and drink it, picking it up with only his teeth. Later, everyone will dance around the tables.

Dianna's *is* Petros, swarthy, long-haired, grinning, wheeling, dealing, raspy-voiced, friendly, calling everyone "cousin," labeled by no less than the *Chicago Tribune* as one of Chicago's most eligible bachelors, a shrewd businessman, who has created a success where others have failed, who wrote a cook book titled *Petros' Famous*

Recipes, which includes two references in different introductions to Dianna's being "God's gift to Chicago." Maybe it is.

Petros, one of five brothers and four sisters, from the town of Nestani in Greece, agrees with a policy shared by all other owners of restaurants in Greek town. If you order a bottle of wine and can't finish it, you can either pay for it and take it home or be charged for however much you drink and leave the rest.

As you leave, be sure to browse through the alcove in front of the cash register, where we see many pictures of Petros kissing the famous. Also, notice the big sign which says, "Welcome Home, God Bless America and ALL Greeks."

Greek Islands

We next walk to 200 S. Halsted, the Greek Islands Restaurant, a personal favorite of mine. I have not eaten in every restaurant in the world, America, Illinois or even Chicago. But, of the restaurants I have tried, the Greek Islands is, without question, the best.

I realize that reads like very, very high praise indeed, but I have never had a bad meal at the Greek Islands Restaurant. Neither have I ever had a bad evening. The feeling, the food, and the pure fun of the place combine to make it the best.

Don't take my word for it. James Ward, an often acerbic restaurant critic for the *Chicago Sun-Times,* reviewed the restaurant in 1983, just days after it moved to its present location from 766 W. Jackson. He wrote, "What a revelation! What a delight! Opaa! Opaa! . . . What a setting! What a welcoming ambience! . . . And it's wonderful food, still the best . . . Now in its new home, Greek Islands is everything that a restaurant should be in the true meaning of the word 'restaurant': This splendid, spacious establishment 'restores' the psyche as well as the soma, the spirit as well as the tum-tum. And now there's room to dance in the aisles of the Greek Islands—and dance you should!"

This 350-seat restaurant is a joyous experience. Although it is large, I feel intimate here. Although loud, I feel a sense of energetic quiet.

Order anything. It will be perfect.

My favorites are the taramasalada (fish roe) and tzatziki (yogurt, cucumbers and garlic) before dinner, gyros and a Greek salad, then the lamb chops (unsurpassed) and either the sea bass or red snapper (whichever the waiter says is fresh) washed down with the dry Corinth white wine.

Sometimes, I just give up and tell the waiter to order whatever he wants for me, often with some help from Nick or Gus or any of the managers. Do not worry, they will not pad the bill, they will not

Nick Sguros, manager of the Greek Islands, and his happy customers

automatically order the most expensive items, and your meal will be the best.

I remember the night Anthony Quinn and the cast from the musical "Zorba the Greek" were eating in the balcony above the kitchen area and the waiters continually brought Quinn plates and glasses to break a la Zorba. But the plates were so sturdy that they often did not break and had to be slammed to the floor again and again.

The Greek Islands is a happy place, where the Roditys wine flows, where the conversation comes easy, where the eternal truths seem to be discovered in the midst of laughter. I have gone there to cry, sing, laugh, settle differences, fall in love, introduce fiances to parents, joke with co-workers, eat, drink and celebrate being alive.

What better place to end the Greek Town Pub Crawl with a glass of wine in hand, toasting today and tomorrow, and just loving the fact that life can be this good.

Opaa!

22 OLD TOWN PUB CRAWL

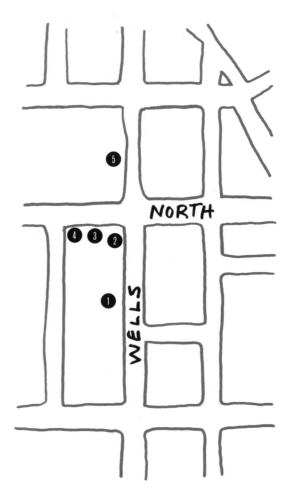

1. Barbara's Bookstore
2. Zanie's
3. Cafe Azteca
4. Old Town Ale House
5. Second City

Time: More than two hours.
To get there: The 22 and 36 CTA buses stop at North Avenue and Clark Street, two blocks east of North and Wells, where the pub crawl begins. The 156 LaSalle, 11 Lincoln, Express 135 and Express 136 buses stop at North Avenue and LaSalle, one block east of North and Wells. If you drive, park in a lot on Wells Street rather than attempt to find a space on the side street. The streets east of Wells never have spaces and those west of Wells can be dangerous to non-neighborhood residents.

The Ups and Downs of Old Town

In the '50s, Old Town housed real artists living inexpensively in storefronts.

In the '60s, Old Town became a freak show. People with long hair congregated there, and tourists and suburbanites came to observe and feed them.

After the riots in the wake of Martin Luther King's murder in 1968, when gangs from nearby Cabrini Green public housing roamed through Old Town smashing and grabbing at will, the area went into a swift decline. During the '70s, Old Town turned mean, dangerous and unsafe.

Wells Street became the place to get ripped off while trying to buy dope or the home of strip joints where conventioneers would get ripped off trying to buy sex.

But, in the '80s, Old Town has started a comeback. The street still has its tough areas, which is why this walk does not take you too far south on Wells Street. And there are areas to the west where no one should walk alone at night. But better restaurants are opening on Wells, some of the older establishments remain, Second City still flourishes here offering improvisational comedy, and there is enough going on to once more include this walk in this book.

We begin at Clark, North and Wells, where the bus probably has stopped. Across the street, you can see the Chicago Historical Society and the Chicago Latin School, two institutions mentioned in the Lincoln Park Walk.

Cross to the south side of the street, take a right and head west on North Avenue, passing the Metropolis Cafe, 165 W. North Avenue, which offers good, health-oriented food.

When you reach Wells Street take a left. The Trattoria Pizzeria Roma, at 1557 N. Wells, has quite suddenly become a very popular, small Italian restaurant. On a good night, you can see patrons waiting in line and holding brown bags with wine bottles because you bring your own booze here.

The Town Shop Apartment Store, 1561 N. Wells, is a crowded shop with mugs, decorative toilet seats (yes, there is apparently a great need for such things), and mobiles hanging low enough to bump most foreheads.

Incidentally, Wells Street is named after Billy "Black Snake" Wells, who died in the Fort Dearborn 1812 Massacre. Billy was captured by the Miami Indians at age 12 and was raised by Little Turtle, chief of all the Miamis. He fought with the Indians in 1790, probably killed several white men and felt guilty about that. He then fought with the white men against the Indians and finally acted as a go-between for both sides.

Wells Street scene south of North Avenue

He showed up at Fort Dearborn because he was concerned about his niece, Rebekah, who had married Capt. Nathaniel Heald, who was in charge of the fort. During the massacre, Wells rode back to Rebekah with a message for his wife, "Tell her I died at my post, doing the best I could. There are seven red devils over there that I have killed." That's a lot to say with a bullet or arrow in your lung, but Wells is supposed to have said it.

Moments later his horse was wounded. It rolled on Wells, trapping him. Wells shot one more Indian and then held up his head and shouted, "Shoot away." The Indians took his advice, beheaded him and then ate his heart as a tribute to his bravery.

In 1870, Wells Street was so disreputable that folks thought it dishonored old Black Snake's name. So the street became Fifth Avenue. Then in 1918, despite the protests of businessmen who liked the idea of Chicago having a Fifth Avenue the way New York did, the name was changed back to Wells Street. In view of its current state, perhaps it's time to change it back to Fifth Avenue.

At 1517 N. Wells, you'll see Uno's Bizarre Bazaar, a huge, garish emporium which boasts that it is the "largest head shop in the Midwest." The place has 125 different brands of cigarette papers, which doesn't mean that Chicago has a lot of cowpokes who like to roll their own the way John Wayne did.

244

The farther south you walk on Wells the closer you get to the crime-ridden neighborhoods. Therefore, let's cross Wells at Schiller and retrace our steps but on the opposite (west) side of Wells Street.

You will stroll by Barbara's Bookstore, 1434 N. Wells Street, one of the original Old Town establishments. Barbara's has been here through the good times and the bad, the store is always a good place to stop, and we really should buy a book here just to encourage the kind of determination it takes to anchor the best intentions of this neighborhood.

You'll see Ripley's Believe It or Not Museum a little farther north at 1500 N. Wells. Here you can find the world's longest gum wrapper chain, the catacombs and even the world's largest hair ball (six pounds, 30 inches around). By now, if you have been walking through Chicago, you must know that the city has a fetish for being the best, the first, and the world's tallest or largest. Frankly, the world's largest hair ball is pushing the point to the extreme. Admission is $4.50 for adults and $2.50 for those 12 and under.

Nearby, the Crate and Barrel, another Wells Street veteran at 1510 N. Wells, sells candles, pots and baskets.

Continuing north, do stop in The Up Down Tobacco Shop, at 1550 N. Wells, just to smell the heady atmosphere, if nothing else. The owner, Mrs. Diana Gits, has a smokers paradise here and, even if you do not puff, you will appreciate the aromas here, especially of her sample pipe tobaccos. Each year she runs a pipe smoking contest, and she will proudly show you the world's largest humidor, a 40-foot storage space for cigars.

Zanie's, Cafe Azteca, and Old Town Ale House

Zanie's, at 1548 N. Wells, is one of Chicago's premier comedy night clubs. Many of the performers here are unknown at the moment, but most will shortly appear with Johnny Carson or David Letterman. If you haven't heard of the current stars of Zanie's, don't be put off. The standards here are very high, the comedy is always good, and you might just see someone just before he or she becomes a star.

When you get to Wells and North, turn left and go west to Cafe Azteca, at 215 W. North Ave. Every once in a while, the owner, Federico Camacho, plays marimba or guitar for the guests. If the weather permits, try to sit in the garden with the overhanging peach, pear, apple and jacaranda trees where the city seems far away even though Wells Street is on the other side of the wooden fence. Order the Mexican beer and try the kamoosh, which is Mexican pizza.

You'll find the Old Town Ale House at 219 W. North Avenue, home of some of the most bizarre people in Old Town. It's almost as if the Beat Generation beached here 25 years ago and never moved. The wall mural features faces of Ale House regulars. These regulars

Diana Gits, owner of Old Town's Up Down Pipe Shop, shows off a $5,000 Meerschaum pipe

include the dean of the writers of angry letters to local newspapers, a foot fetishist, Second City regulars, and a man who enjoys imitating Kate Hepburn.

Second City

Return to Wells Street and walk north. Second City, home of improvisational theater in Chicago, is at 1616 N. Wells. It is justly famed for helping the careers of Shelley Berman, Mike Nichols, Elaine May, Alan Arkin, Paul Sand, Severin Dardin, and Valerie Harper.

It is a little-known fact that after the regular shows (at 11 p.m. Sunday thru Thursday and 1 a.m. on Saturdays) you can watch the improvisations and pay no cover or minimum. If it is late and you feel like taking a chance, you will see future Second City revues gestating. Sometimes the skits fail, but after all they are making things up as they go along. More often than not, they succeed, wildly, with the audience and the actors discovering the humor in the situations as they develop. Later, the skits will enter the regular shows.

Before going on, do look across the street at the Walgreen's, where the first of the infamous tainted Tylenol capsules was bought in 1982 by Paula Prince, a flight attendant who died of the poison. Another poison capsule was bought at the Dominick's at 230 W. North, a half block away. Eventually, seven people were killed by the tylenol terrorist. These murders are still unsolved crimes.

More Walking and Shopping

Continue north, passing Piper's Alley, once the home of many small shops and restaurants and now nearly deserted.

Crown Books, at 1660 N. Wells, is part of a large chain of discount books. I am always amazed at the prices of hard-cover best-sellers here. This a good place to get that gift book you've been meaning to give a relative.

Continuing north, walk and marvel at the decorated doors on the townhouses here, the new antique-looking ironwork and the general feeling that we are not on the edge of a neighborhood in the midst of rehabilitation.

Coffee Corner, at 1700 N. Wells, is another place to go for the aromas. Here you will inhale the scent of freshly ground coffee mixed with the luscious deserts.

You'll next pass several small shops. A Joint Venture, 1704 N. Wells, is devoted to whimsical tchotchkes (I don't think anyone can spell that word or define it, but I'm pretty sure we all know what it means). The Design Source at 1710 N. Wells has old and new furniture and accessories which are not as expensive as they look.

Wells Street ends at Lincoln Avenue a diagonal street. Walk northwest on Lincoln for a couple of blocks, past this row of townhouses which has already been through renovation. Isn't it wonderful to see a neighborhood go from near slum to old fashioned charm?

This part of the walk takes you past one side of the Old town Triangle, which was originally known as the Cabbage Patch, although celery was the big local crop. Johnny "Tarzan" Weismuller went to school here.

Chicago radio soap opera actors once tended to live at Whiskey Point, 1852-56 N. Lincoln. This light and darker gray apartment building once housed the stars of "Backstage Wife" (the story of an

Iowa stenographer married to Broadway star Larry Noble), Oxy-dol's. "Ma Perkins," "The Romance of Helen Trent" (which proved that "romance can live on at 35 and even beyond"), "The Guiding Light" and "Jack Armstrong, All-American Boy."

Armitage-Lincoln Restaurants and Bars

If you continue this walk, you will shortly get to the corner of Armitage and Lincoln. There you will see the Ultimate Sports Bar and Grill, 356 W. Armitage with a basketball shooting lane, a boxing ring with dining tables inside the ropes, and lots of athletic memorabilia on the walls.

Just to the east, at 340 W. Armitage, is Geja's Cafe. Walk down a few steps to the tiny courtyard to enter Geja's, which is a fondue/wine/cheese bar with a tradition of having live flamenco guitarists performing for the customers. It is just the place for an intimate glass of wine with a very, very close friend.

If you continue strolling to the east, you'll find the Park West, a 750-seat nightclub at 322 W. Armitage, often voted the best place to see rock music in town. A porno movie house, which got into trouble after it played "Deep Throat," was once here. Today, the Park West features the best sound and light system in town, fine sight lines and a parade of acts who have just released their first album and are about to become superstars.

The Chicago Bears came to the Park West to record their 1985 "Super Bowl Shuffle" rap song.

Next, cross the street at Clark and return to Lincoln Avenue by walking along the south side of Armitage. You will pass Gamekeepers Taverne and Grill, which is across the street from the Ultimate Sports Bar. Gamekeepers is a singles bar, a place to meet someone who probably will alleviate a night's loneliness but may offer a lifetime of romance.

In 1986, Cosmopolitan magazine named Gamekeepers one of the "top ten bars in America" calling Gamekeeper's "a staggering success," and a "romantic meeting place" where "everybody looks great." That same issue had stories on "The Nonorgasmic Woman. What Is She Supposed to Do?" And a look at the possibility of loving him "in another life."

Take a left on Lincoln Avenue, retracing your steps back to Wells, only this time you are walking on the north side of Lincoln. Renalli's at 1925 N. Lincoln, has won some pizza contests, which is not easy to do. It is known for its outdoor cafe, where you can choose from a wide selection of beers and enjoy a pizza.

Continuing down the street past the Moveable Feast, at 1825 N. Lincoln, which features dozens of delicious sandwiches.

And this is a good spot to end the walk, unless you want to continue south on Wells to the Exit, at 1653 N. Wells, a punk bar. At one time, I lived nearby. It was frightening to drive home late on Saturday night and try to avoid the stoned, drunk Exit fans wandering about with their pink and green hair at 2 a.m. If that is the crowd you are yearning to find, dye your hair orange and slam into the Exit. Or just go home and rest a while.

23 ARMITAGE-HALSTED WALK

BAR CRAWL AND ANTIQUE SEARCH POTPOURRI

1. Old Town School of Folk Music
2. Gare St. Lazare
3. Cafe Ba-Ba-Reeba!
4. Grant's Tavern

Time: About an hour, less if you pass all the antique stores, more if you are a serious shopper or if you find a saloon you can call home.

To get there: The Ravenswood elevated train, which leaves from the Loop, stops at Armitage. The Number 8 Halsted bus will stop at Armitage and Halsted and you can walk a couple of blocks west to the elevated tracks to start the walk.

Overview of Armitage

This area has a little bit of everything. You might even want to take this walk twice, once during the day to stroll by the many shops and again at night when the bars are jumping.

Or you could take this walk at around 3 p.m. on a nice Saturday, as I once did, finding that everything was open and ready for business.

As with so much in Chicago, this area changed over the last few years, moving from one of the toughest places to one of the nicest. The area high school was once called Waller High, it was the home of many gangs. Once a student brought a carbine to school and took over the auditorium. Now part of Waller has become Lincoln Park Academy, the home of the program which puts some students on equal footing with the best minds of their age around the world.

The walk begins with a stroll to the east (the address numbers will be going down if you are heading in the right direction). Hibbeler's 1895 Restaurant, at 917 Armitage, features dishes of Alsace-Lorraine, an area in France. Quiche Lorraine is naturally on the menu.

Old Town School of Folk Music

The Old Town School of Folk Music, at 909 W. Armitage, is a must stop. If you think that folk music died when the Kingston Trio's record sales faltered, think again. It is alive and well in Chicago, and this school is vital for its preservation.

Such folk singers as Bonnie Koloc, John Prine and the late Steve Goodman learned guitar here. Goodman is known for writing the best train song ever, "The City of New Orleans," for writing a tribute to the Lincoln Park Towing Company, which protects many local parking lots by grabbing unwanted cars from the area; and for writing a perfect country song which combined mom, trucks, prison, dogs, the rain and many other elements.

The Old Town School of Folk Music is a great place to just visit for a while. There are always fascinating people hanging around there, the music you hear is sure good, and maybe the exprience will get you interested in that old banjo or guitar which has been gathering dust for years. Michael J. Miles, OT's program director, boasts, "I can send you home after a hour lesson, you would learn at least two chords and you would be able to play hundreds of songs, too many for anyone to know all the words to them!"

The school is interested in blue grass, blues, Hispanic and Eastern European music. It wants to preserve our heritage through music, and it does so through lessons, group sings, and festivals.

Just east of the school or to the right as you leave, Max's Music is named after the owner's Michael Bronner's father, who was a classi-

251

cal musician. It sells new and used guitars, amplifiers and other accessories.

Continue walking east, cross Fremont and enter the Gare St. Lazare, at 858 W. Armitage. There is a quiet, almost contemplative bar. Walk through it, towards the back to find a wonderful, hidden, comfortable French restaurant, which lists its daily specials on a large blackboard to the rear of the dining room. The wine selection is superb and the atmosphere is most romantic.

Turn Down Halsted

Next, continue walking east, to Halsted, passing Chewy's, a candy shop with chocolate-covered Gummy Bears, and Benton Hartt's, another candy shop with hand-dipped, chocolate-covered Oreos.

If you take a right and go south on Halsted, you will see the Manhandler Saloon, at 1948 N. Halsted, probably the most aptly named gay men's bar in town. Village Green is next door and it sells flowers and firewood. Or stop in Les Desserts for a croissant and coffee.

You will also see Women and Children First, at 1967 N. Halsted, a book store specializing in feminist publications. Even the greeting cards sold here are chosen from the feminist perspective and the owners, Ann Christopher and Linda Bubon, have a children's section devoted to anti-sexist books.

Returning to the corner of Armitage and Halsted, Gepperth's Market is an old-world, European-style grocery store with home-made sausages, fresh cornish game hens, and nitrite-free bacon. A sign there once read, "Just in time for mother's day—double-yolk eggs!"

Nick's, a popular local bar with a good juke box, is across the street from Gepperth's.

But we will continue walking north. Ringolevio, at 2001 N. Halsted, is a high-tech, unisex sportswear shop. Bellini, next door, is babyland for yuppies, with $700 cribs.

Across Halsted, there is The Store, a singles bar, and Expectations, for elegant maternity clothes.

The Beaumont Garden Cafe, at 2020 N. Halsted, does have a garden. Well, it's really an outdoor bar, usually under a tent in the back of the saloon. If the interior of Beaumont's is too loud (or if you are tired of brass, stained glass and instant antiques), the back beer garden is a bit quieter.

Cafe Ba-Ba-Reeba!

Cafe Ba-Ba-Reeba!, at 2024 N. Halsted, is a Spanish tapas bar, a concept which came to Chicago after success in New York, Houston, San Francisco and Los Angeles.

The theory goes that we have become a nation of "grazers," people who would rather "graze" at several light snacks throughout the day than sit down to a huge meal.

Tapas are Spanish appetizers which, legend says, were created when Spanish bar owners would give customers a piece of bread to cover the wine glass so flies wouldn't fall into the vino. The smarter saloon keepers would also put a piece of salty meat on the bread, making their patrons thirsty and producing more wine sales. Thus, a new group of appetizers were created.

Since Ba-ba-Reeba opened in December, 1985, Chicagoans have learned to enjoy little dishes with thinly sliced octopus, squid stuffed with ground squid, mussels marinated in vinaigrette, baked fennel, goat cheese tarts, grilled Spanish blood sausage, and clams in white wine sauce.

Continuing north, you will pass Aged Experience, an antique shop with chairs hanging from the ceiling.

Salamander, at 2040 N. Halsted, is a clothing store.

If you walk through a corridor to the rear of 2044 N. Halsted, you will discover a small French restaurant calles Les Plumes, which has peach walls, white table cloths and wood trim. Its cuisine is described as not as light as nouvelle and not as heavy as classic French cooking—the in-between French restaurant.

Passing the interesting clutter in the antique shop at 2044 N. Halsted, the Halsted St. Fish Market is at 2048 N. Halsted. Look up to see the bow of the S. S. Upper Deck sticking over the sidewalk. The restaurant claims it has "20 different varieties of fresh fish and shellfish" and the S. S. Upper Deck is a fine place for outdoor dining, weather permitting.

Finables is next door and this is a small shop with imported French linens, handrolled beeswax candles and expensive costume jewelry.

Cross Dickens to the Cafe Bernard, a French restaurant with fresh fish daily, with excellent onion soup and a variety of fine chicken dishes.

Continuing north, the American West Gallery specializes in native American art, and features Navajo pottery, drums and paintings of deserted buttes.

Nookie's Too, at 2114 N. Halsted, is a clean diner; while Contemporary Statements, at 2116 N. Halsted, is a greeting card store.

Kirin Garden, at 2122 N. Halsted, is a Mandarin and Szechwan restaurant near The Gap, a jeans store.

Grant's Tavern

Grant's Tavern, at 2138 N. Halsted, was praised by the *Chicago Tribune* for having "an extra-ordinary women's room." It also has a small pool table in the back and a magazine rack towards the front—

the rare indication that people who go to saloons might also read.

Continuing to move to the north, Saturday's Child, at 2144 N. Halsted, is a fine toy store, which has Greta Garbo and Carmen Miranda paper dolls. My Own Two Feet, at 2148 N. Halsted, is a kiddie shoe store where tiny, tiny baby shoes can cost $30.

Bun Stuffers, at 2150 N. Halsted, can make a hamburger 21,090 different ways. Jerry Karp, the co-owner, explained that they have three different buns, 10 ingredients, and 38 stuffings (help yourself from the stuffing bar), resulting in the huge number of statistical combinations. They can make hamburgers from lamb, veal, chicken, turkey, beef, salmon, tuna, cheese and vegetables. Wouldn't the hamburger then be called a tuna-burger?

Glascott's, at 2158 N. Halsted, is a long, open, friendly singles bar.

Next, cross Webster to the east side of the street and enter Carlucci, 2215 H. Halsted, an excellent Italian restaurant in a converted auto body shop. Notice the beautiful entranceway, which looks like old marble and isn't. This restaurant has a garden which is open in the summer.

Continue walking north, noticing the different doors and doorways, the stained glass and the wrought-iron railings on the homes here. The neighborhood has been recently rehabilitated.

There is a lot at the corner of Belden and Halsted which is devoted to gardens. This is worth noting, because real estate prices in this neighborhood have gone up and still there is room for gardens. For now.

Just after you pass a sign indicating DePaul University, you will reach Fullerton, Halsted and Clark.

This ends the walk and you can take the number 11, Lincoln Avenue, bus downtown or walk left (west) a few blocks to the elevated station for a quick trip to the Loop.

However, if you wish to continue, the North and the South Lincoln Avenue Pub Crawls begin at this corner.

24 SOUTH LINCOLN AVENUE PUB CRAWL

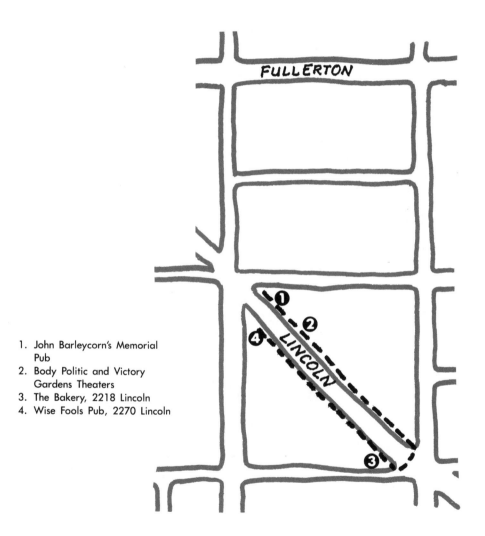

1. John Barleycorn's Memorial Pub
2. Body Politic and Victory Gardens Theaters
3. The Bakery, 2218 Lincoln
4. Wise Fools Pub, 2270 Lincoln

Time: An entire evening. Some people make this walk their life's work, but that's a bit excessive.
To get there: Take the CTA subway to Fullerton and walk east to Lincoln, a diagonal street. By car, take Lake Shore Drive to

Fullerton, then west to Lincoln and circle the blocks for about an hour before finding a parking space.

John Barleycorn and Redamaks

Lincoln Avenue is the place to go for a mellow drink. It's the lively street Wells Street once was, and it's the place young Chicago goes to for a good time.

This pub crawl begins at Fullerton and Lincoln. Lincoln is a diagonal street, so the directions may seem a little complicated. Walk southeast on the east side of the street past the hospital until you reach the John Barleycorn Memorial Pub, at 658 W. Belden. What a bar!

Classical music constantly plays for the patrons. A screen on one wall reflects Barleycorn's collection of art slides. Another wall boats a screen where silent film comedies may be seen. There's Miller's light and dark, Bass Ale, Guinness Stout and Heineken's on draught, model boats and moose head on the walls, and the hamburgers are good! A tavern for the true aficionado of fine boozy ambience.

The Read Barron (sic), at 2265 N. Lincoln, is a bar which seems to be losing energy. Once it offered a 22-piece swing band in a back room which had seats for only 54 people. Now, on some Saturday nights, it is nearly empty, although there are times when local rugby teams go there to drink, meaning that you will see a large group of stripe-shirted, rowdy males, proud of their wounds, beer bottles in hand hooting continuously at passing females.

Redamaks, at 2263 N. Lincoln, is an extension of a great little hamburger joint in southwestern Michigan (the original Redamaks has expanded so much that it can no longer be called "little"). The Chicago incarnation favors high tech glitz rather than stuffed deer heads in the decor.

At one time, the Oxford Pub was here and it was the home of the wildest late-night drinking in town. The place jumped from 2 to 4 a.m. It also sponsored something called "coffin races" in the spring. Alas, it could not outrace the grasp of the tax man, and so it disappeared.

But Redamaks is no place to mourn the passing of the old. It offers fine hamburgers and fast service, although some have commented that nearly everything on the menu seems to be deep fried. Once, a waitress was asked if the soup was "deep fried."

Body Politic and Victory Gardens Theaters

The Body Politic and Victory Gardens Theaters, at 2261 N. Lincoln, usually have three productions going on at once. These off-loop

256

Redamaks and Body Politic and Victory Gardens Theaters

theaters will experiment, try new playwrights, discover new actors and actresses, and succeed. Stop by and ask about the current plays, and then go—you will not see a bad production.

These two theaters have been called the soul of Lincoln Avenue. It is amazing how important a theater can be. People who attend theaters want dinner close by and are often willing to go out for a snack or a drink after the curtain, meaning that a theater keeps the street alive through the night.

The theaters also sponsor the Lincoln Avenue Street Fair in early summer, when there is food, music, performances and the owner of a local bar dressed in his huge bunny costume selling carrots.

Look up at 2251 N. Lincoln. There is the front half of a '50s Chevrolet sticking out of the wall above you indicating that you are at Jukebox Saturday Night. Years ago, this was a cowboy bar with the first mechanical bull in Chicago. Today you can enter a time warp, with disc jockeys playing '50s tunes, a large and active dance floor and walls decorated with '50s rock memorabilia. If you are a guy, slick the back of your hair so it looks like a duck's behind. If you are a gal, wear those big skirts with fat, cinch belts, and dance to "It's My Party and I'll Cry If I Want To" or "The Duke of Earl."

Nearby, we can find the 2350 Pub, which is actually at 2249 N. Lincoln. It carries this name because once upon a time it was a 2350 N. Clark St. There is a friendly bar, with the required amount of

A '50s Chevy sticks out of the wall at Jukebox Saturday Night

wood. Just beyond the bar area there is a restaurant which serves a delicious onion ring loaf.

Continue south to the Drake-Braithwaite Funeral Home, 2221 Lincoln where the seven victims of the St. Valentine's Day Massacre of 1929 were taken.

Police asked the only survivor of the Massacre, Frank Gusenberg, who shot him. Before he died, Gusenberg said, "Nobody shot me," either a tribute to the gangland code of silence or a terribly mistaken diagnosis on his part. Later, in the Drake-Braithwaite Funeral Home, both Mrs. Lucille Gusenberg and Mrs. Ruth Gusenberg arrived, claiming to be Gusenberg's wife. Lucy and Ruth had many fond memories to share.

The Bakery

Cross Lincoln Avenue and notice The Bakery, 2218 Lincoln, named as a Holiday Magazine award winning restaurant every year—save one—since 1964, and voted one of Chicago's Top 10 restaurants. Try

Chef Louis Szathmary's excellent duck with cherry sauce or his beef Wellingtion. Call 472-6942 for reservations. Or stop by, make a reservation, continue the walk and come back later for dinner.

Chef Louis is one of the gentlemen who civilizes Chicago by his presence. And he's got a thousand stories. Ask him about the time he cornered the market on Illinois champagne by buying the entire stock of a bankrupt winery in Monee, Illinois. Ask him about the Chicago chefs who invented shrimp De Jonghe or crepes suzette, two dishes created closer to State Street than to the Champs Elysses. Ask him why the Bridgeport neighborhood of Chicago is named after Bridgeport, Connecticut. And ask him about one early owner of the Playboy Mansion, who put human beings and horses on the black-and-white marble squares of the ballroom and played chess.

Continue walking, staggering or leaning north.

Sterch's

In the land of singles bars and glitzy hamburger joints, you will find something unique at 2238 N. Lincoln Avenue. Sterch's is a sleazy, delightful neighborhood saloon owned by Bob Smerch, who has said that he was once a carnival operator, a Paraguayan paratrooper, a lumberjack, art gallery owner and medical researcher working on rabbits (which may be why he dresses like a bunny for the street fair).

Back in 1971, this was The Volstead Act, a bar suffering from a "personality disorder," according to Smerch because it was a combination Indonesian restaurant, chess club and "artsy-fartsy lounge." After he bought the place, he corrected that problem by carefully creating a sleazy, friendly place.

Smerch is one of the great talkers in Chicago, a guy who will show you "the best invisible-deck card trick in the universe," and a proprietor who owns "the last stronghold of the Bohemian, beatnik and mad dog Chicago drinkers," according to Dennis McCarthy's "The Great Chicago Bar & Saloon Guide." We have a few more blocks to go before we stop, although the friendly confines of Sterch's may be attractive enough to end the walk right there.

More Shops, Sandwiches, and Muffins

Continuing north, we pass an area of small shops which tend to change owners and intent quite frequently. A few years ago something called "Space Shoes" was here and, after making a plaster cast of your foot, they would create the shoe just for you. They are gone now, replaced by Natural Selection, at 2258 N. Lincoln, a gift shop.

The Potbelly Sandwich Works, at 2264 N. Lincoln, offers vegetarian submarine sandwiches, a free juke box sometimes playing "When a Man Loves a Woman" by Percy Sledge and chocolate chip cookies which rival Mrs. Field's.

Live performance at Wise Fools Pub

The Wise Fools Pub, 2270 N. Lincoln, is a blues and jazz club with a long bar for drinking and a comfortable room for listening.

Jerry's, at the corner of Orchard and Lincoln, was once a sleepy neighborhood bar. Today it is a video-disco bar in a triangular building. It's got large windows facing the street making it easy to look inside to see if this is the sort of place you find inviting.

The last sight on the walk is the White Elephant Resale Shop, at the corners of Lincoln, Halsted and Fullerton. It's probably closed if you are on a night-time pub crawl, but look in the window. Perhaps you will see just the collapsible top hat you need for $25.

If you have stopped at each of the places mentioned during this pub crawl for a drink or two, it is probably time to stagger home and lie down. If not, you may want to go back and review some of your favorite spots.

25 NORTH LINCOLN AVENUE PUB CRAWL

1. Three-Penny Cinema
2. Red Lion Pub
3. Holstein's
4. Apollo Theatre
5. Biograph Theater

Time: Come on now, be reasonable. How long will it take you to drink enough to call it a night and then crawl (not drive!) home? Let's say an hour for speed drinkers and until dawn tomorrow for people who like things to build slowly.

To get there: The CTA subway stops at Fullerton. In addition the Number 74 Fullerton bus plies the street. If you use the subway, get off at Fullerton and walk east a couple of blocks. By car, take Lake Shore Drive to Fullerton, go west to Lincoln and then good luck in finding a place to park. This is one of Chicago's most congested neighborhoods. If you live here long enough, you might inherit a parking space when and if your best friend dies. Once you get a parking space, immediately convert it into a condominium.

North to Three-Penny Cinema

The area north of Fullerton along Lincoln Avenue is supposed to be more relaxed than the area south of Fullerton. At least, that's what its denizens say.

It just might be that you have to live there to understand the subtle differences.

Suffice it to say that this is the shortest walk in distance because once you are north of Fullerton you'll tend to stay there. It's an interesting couple of blocks.

This walk begins at the intersection of Lincoln, Fullerton and Halsted. Lincoln is the diagonal street and you want to be on the west side of Lincoln, heading north. You know you are going in the right direction if you are walking past the Seminary Restaurant, which was recently remodeled, with a few ferns and fixtures added, bringing this restaurant up to mediocrity, which is a vast improvement from what it was before.

The Three-Penny Cinema, at 2424 N. Lincoln, has had a checkered history, beginning life as an avant-garde movie house which often showed radical, politically conscious films. Later it became an x-rated film house, meaning that some people got angrier at the theater then than when it was involved in politics, which made folks angry enough. Now, although in need of remodeling, it has settled down, showing an occasional cult film and offering first and second run attractions.

Continue going north. Uncle Dan's Army Navy Surplus Store is the Lincoln Park camouflage headquarters.

Red Lion Pub

The Red Lion Pub, at 2446 N. Lincoln, is a fine place for shepherd's pie, steak and kidney pie, scones, fish and chips, and beer. John Cordwell, the owner, is central casting's idea of a British gentleman, generally walking about with an ascot, politely kissing the ladies, and happily telling stories about Nigeria, World War II and his first wife.

Cordwell insists that this is a "pub" and not a tavern, meaning that it is a place for people to talk to each other. Sort of a neighborhood living room, except that it has a wonderful deck out back.

John is chairman of the board of one of the city's top architectural firms, Solomon, Cordwell, Buenz & Assoc. Inc. But, when it came time to create a "pub," Cordwell claimed that "it was designed to look as if an architect had nothing to do with it."

For a while, the Commonwealth Club met here. It was a chance for local Englishmen to tell dirty stories to each other. Then, women demanded to join, so the name was changed to the Red Lion Club, which meets once a month so men AND women can tell dirty stories to each other.

Books, Folk Music, and Dancing

Continue north, stopping at Guild Books, 2456 N. Lincoln, which has a knowledgeable staff, and a fine selection of periodicals. Many authors stop here to autograph their books.

Holstein's, 2464 N. Lincoln, is the mecca for folk music. If you think it died some time back in the '60s, you are wrong. It is alive and well here, where banjos and string guitars still accompany the performers. Be sure to tell one of the owners, Ed Holstein, how good he looks. He lost over 100 pounds in the last few years. Fred, his brother, is the best leader of a group sing in America. He also attended the same high school I did and had the same difficulties with the music appreciation teacher, but he overcame them to become a thoroughly professional folk singer.

The Earl's Pub, at 2470, was formerly Somebody Else's Troubles, but in either guise it is a warm, friendly bar which also features entertainment.

Jackie's at 2478 N. Lincoln, is a posh little French restaurant. The Lincoln Avenue Deli, at 2526 N. Lincoln, offers good bagels.

The Latin Village Supper Club, 2528 N. Lincoln, has great salsa music. There is a Latin menu, and a well-dressed crowd of people who come to dance. The place to go to refresh your memory of the cha-cha.

Apollo Theatre, Blues, and Used Books

If you walk a little further, nearly to the elevated tracks, you will find the Apollo Theatre, at 2540 N. Lincoln. "Pump Boys and Dinettes" was the long, long running attraction here and it may very well still be there when you read this book. It's a delightful collection of country songs performed by supposed gas station attendants (pump boys) and waitresses (dinettes).

Next, cross the street and retrace your steps. Irish Eyes, at 2519 N. Lincoln, has a dart room, and Irish entertainment without cover or minimum on weekends. No, you cannot go from the cha-cha at the Latin Village to the jig at Irish Eyes without some refreshment in between.

Lilly's, at 2513 N. Lincoln, is one of the best blues bars in the city. Especially on weekends, this is the place to go to hear the men who made the blues. Go here if you want to hear what music was like before everyone plugged in and got amplified.

You will next walk by a series of book stores. Children's Bookstore, at 2464 N. Lincoln, has story telling for children on Saturdays. J. L. Clark's Bookstore, at 2463 N. Lincoln, offers used books.

But the very best used book store in the city, in my estimation, is Booksellers Row, at 2445 N. Lincoln, where all the books are in fine shape, where just the book you have wanted for years can be located and where, apparently, the people who work there have also read every book ever written.

After finding just the book you've been looking for for years, continue south. Vie de France, at 2441 N. Lincoln, is a clean, bright cafe which sometimes has problems. Once I ordered a bottle of white wine, but I was told that there was only one bottle left, that it had to be apportioned out to all the customers that night and that any one customer could only order one glass. It is amusing to think of a French restaurant facing an entire evening with but one bottle of white wine, which had to be rationed. It was like Humphrey Bogart in the film "Sahara" with only one canteen of chablis for the entire tank crew.

Biograph Theater

You will next pass the Biograph Theater, at 2433 N. Lincoln, which is actually three movie theaters—the Biograph, Roxy and Ritz Theaters, showing some of the best foreign or art films around. Check it out. Chances are (1) you may not have heard of the movies being offered and (2) they will be excellent.

Gangster history buffs will recall that the Biograph was the place where John Dillinger was shot. The notorious "Lady in Red" had betrayed him to federal authorities and at 10:40 p.m., July 22, 1934, after watching "Manhattan Melodrama," Dillinger stepped into a 16-man ambush. They say that the seat in which he sat on that night is painted silver.

But the commemorations of that bloody evening do not stop with a mere seat. Towards the south end of the theater entrance there is a sign stating, "This property has been placed on the national register of historic places by the United States Department of the Interior."

Next walk past a couple of stores to Fiesta Mexicana, at 2423 N. Lincoln. Do walk through the restaurant to the patio, with its green, white and red umbrellas.

This ends the North Lincoln Avenue pub crawl, unless you want to continue past the little, triangular park to the south of Fiesta Mexicana and buy a newspaper or a magazine from the well-stocked newsstand there.

Or you might go back to one of the folk-song or blues bars you passed to catch an act that seemed intriguing.

Biograph Theater—art films where John Dillinger was shot

ON THE ALMOST WILD SIDE

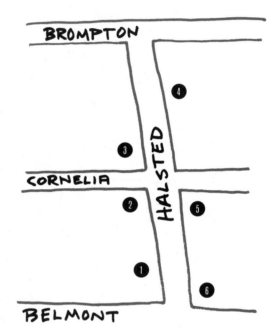

1. Pumpkin Patch Antiques
2. Pergolisi Coffee House
3. Goodies
4. The LARC and The Hawk
5. Chicago Diner
6. Helmand Restaurant

Time: About one hour, more if you stop to eat.
To get there: The number 77 Belmont and the number 8 Halsted CTA buses each stop at Belmont and Halsted. The Howard elevated trains stop at Belmont about three blocks west of Halsted. Just leave the train station and take a right, heading towards the Lake. If you are driving, get off the Outer Drive at Belmont and go west to Halsted. Parking will probably be a problem because this is a most congested neighborhood.

Antiques, Health Food, and a Coffee House

Four years ago, this North Halsted walk was not included in a rewrite of this book because there wasn't enough there. But that's changed. A walk along N. Halsted Street today is a stroll through an area that is just becoming. We're not quite sure what it is becoming, and perhaps the neighborhood itself isn't sure. But whatever it is, it's fascinating, energetic, changing and fun with dozens of antique stores, silly odds and ends stores, and a friendly group of shop keepers and restaurant owners.

There is a Chicago feel to the area, with its profusion of ethnic restaurants, vintage clothing shops and gay bars attracted to the street because of the low rents.

Begin on the west side of Halsted at Belmont and walk north past several sure-to-be rehabbed three flats. The Pumpkin Patch, at 3250 N. Halsted, is the first of several antique stores you'll pass. Gary Culler, the owner, claimed that his Pumpkin Patch was created years before the cabbage patch kids came along. He says he probably has the largest collection for sale of royal Bayreuth China in the city. The brightly colored cream pitchers and sugar bowls are on the back wall.

The giant panda holding a bright, red heart sitting on a chair near the front of the store was not for sale. Gary found it and was waiting for a child to reclaim it. Otherwise, it was destined to join his personal panda bear collection at home.

Continue strolling north, walking past Tony DiFiglio's Antiques, at 3324 N. Halsted, with its selection of silver jewelry. Nookies Tree, at Halsted and Buckingham, is a bright clean place for lunch.

The Boomerang, 3352 N. Halsted, with its distinctive blue and peach sign, has apparently decided to stop time in the '50s and offers furnishings from that era.

The Bread Shop, in the brown building at 3400 N. Halsted, has health food pizza by the slice, meatless stew and, of course, over 20 kinds of fresh-baked bread. It also has hot vegetarian meals to go, something not easy to find if you are in the market for such food.

The Pergolisi Coffee House and Art Gallery, 3404 N. Halsted, is a survivor and throwback to the great coffeehouse days of the '60s, when there was a profusion of such places and when they became the ideal shelters for starving poets and folk singers. The Pergolisi is the perfect place to go to read a newspaper and to get upset about where the world is going.

Raymond's Antiques, 3418 N. Halsted, had a selection of old postcards for fun browsing.

Used Jewelry, Whoopee Cushions, and more Antiques

The 3434 (Halsted) Shop claims to specialize in "20th Century

Design. The unique, the good, the bad and the ugly." That about covers it.

The Brokerage, at 3448 Halsted, sells lots of jewelry to this book's researcher, Donna Neuwirth, who noted that each time she has been in the shop someone is bringing in new items for resale. But be careful, even the graceful Donna says, "I feel like a bull in a China shop here."

Next walk to Goodies, with the black and white striped awning at 3450 Halsted, for goodies. Where else can you go to find rubber vomit, whoopee cushions, beanies with propellors on them, wind-up Godzillas, glasses with eyeballs on springs, or a selection glasses with noses and mustaches attached? It is the store of your mis-spent youth, the place where every small prize in all the gumball machines in history are sold.

The owners admit that the store is a collecting hobby which "just got out of hand." Now they buy stuff that has been languishing in warehouses and old department stores for the last four decades or so and then sell it to those of us who have a silly streak a mile wide. Come on now, how long has it been since you stuck your fingers into "Chinese handcuffs," that tube of paper which refused to release you as long as you were pulling in opposite directions but would relent the moment you relaxed or moved towards your partner-in-silliness?

At 3458 N. Halsted, you will find Christopher Street, a gay bar and one of several in this neighborhood.

Walk one more block, past the European car repair shop, to Brompton, then cross the street to the east side and retrace your steps back to Belmont. You'll see the Bankok Restaurant at Brompton and Halsted, featuring an all-you-can-eat buffet of Thai food for under $8.

Las Mananitas, a Mexican restaurant, is next door. It is a continuing pleasure to marvel at the juxtaposition of foods and nationalities in Chicago neighborhoods—a Thai restaurant sharing a wall with a Mexican restaurant. Try the Bohemia beer in Las Mananitas.

When you stop by Flashy Trash, at 3521 N. Halsted, ask for the always energetic owner, Harold Mandel, a former actor who now sells antique lingerie. He has created the one-stop shop for girls (and, in this neighborhood, boys) who want to dress like Madonna. Mandel, who talks faster than a machine gun shoots, will proudly show you his antique watches, proclaim that in the future he will offer more "never worn" clothes and take you on a whirlwind tour of his shop.

J. Russell Andrews Antiques, at 3519 N. Halsted, is the place to go for rhinestone jewelry. He should know because he is the past president of the Oriental Arts Society of Chicago. He began his business about three years ago, buying 15 pieces of jewelry and selling 12 of them in one weekend. Since then, Andrews has offered designer pieces by Schiaparelli, Hattie Carnegie and Kenneth Jay Lane. He has rhinestone earrings resembling chandeliers.

Experts say that, when considering rhinestones, remember that only $15 to $20 separates the best from the cheap and look for hand-set stones in pronged settings. (I must admit that I wouldn't know hand-set stones if they jumped at me, but I am told that is what any rhinestone aficionado should notice.)

The LARC and The Hawk, at 3452 N. Halsted, are actually two antique shops in the same space. LARC, standing for the Lakeview Antique Resale Center, is owned by Bill Wilson and Rick Vacek, who specialize in rhinestone jewelry and crystal. They were repairing some jewelry for the Governor when we last stopped by. The Hawk is the nickname of Mark Sanders and it is also his name when he publishes poetry. In fact, his half of the store supports his poetry habit. He claims to have the largest selection of silver jewelry on North Halsted.

Wheel and Deal, at 3515 Halsted, is a store which sells the strangest of the strange. In fact, its motto is "we like the unusual."

The owners, Kalon, formerly a clerk in a book store, and her husband, Steve Sloan, a carpenter, were selling three gigantic (five times life size) kings' heads from the Adventureland amusement park when we last visited Wheel and Deal. The shop features toys for collectors, a gold Martian head which opens into a bar, and shelves of "black Americana" with statues of black children and Aunt Jemimas in embarrassingly cute poses.

As we left, Kalon said, "We spend our lives shopping." They do.

At the corner of Cornelia and Halsted, take a quick left and walk about 20 yards east to Cornelia's, which sometimes has a sidewalk cafe, which always has flowers in the boxes out front and which is as clean and bright as any restaurant in town. It is only open during the day on Sundays for brunch, otherwise you have to wait until 5 p.m. for cocktails and American nouvelle cuisine featuring fresh fish, steaks and crab.

The Roan Galleries, at 3457 Halsted, features the considerable personality of Tony Roan, the owner, who left Portugal to travel and came to Chicago to live. In addition to antique furniture, look at the ceremonial masks which mysteriously decorate several walls of his crowded shop. Some seem friendly. Many glower.

When you stop by Hobby Heaven, at 3451 Halsted, ask the owner, Doris Kaye, about how Halsted street has changed over the years. She has lived above her shop since 1947 and she will tell you that only four or five years ago this area was "a dead street." Then she will map the changes, "When I bought this building, the neighborhood was German and Polish, then it went hillbilly, then Puerto Rican and now it's gay." There is no telling what group will come through next, although Doris, with her French and Chippewa Indian Heritage, will remain.

She sells kits for embroidery, decoupage, needlepoint, beading, rug hooking and so on. And she's glad to get the passerby started in any of those crafts and more.

The owners of Formerly Yours Antiques, at 3443 Halsted, were standing around one day a few years ago trying to figure out how they could avoid working for someone else. At that moment, a man from Colorado, who did not leave so much as his name or forwarding address, came up to Ronald Holzman and Jamie Conly, and began to lecture them on how to become antique furniture brokers. They never saw the stranger again, but from that conversation, this antique store was born. Visit the store but avoid conversations with strangers from Colorado unless you want to change your life.

Cheap Eats, Expensive Eats

The "best of the cheap eats," according to the *Chicago Tribune*, can be found at the Chicago Diner, 3411 Halsted, which is decorated to look like a neon-lit diner from the '50s with an '80s twist. This is purely a vegetarian restaurant with the avowed intention of weaning all of us from from red meat to white (chicken, turkey) to fish and finally to no meat at all. The staff does not preach, although the restaurant is capable of meeting the needs of all the various vegetarians in our midst—those that eat dairy foods and those who do not, those who eat sugar and those who do not.

The men's room, at 3359 N. Halsted, is another bar which primarily caters to gays, although anyone of any sexual persuasion is welcome.

The Gallimaufry Gallery, at 3351 Halsted, takes its name from a Shakespearean word meaning a mixture of things. Michael and Pat Merkle have had this shop for 11 years, but kept their day jobs for seven of those 11 years. They feature handmade items, especially earrings.

Aunt Edie's Glass, at 3339 Halsted, has Depression era glass. It's a place I enjoy looking at from the outside, but will send someone less clumsy inside to report on the delicate glass there.

If you have walked enough and want a quiet place to sit and eat, try Wicklines, at 3335 Halsted, where the muffins are delicious, where the classical music plays in the background, and where the stained-glass and wood decor is restful. This restaurant does not have a liquor license, so either bring your own wine or dash across the street

270

to the nearest bar-liquor store for the proper accompaniment to your fresh quiche.

Past the Sherwin-Williams Paint Store, you will next see, Yoshi's Cafe, at 3257 N. Halsted, a Japanese restaurant with a French flavor and prices to match—main courses are in the $16 to $17 range.

Walk another block and a half to the large green awning at Belmont and Halsted. This is the Helmand Restaurant, which features Afgan food, meaning you can try aushak, mantwo, or bowlawni. Don't be frightened just because you do not know what those dishes are. The prices are reasonable, the staff is friendly and they will explain their menu.

The food is delicious, if you like mild, lightly spiced curries. By all means try the eggplant appetizer which is outstanding. And, while you eat, reflect on the long, long trek it must have taken to come all the way from Afganistan to Belmont and Halsted.

Also, think about this vital, constantly changing neighborhood. Some of the restaurants and stores mentioned above may be gone when you visit, but others will replace them.

Here's hoping that you either find the antique of your dreams, the beloved whoopee cushion of your past or the ethnic food discovery you've been wanting.

Architecture, Museums, Sightseeing

Adler Planetarium, 155
Alta Vista, 195-96
Apparel Center, 90
Archbishop's Residence, 110
Art Institute, 8-10
Auditorium Theatre, 5-6

Balbo Column, 182
Beaubein Court, 15
Bridgeport, 212
Brookfield Zoo, 169-77
Buckingham Fountain, 2

Calder, Alexander, *Flamingo* stabile, 72
Carl Schurz High School, 193
Central District Filtration Plant, 180
Chagall, Marc, *Les Quatre Saisons* mosaic, 74
Charnley House, 106
Chicago Board of Trade, 69
Chicago Cubs, 11, 23, 193-94
Chicago Fire, 34-35
Chicago Fire Academy, 204
Chicago Historical Society, 116
Chicago Loop Synagogue, 76
Chicago Mercantile Exchange, 87
Chicago Metropolitan Correctional Center, 70
Chicago Public Library Cultural Center, 11
Chicago Sun-Times, 20
Chicago Temple Building, 76
Chicago Theological Seminary, 141
Chicago White Sox, 210
Chinatown, 212-13
Christ of the Loop, 76

Civic Opera House, 87-88
Coliseum, 206
Columbia College, 4
Comiskey Park, 210
Continental Illinois Bank and Trust, 70
Couch Mausoleum, 118
Court of the Golden Hands, 105
Court Theater, 145
Crosby's Opera House, 61

Daley, Richard J., Center, 78; house in Bridgeport, 211-12
Dearborn Street Station, 202
Diversey Harbor, 184
Doane Observatory, 157
Dubuffet, Jean, *Monument with Standing Beast* sculpture, 79

Everleigh House, 213

Farm in the Zoo, 118
Federal Government Center, 72
Field Museum, 148
Fine Arts Building, 7
First National Bank Plaza, 74
Fisher Building, 72
Fourth Presbyterian Church, 40

Gage Building, 10
Getty Tomb, 198
Glessner House, 207-08
Graceland Cemetery, 196-98
Grant Park, 2-3

Heald Square, 67
Holy Name Cathedral, 31
Hull House, 204
Hutchinson Street, 200

Illinois Center, 17
Illinois Institute of Technology, 209-10
International House, 138

John Hancock Center, 37

Karoll Building, 60
Kimball House, 207

Lane Technical High School, 193
Latin School, 117
Lincoln Park Conservatory, 124
Lincoln Park Zoo, 120
Logan Square, 193
Luxor Baths, 192

Madlener House, 112
Mandel Building, 25
Manhattan Building, 72
Marina City, 83
Marquette Building, 73
McCormick Place, 215-16
Medinah Temple, 228
Meigs Field, 155, 182
Merchandise Mart, 90
Miro, Juan, sculpture, 78
Monadnock Building, 72
Moore, Henry, *Nuclear Energy* sculpture, 145
Morton Thiokol Building, 88-89
Museum of Contemporary Art, 26-27
Museum of Science and Industry, 158-68

Navy Pier, 181-82

Oak Park, 125-35
Oak Street Beach, 180
Oldenberg, Claes, *Batcolumn* sculpture, 76
Orchestra Hall, 8
Oriental Institute, 141

Patterson-McCormick Mansion, 109
Peace Museum, 100
Petrillo Bandshell, 2
Picasso, sculpture, 78
Playboy Mansion, 112
Printers Row, 203
Prudential Building, 15

Quigley Preparatory Seminary North, 39

Railway Exchange
Building, 7
Randolph Street Gallery,
189
Regenstein Library, 143
Renaissance Society, 142
Ripley's Believe It or Not
Museum, 245
River City, 203
Robie House, 141
Rockefeller Chapel, 140
Rookery, 70
Roosevelt University, 7

St. Peter's Church and
Friary, 76
Sears Tower, 85-87
Second Presbyterian
Church, 209
Shedd Aquarium, 152
Soldier Field, 216
Spertus Museum of
Judaica, 4
Standard Oil Building, 15
State of Illinois Center,
79-80
Stock Yards Gate, 212
Streeterville Plaza, 38

Totem Pole in Lincoln
Park, 184
Tree Studios, 228-29
Tribune Tower, 24-25

Unity Building, 78
Unity Temple, 134
University of Chicago,
136-46
University of Illinois at
Chicago, 206

Water Tower, 33-35
Waveland Golf Course,
186
WBBM-AM-TV, 27
WFMT, 17
WGN-TV, 193
Wicker Park, 192
Widow Clarke House, 209
WLS-TV, 65
WMAQ-AM-TV, 90
Wolf Point, 89
Wright, Frank Lloyd,
Home and Studio,

130-33; and architecture
in Oak Park, 125-35
Wrigley Building, 20
Wrigley Field, 193

Restaurants, Bars, Hotels

Allerton Hotel, 30
Acorn on Oak, 53
Ambassador West and
East Hotels, 112
Americana Congress
Hotel, 4-5
Arnie's, 219-20
Astor Tower Hotel, 104

Bagel Nosh, 218
Bakery, 258
Beaumont Garden Cafe,
252
Biggs, 223
Billy Goat Tavern, 23
Bootleggers, 222
Bread Shop, 267
Brehon Pub, 233
Bun Stuffers, 254

Cafe Azteca, 245
Cafe Ba-Ba-Reeba, 252
Cafe Bernard, 253
Cafe Jasper, 228
Cape Cod Room, 40
Carlucci, 254
Carson's for Ribs, 233
Charlie Chaing's, 226
Chez Paul, 227-28
Chicago Chop House, 230

Chicago Diner, 270
Christopher Street, 268
Ciel Bleu, 42
Conrad Hilton Hotel, 3
Cornelia's, 269
Courtyards of Plaka, 237

Deli on Dearborn, 203
Dianna's Opaa, 239
Ditka's, 233
Dixie Bar and Grill, 234

Don Roth's River Plaza
Restaurant, 22
Drake Hotel, 40

Earl's Pub, 263
Ed Debevic's, 232
Edwardo's Pizza, 223
Eliot's Nesst, 219
Exit, 249

Gamekeepers Tavern and
Grill, 248
Gare St. Lazare, 252
Geja's Cafe, 248
Gingerman, 222
Gino's East, 31
Glascott's, 254
Grant's Tavern, 253
Greek Islands, 240
Green Door Tavern, 100
Guadalaharry's, 219

Halsted Street Fish
Market, 253
Hard Rock Cafe, 230
Harry's Cafe, 219
Helmand Restaurant, 271
Holstein's, 263
Hotel Continental, 26
Hotsie Totsie Yacht Club
and Bait Shop, 224
Houlihan's Bar and
Restaurant, 223
Howard's Knight Tap, 227
Hunan Palace, 221
Hyatt Regency Hotel, 18

Italian Village, 74
It's Greek to Me, 239

Jackie's, 263
Jerry's, 260
John Barleycorn Memorial
Pub, 256
Jukebox Saturday Night,
257

Kirin Garden, 253
Knickerbocker Hotel, 40
Kronie's, 219

Las Mananitas, 268
Latin Village Supper Club,
263

La Tour Restaurant, 33
Lawry's, 28, 227
Lenox Restaurant, 228
Le Petit Cafe, 222
Les Plumes, 253
Lilly's, 263
Limelight, 229-30
Lino's Ristorante, 233
Lodge, 222

Manhandler Saloon, 252
Maple Street Pier, 221
Maxim's Restaurant, 104
Mayfair Regent Hotel, 41
Medici, 146
Melvin's, 221
Metropolis Cafe, 243
Mirabell Restaurant, 193
Moe's Deli, 228
Moonraker, 203
Morton's Steak House, 221
Mother's, 223
Moveable Feast, 248

Nick's, 252
Ninety-Fifth, 37
Nookie's Too, 253

Oak Tree, 49
Ohba, 228
Old Town Ale House, 245

Palmer House, 56-58
Park Hyatt Hotel, 33
Parthenon, 238
Pat Harrah's, 221
Pergolisi Coffee House
    and Art Gallery, 267
Pigouts, 193
Pizzeria Uno and Due, 228
P.O.E.T.S., 221
Potbelly Sandwich Works,
    259
P.S. Chicago, 224
Pump Room, 112

Raccoon Club, 235
Ranalli's, 248
Ranalli's Off Rush, 223
Read Barron, 256
Redamaks, 256
Red Lion Pub, 262
Riccardo's, 22

Richmont Hotel, 226
Ristorante Zio, 221
Ritz Carlton, 36-37
Roditys, 239
Rookery, 224

Sayat Nova, 26
Scoozi, 101
She-Nannigans, 223
Sheraton Blackstone
    Hotel, 4
Snuggery, 222
Sterch's, 259
Store, 252
Su Casa, 228
Sweetwater, 219
Szechwan House, 28

Trattoria Pizzeria Roma,
    243
2350 Pub, 257

Ultimate Sports Bar and
    Grill, 248

Vie de France, 264

Waterfront, 221
Wells Street Deli, 233
Westin Hotel, 40
Wicklines, 270
Wise Fools Pub, 260

Yoshi's Cafe, 271
Yvette, 224

Theaters and Live Entertainment

Apollo Theater, 263
Biograph Theater, 464
Body Politic and Victory
    Gardens Theaters,
    256-57
Chicago Theater, 65
Esquire Theater, 51
Hot Tix, 60
Old Town School of Folk
    Music, 251
Park West, 248
Second City, 246
Three-Penny Cinema, 262
Zanie's, 245

Shops and Galleries

A Capriccio, 48
Aged Experience, 253
A Joint Venture, 247
American West Gallery,
    253
Animal Kingdom, 193
ARC Gallery, 99
Artemesia, 97

Barbara's Bookstore, 245
Bellini, 252
Benetton's 44
Betsy Rosenfield Gallery,
    94
Bookseller's Row, 64
Boomerang, 267
Bottega Glasseia, 51
Bottega Veneta, 45
Brokerage, 268
Bud Holland Gallery, 95

Carson Pirie Scott, 59
Chewy's, 252
Clown, 51
Coffee Corner, 247

Dart Gallery, 94
Design Source, 247
Donald Young Gallery,
    100
Douglas Dawson Gallery,
    98

E. Houk Gallery, 94
Esther Saks Gallery, 93, 96
Exhibit A, 98

Feature, 100
Finables, 253
Flashy Trash, 268
Formerly Yours Antiques,
    270

Gallimaufry Gallery, 270
Gepperth's Market, 252
Gianni Versace, 46
Gilman Gallery, 95
Goldman/Kraft Gallery, 96
Goodies, 268
Gucci, 31
Guild Books, 263

Hammacher Schlemmer, 28
Hansen Galleries, 94
Hobby Heaven, 269
Hokin/Kaufman Gallery, 94

Ilona of Hungary, 49

Jean Charles, 49
Jeraz, 46
J. Rosenthal Gallery, 95
J. Russell Andrews Antiques, 268

Kroch's and Brentano's, 58-59

LARC and the Hawk, 269

Marianne Deson Gallery, 100
Marshall Field & Co., 62
Medinah Barber Shop, 229

Morrie Mages, 232
Musicraft, 49
My Own Two Feet, 254
My Sisters Circus, 49

N.A.M.E. Gallery, 98
Neal Gallery, 94
Neiman-Marcus, 31
Neville/Sargent Gallery, 94

Oak Street Bookshop, 49-50
Objects, 98

Peter Miller Gallery, 100
Phyllis Kind Gallery, 96
Pierre Deux, 44
Piper's Alley, 247
Prairie Lee Gallery, 96
Pumpkin Patch, 267

Rhona Hoffman Gallery, 94
Richard Gray Gallery, 96
Ringolevio, 252
Roan Galleries, 269
Romano Gallery, 229
Roy Boyd Gallery, 93

Salamander, 253
Saturday's Child, 254
School of the Art Institute Gallery, 98

Sharper Image, 74
Struve Gallery, 96
Stuart Brent Bookstore, 30
Stuart Chicago, 51
Sugar Magnolia, 51

Tiffany, 31
Tuscany Studio, 233

Ultimo, 51
Uncle Dan's Army Navy Surplus, 262
Uno's Bizarre Bazaar, 244
Up Down Tobacco Shop, 245

Village Green, 252

Walter Bischoff Gallery, 100
Water Mark, 45
Water Tower Place, 36
Wheel and Deal, 269
White Elephant Resale, 260
Wieboldt's, 60
Women and Children First, 252

Yolanda Saul Gallery, 96

Zolla/Lieberman Gallery, 99